lululemon
and the future of technical apparel

By the founder

CHIP WILSON

Time is Tight Communications Ltd

CONTENTS

"*In the end, it is impossible to have a great life unless it is a meaningful life. And it is very difficult to have a meaningful life without meaningful work. Perhaps, then, you might gain that rare tranquility that comes from knowing that you've had a hand in creating something of intrinsic excellence that makes a contribution. Indeed, you might even gain that deepest of all satisfactions: knowing that your short time here on this earth has been well spent, and that it mattered.*"

—**Jim Collins**, *Good to Great: Why Some Companies Make the Leap . . . and Others Don't*

To all past, present, and future employees of lululemon,
and my wonderful family and friends.

LULULEMON VISION
(Defined as an unwavering commitment
to the number one principle)
"Elevating the world from mediocrity to greatness."

MISSION STATEMENT
Providing components for people to live a longer,
healthier, and more fun life.

NUMBER ONE PRINCIPLE
The store Educator is the most important person, and all
decisions are made with this in mind.

NUMBER ONE GOAL
Within six months of hiring, a person will have taken
the Landmark Forum and be coached on how to set
their two-, five-, and ten-year goals, which include
two for each of health, business, and personal.

CORE VALUES

QUALITY

Our customers want to buy our product again.

PRODUCT

We create components designed by athletes for athletes.

INTEGRITY

We do what we say we will do when we say we will do it.
If we cannot keep our promise, we immediately contact
all parties to set new by-when dates.

BALANCE

There is no separation between health, family, and work.
You love every minute of your life.

ENTREPRENEURSHIP

We treat and pay employees as though they run
their own businesses.

GREATNESS

We create the possibility of greatness in people
because it makes us great.
Mediocrity undermines greatness.

FUN

When I die, I want to die like my grandmother
who died peacefully in her sleep.
Not screaming like all the passengers in her car.

INTRODUCTION:
WHY I AM WRITING THIS BOOK

This is a book about ordinary people who took an opportunity to be creative, to be innovative, and to maximize their potential. My part in this story comes from the learnings gleaned from thousands of mistakes. I set the culture, business model, quality platform, and people development program, then got out of the way. Lululemon's exponential growth, culture, and brand strength have few peers, and it is because of those employees who choose to be great.

This book is also about missed opportunity—five years of missed opportunity. I was playing to win, while the directors of the company I founded were playing not to lose. There is a big difference. Lululemon invented a new context for apparel and how we think about dressing. In 2013, just when five years of exponential growth was in its infancy, when the way people dressed was at the precipice of the most significant change in history, lululemon self-imploded. The company went from owning 95 percent of the women's technical apparel market in 2011 to 10 percent in 2018. It is this part of the book from which I hope entrepreneurs will learn.

There are two parts to a successful business. First, there is the product and customer—the two aspects that started the business in the first place. This is the part the entrepreneur knows better than anyone else in the world.

Second, there is the business of public board governance. It includes the Machiavellian power moves and survival struggles of top executives and board members. This is generally not something the entrepreneur knows very well—certainly not as well as he or she knows the product and the customer. In this regard, my story is not unusual. The more I speak to successful entrepreneurs, the more I see that what happened to me is quite common.

I believe every person in life has a different genetic makeup and unique expertise that the world needs. My expertise was seeing athletic and apparel trends. With my first company, Westbeach, it was the rise of the surf, skate, and snowboard culture from 1979 to 1997. In 1998, I had the same sense that something big was about to happen with yoga.

I had no way of knowing just *how* huge yoga would be—and how lululemon would explode like nothing else. The little company that I founded in Kitsilano, Vancouver, would go on to redefine how a generation of people dressed and lived. The financial rewards for my family and me would be enormous, but at the time I was rolling the dice. I could have just as easily lost everything multiple times. The journey was exhilarating and terrifying. I was forty-two, I had a young family, and I bet the farm.

After a thrilling fifteen-year ride at lululemon, I got hit by a proverbial "sensational media" bus. The need of the media to create fiction for advertising revenue was just gaining traction. I became gun-shy of discussing my thoughts and played defense for the first time in my life; being authentic was no longer acceptable or possible. However, I am no longer concerned with negative media because I choose not to acknowledge comments from writers of fictional sensationalism. I am out to live a great life—and to be great, one must have a point of view.

This is the story of that journey and an account of what I've learned.

Chip Wilson, 2024

2024:
THE NEXT CHAPTER

At my house, one of our favorite pastimes is Dinner Questions. Everyone at the table gets to ask anything they want, and we all do our best to answer. With five boys, it can get raucous. Sometimes one question becomes a conversation for the whole night.

I don't know about you, but I have a lot of questions about where things are headed—not just in the athletic apparel industry but the entire world. Maybe a few answers, too.

Since the last edition of this book, we've emerged from the pandemic into a new normal of economic uncertainty and rapid technological change. I've kept doing what I've always done—watching, reading, and extrapolating. How will what's happening in apparel today play out tomorrow? Like a sci-fi author, I try to take things to the limit.

I do that by following the Chip Ratio: 20/60/20.

Think of any company that makes products. Every year, 20 percent of its new ideas and designs really push the envelope. If an idea works as a product, it joins the 60 percent: core offerings like lululemon's little black stretchy pants or Nike's Air Jordans. Then there's the other 20 percent. That's all the stuff you wish you didn't make anymore because it's a bit tacky or dated. But hey, it's selling so well that it fuels the rest of the business.

As an entrepreneur, I've always been willing to risk 20 percent of my time and money to find out what's next. It isn't a bad way to look at life either.

On that note, I've been going through some changes. I'm trying to step back and figure out a different way of living, so I'm not just taking on projects to fill my time. At my age, with money no longer a worry, family and health matter much more than what new business I'm launching. I also suffer from a medical condition that constantly reminds me life is precious.

But I'm an optimist who has always set and written down goals. In fact, I just redid them the other day. I turn seventy next year, and I aim to live to 156. It really doesn't matter if a goal is unachievable. The most important thing is having one.

And I haven't stepped away from the apparel business. Far from it. In 2019, I joined a consortium to take Amer Sports private. I was fulfilled as co-owner of Amer Sports, whose brands include Arc'teryx, Peak Performance, Salomon, Atomic, and Wilson. Besides serving on Amer's board, I am chair of the Brand Product Committee.

Amer is my third bet on China, which is well on the way to becoming the world's biggest market for technical apparel. With my Chinese partner, Anta Sports, I'm convinced that we're just at the start of the growth curve.

COVID put Amer on the back foot. We'd been planning to change all our CEOs from old-school, wholesale folks to direct-to-consumer types, but that was shelved because we needed to cut costs. Also, the fact that we couldn't get out and build relationships in person left us treading water when it came to elevating the business to the next level.

But as people flocked outdoors during the pandemic, sales took off, even though our retail stores were struggling like everyone else's. In 2023, Amer's growth in Greater China surged more than 60 percent, led by Vancouver-based Arc'teryx.

We took Amer public again in February 2024, when I bought more than $320 million worth of the company's stock. Combined with the 20 percent stake I took in 2018, that's real money.

I've found a kindred spirit in Anta's chairman, Ding Shizhong. We're both entrepreneurs who built apparel companies from the bottom up—in his case, by growing a small shoe manufacturer into the world's largest sports equipment player. We also both understand that for any successful retail company, 50 percent of its value lies in how customers feel about the brand.

For Amer, that means setting the business apart by using push technology to reach people. It also means making quality products and ensuring that our stores look premium, not stuffing them to the rafters with goods. And hiring the right people to work in those stores—athletic types who live and reflect the brands we sell.

I see three big opportunities for Amer: (1) expanding our offerings for women, (2) creating a product mix that attracts consumers year-round, and (3) going direct-to-consumer.

And I'm bullish on China, where health and fitness have become serious pursuits. Chinese consumers used to be happy wearing street clothing with an athletic logo, a trend that Anta capitalized on by snagging the license for Fila. That all changed about a decade ago when people started following North American trends by actually getting in shape—correlating fitness to a long, fun life. The Chinese movement to elevate athletes as heroes created demand for real athletic apparel. Also, the Chinese government is promoting health and fitness—by declaring them a priority and building new sports facilities.

And of course, sports has a global appeal. If there's anything that can bring the world together, it's the Olympics and other sporting events.

Then there's China's unrivalled manufacturing prowess, thanks to the economies of scale created by serving a domestic market of 1.4 billion people. Just look at what's happening with electric cars. BYD can make a better, cheaper vehicle than Tesla—and deliver it anywhere around the globe at a rock-bottom price.

China holds the same commanding position in technical clothing, with the added advantage that there's no longer any apparel production to speak of in North America and Europe. On top of that, governments around the world probably won't increase duties on Chinese clothing like they're doing with Chinese EVs.

Sure, the culture is different in China. As I've learned on my frequent visits, people there have their own way of doing things. But fundamentally, the Chinese have the same ratio of people with integrity to those lacking it as exists anywhere else. The rules are pretty straightforward, too. If you become wealthy, you'd better not flaunt it. And whether you're rich or poor, don't criticize the government. In my experience, China is also the most entrepreneurial country in the world, well beyond even the US.

So I'll keep divesting from lululemon and buying into Amer, where I have more control and impact. I also love being part of a global business—seeing how the world operates and thinking about geopolitics and economics and trade, as well as how popular culture and buying patterns are changing. Those things all fascinate me.

My health is a preoccupation, too. I was diagnosed with facioscapulohumeral muscular dystrophy (FSHD) in my early thirties—after discovering that I could no longer swim across the pool only four years after completing an Ironman competition. But until a decade ago, I was in denial about this progressive genetic disease, which weakens the muscles of the face, shoulders, and upper arms, as well as those in the legs and elsewhere in the body.

Since then, I've been making up for lost time. In 2022, I founded SOLVE FSHD, committing $100 million to finding a cure for the disease by the end of 2027.

To be clear, I'm not just doing this for my own personal gain. Worldwide, an estimated one million people suffer from FSHD, enough to make a treatment profitable for drug companies.

To that end, until recently, only one business was chasing a cure. Now, partly thanks to the support of SOLVE FSHD, where I chair the board, there are about forty companies and academic researchers on the case. We're in constant contact with them as they pursue effective treatments. It's one of those things where you have to put a lot of shots on goal, or you're never going to score.

For me, it's also about being willing to risk that 20 percent. And I'm not just talking about money. As someone my age who's suffering from the disease, I'm willing to be a bit of a guinea pig. So if I think a potential treatment is relatively safe, I'll try it.

Because I've been an athlete all my life, I'm in better shape than many other people might be at this stage of the illness. For me, it comes back to longevity. I need to ensure that my body is as healthy as possible so the muscles I have left keep working.

Probably the cleanest potential FSHD therapy is gene editing—regenerating muscle by making changes at the genetic level. In the entire realm of muscle cures and regeneration, there are probably one hundred possible solutions— with more coming every day.

I've been taking follistatin, a protein that inhibits the

body's cap on how large muscles are able to grow. My dose is a low-risk version, but there's another form of follistatin that offers a very good chance of providing more muscle.

The catch: It comes with big risks. If I took it, I might not be able to do a future treatment that solves FSHD, because it creates antibodies that would reject any new medicine.

I'm also working with a chiropractor who does electrical stimulation of my weakest muscles. And with a trainer, I'm using a PoNS (Portable Neuromodulation Stimulator), a headphone-like device worn around the neck that lets me do balance exercises. Because most people with FSHD die from falling, we're seeing if this machine can improve my balance by resetting my neuroplasticity, allowing my stronger muscles to compensate for the weak ones.

To keep tabs on the effectiveness of these therapies, I wear digital "Plantiga" pods in the soles of my shoes that track my walking. The information collected can be used to analyze and compare my movements over time. Unfortunately, there's still no blood biomarker for FSHD. But if the length and speed of my step improve, it could help to signal a cure.

No matter what happens, I remain optimistic. If I want to make it to 156, I need to get my brain focused on that goal, and my body will follow.

After all, I have a lot to live for. Family is everything to me. I recently became a grandfather for the first time, of beautiful twin girls. My three youngest boys just finished their first year away at university, which has been a big change for all of us. As I write this, they're home for the summer, so I'm trying to be around when they are, so we can enjoy some quality time together. If we can spend some weekends as a family, at our beach house on the Sunshine Coast near Vancouver, even better.

In recent chats with my kids, I made an eye-opening discovery. They have long felt that I would be disappointed in them if they didn't follow in my footsteps—like that open door was a directive, not an option. I've never expected any of them to join me in the business. I show my love by giving them opportunities based on what I see as their aptitudes, with the understanding that they can take it or leave it. All I really want is for them to be happy with themselves.

Of course, my son JJ shares my passion for technical apparel. Because our institutional knowledge of the industry is likely second to none, I believe we should keep investing in what we know, rather than what we don't know.

To ensure the longevity of those investments, I spend a lot of time planning the family's financial future. When it comes to generational wealth, every family is a snowflake, as they say. There really isn't one right way to do things.

We have a family office, we have a fiduciary board for our real estate holdings, we have an advisory board, and we have trustees. If something were to happen to me, there are wills and trusts. We have mechanisms in place to ensure that the business will keep running smoothly—and that my wife, Summer, and the kids have a choice about stepping in.

I also keep setting financial goals for the family. For example, with diversification in mind, I plan to have 30 percent of our wealth in real estate by 2032.

I love all the routine things we do as a family, whether it's dinner or weekends away. Every two years, we have a big reunion on the Sunshine Coast with about sixty people. But with the boys, we also set aside 20 percent of our time to do crazy stuff. I've always tried to give them the gift of travel by taking them everywhere. Now that nearly every tourist destination in the world has a Starbucks and a McDonald's, we like to go hiking in places that are off the beaten track.

We've made two trips to Peru, where we followed the Inca Trail to Machu Picchu. We've done the Copper Canyon in Mexico. Morocco is one of our favorite places to hike, and we've trekked all 600 kilometers of the Camino Portugués, from Lisbon to Santiago de Compostela.

As far as I'm concerned, there's no such thing as balancing work and family. That might have been possible back in the early 1990s, when you left your family to go to work in the morning and came home to be with them in the evening. But because of technology—not to mention the rise of remote work—everything has blended together.

To get the most out of family life and do my best work, I need to use my time effectively—and prioritize health and wellness. I still travel a lot for work, but thanks to the luxury of having a private jet, I'm able to be in many different places in a relatively short period of time. And no matter where I'm going, I arrive rested so I can be fully present.

As a family, we're also continuing our philanthropic efforts. In 2022, through the Wilson 5 Foundation, we committed $100 million to the BC Parks Foundation. With the biggest private donation to conservation in Canadian history, the goal is to put 30 percent of British Columbia into parkland by 2030. The provincial government is on board now, along with several First Nations.

Most of that 30 percent will be in northern BC, which remains sparsely populated. Basically, we're buying out the forestry and mining rights, and the province will lease land for $1 to the First Nations, who will manage it like a national park. That way, it can't be returned to industry through some future legal change. The long-term plan is for the First Nations people to create tourist-based businesses so people can experience one of the last untouched places on Earth. As time goes on, that land will only become more valuable.

Although I spend two months a year in Sydney, Australia, BC is my home. To me, it's still the most beautiful place in the world. Only Sydney and Vancouver have the perfect combination of sophisticated urban living in the midst of nature.

Yes, I'm disappointed every time a New Democratic Party (NDP) provincial government gets elected in Canada, which stops the flow of investment and encourages people like me to move their money to the US. But Vancouver is still Canada's gateway to Asia—for China in particular.

And I'm still very active in real estate in Vancouver, where my company owns about fifty properties. We used to invest a lot in offices as well as family housing, but that's changed because demand for rental apartments has skyrocketed. To diversify our portfolio, we've been buying select properties in Seattle, too.

BC is also the best place in the world to design technical apparel. That's partly thanks to our varied climate and geography, with the mountains and ocean serving as both inspiration and proving ground for new designs and technologies. It's almost become a cliché, but there aren't many other spots where you can snow-ski in the morning and go kitesurfing or play beach volleyball in the afternoon.

The fact that Vancouver is one of the world's newest major cities has also driven innovation. When the city really started to grow, urban planning was just coming into vogue. The smart decision to put aside so many parks and build bike paths along the ocean makes Vancouver very special. For four or five months of the year, it's so gorgeous that people stay outdoors well into the evening. And because it's so easy to cycle to work, take off in the middle of the day for a hike, or shoot up to Whistler for the weekend, there was demand for new types of clothing.

As Vancouverites exerted themselves going to work and back, they probably ditched the suit and tie before anyone else. The replacement: office clothing you could actually move in. Then things got really interesting as local athletic apparel companies started making business-appropriate attire out of technical fabrics.

Along the way, I noticed a bottleneck to continued growth and innovation. People graduating from local fashion design schools didn't know how to make technical apparel. That's why Summer and I donated $12 million to establish the Wilson School of Design at Kwantlen Polytechnic University, which opened in 2018.

Besides offering a Technical Apparel Design program, the school provides scholarships for top students to visit Asian factories where they can learn how to make this clothing. After all, technical apparel involves a completely different process. It requires bonding and glues as well as specialized fabrics.

If I had to do it all over again, I'd probably open my own design school. I am not sure the unions will allow education to move as fast as the world is changing. Still, I'm pleased with the results so far. Every year, ten outstanding grads of the Wilson School of Design go to companies like Arc'teryx, Veilance, Aritzia, lululemon, Westbeach, Reigning Champ, and flotation specialist Mustang Survival—one of several smaller local players that have carved out a niche in technical clothing.

With annual growth of 40 percent, Arc'teryx is probably the hottest brand in athletics right now. They've made great clothing forever, but when COVID got everyone excited about being outdoors, they really started gaining traction.

In North America and Europe, an Arc'teryx garment is now regarded as an essential piece. In China, its quality makes it a premium luxury product. The life-or-death weather conditions that Arc'teryx clothing is designed for help it to go the distance. When you've owned one of their jackets for five years, you realize it's probably the best money you've ever spent. It still looks brand-new and works perfectly.

I'm also stunned by the innovation at Arc'teryx. Their avalanche airbags and new exoskeleton pants for assisted hiking are just two examples. In response to new European Union regulations, they've created environmentally friendly laminates for their garments. Arc'teryx, which is known for its innovation in footwear and backpacks, also recently launched several new shoes that have been bestsellers.

Arc'teryx understands the value of developing and staying true to its tribe—that core of highly athletic customers who drive broader interest in the brand. That's exactly what we did with lululemon back in the day.

The same goes for upstart sneaker brands Hoka and On, which came out of nowhere to challenge Adidas and Nike. They targeted running-only shoe stores whose owners were fanatical about the sport, making it more likely that their products would be worn by the best runners. When their tribes started talking about the brands, Hoka and On didn't need to do much in the way of promotion. They were already known.

Then there's lululemon, which has done a great job of alienating the core customer that made it such a success. Essentially, it's trying to be all things to all people. When someone walks into a lululemon store, they can't tell what the company stands for. Lululemon sits on the edge of becoming a mom-brand with little time to reverse its trajectory.

If I were lululemon, I'd probably launch a spinoff brand that specializes in business apparel—pants, button-down shirts, belts, and so on—made from technical fabrics. But they're trying to cram too many ideas into a small store, or building impersonal mega stores.

Is lululemon a streetwear brand? An athletic brand? An accessories brand? Their stores look like Disneyland with all those keychains and other trinkets, which have nothing to do with athletics. It cheapens the brand experience. As a result, their original core customer doesn't bother to stop by anymore.

For lululemon, the fundamental problem is that there's no longer a founder-owner on the board. They need someone who lives five years in the future—who can give customers what they don't know they want yet, by taking that 20 percent risk on ideas that push the envelope. Lululemon's stock has dropped so much because the board is numbers-driven and there's nobody looking after the creative side. All they care about is Wall Street.

In that sense, lululemon has followed the same arc as many other entrepreneur-owned businesses that became mature public companies. Along the way, they lose sight of the fact that for any brand, only half of its value is financial. The other half is the subconscious feeling that brand creates for the customer.

With lululemon now, it's all about delivering a low-cost product at the highest price—and maximizing sales so management and buyers can get their bonuses. The folks in charge of building out stores are bonused on how quickly and cheaply they can open them. So they've moved to steel fixtures, budget racks, budget everything. That way, they can find a location, paint it white, and get the place up and running in about two weeks.

Also, because the merchants get a bonus on margin, their goal is to make cheaper stuff and charge a higher price. That inevitably results in the wrong product for the customer—an acrylic sweater with no good reason to be in the store, or a button-down, collared shirt that nobody on the West Coast would wear. A store that used to be 80 percent athletic apparel is now 20 percent athletic—at best. The remainder is everyday clothing with a lululemon logo slapped on it.

Thanks to those missteps, lululemon is losing its premium position to athletic brands like Alo and Vuori. Those retailers have followed Aritzia's lead by opening beautiful, thoughtfully laid-out stores that could be someone's living room, with wood and rugs and good lighting. Lululemon has none of that style and elegance anymore. It's basically the Gap from 1998.

As a result, it's also bleeding market share to Arc'teryx and Aritzia, which already sells its own athletic line.

My prediction? If lululemon continues on its current path, it will join the likes of Club Monaco, Ralph Lauren, and Tommy Hilfiger. These brands used to be "athletic," but in their race to the bottom, they failed to see the new technical apparel market coming and were left in the dust.

And what's the next big thing? I'm keeping my eyes peeled. I probably spend 20 percent of my time looking for new sports, new ways to be physically active, and new longevity hacks. I follow sports closely because they go through a shift every five years, creating new opportunities for athletic apparel. I've got to be on my game and an expert on what's emerging before the mainstream catches on.

The biggest market is the $500 billion street technical industry, which I call "strech," my name for athleisure. It's clothing for people who want to dress sharply but won't put up with fabrics that don't stretch, that stink, that are too tight, or that fail to respond to temperature changes.

Now that men have abandoned ties and leather shoes, the trend is toward sophisticated streetwear that's actually wearable. That's the opposite of the luxury market, where fabrics are stiff and unbreathable because the designers only think about visual appeal. Besides making comfortable clothes, forward-looking strech designers are including details—say, a vintage zipper somewhere on the garment—that create fashion for the street.

But at the same time, everything old is new again. As snowboarding enjoys a revival, I recently bought back Westbeach, the brand I launched in 1979 and sold in 1997. For me, it's the perfect 20 percent play. It gives me an outlet to design clothing that doesn't compete with Amer. Some of my ideas are so far out there that no one's willing to take a chance on them. I don't need to make money on Westbeach, so I plan to have some fun with it and see if I can prove out the business model. Call it a passion project.

For entrepreneurs who are just starting out in the apparel business, life is far from simple. When I launched lululemon, we grew the business organically over several years by building our tribe. Is that approach still viable? Yes and no. If you're making, say, run-of-the-mill T-shirts and hoodies, your best bet is to go direct-to-consumer and try to win on price. If you have a trademarked product that's tough for a competitor to copy, then you can start slower.

But the world is changing so quickly. Ten years ago, you could launch a pure e-commerce business and thrive because online customer acquisition costs were low. Now that those costs have gone through the roof, all bets are off.

Then again, it depends on your audience. Just look at two of the most successful athletic apparel brands right now: Gymshark out of the UK, which targets the workout crowd, and Sweden's MONTEC, which makes ski and snowboard clothing. Both aim for a highly specific market: consumers under the age of twenty-five. Gymshark has some retail stores, but MONTEC is a pure e-commerce play. Marketed to people who are comfortable buying online, its clothing costs are about 30 percent less, but the quality shows up in poor fabrics and manufacturing techniques.

Meanwhile, more e-commerce apparel brands are opening retail locations to supplement their online presence. If they command a premium price for their product, they don't have to make much money from the physical stores, which are a branding tool and an opportunity to omnichannel their products. People can visit them to return items they bought online, and the staff and store design help create a brand feeling.

As online and physical retail blend, I see an opening for virtual store visits by video, where a salesperson can walk you around and assist with selections—much like they would in real life. Another win would be the ability to take a selfie that precisely captures your measurements. Besides ensuring a perfect fit for the customer, that would help retailers reduce the massive cost of shipping, particularly when so many items that get returned. Once fit is solved, the next frontier is enabling online shoppers to "feel" a garment, given that texture is a deciding factor when people buy clothes in person.

Looking ahead, there's definitely a role for brick-and-mortar retail, but as Gymshark and MONTEC have shown, it's market-dependent. If a customer is under twenty-five and the price is right, they'll buy online. Of course, as their clientele ages, Gymshark and MONTEC can morph and omnichannel their product. That poses a big risk to incumbents like Adidas and lululemon, and, of course, to Amer Sports.

For me, all this rapid change makes living five years in the future tougher than it used to be. If there's anything I'm scared about right now, it's that I can't keep up. I missed the social media revolution because I didn't need it, but at least I understand how it changed the world. AI (artificial intelligence) is a whole different ball game. In these early days, we don't even know what we don't know.

But here's the thing: If you're involved in any industry where AI can be applied, you're either going to be left behind without a job, or you're going to roll with it and perhaps become incredibly wealthy.

AI is starting to commoditize the global economy even more, so prices are slowly dropping. And when everyone can go to an AI copilot and ask anything they want, it flattens out the world.

For example, AI could have a huge impact on the apparel industry. Now someone without any technical skills can design a piece of clothing—verbally. Let's say they ask their AI copilot to create a spec sheet for a jacket in several sizes, based on the average design of similar products from Nike, lululemon, and Under Armour. The AI sends those specs to the best apparel factory in the world, with instructions to make 500 pieces in worsted wool. It also arranges prepayment, transportation, and duty, then sets up the shipment in a warehouse and connects with Shopify.

That's like telling Uber you want to go to Dublin. It books your flight and accommodation, picks you up at the airport, and takes you to your hotel. With AI, you don't need to figure anything out anymore. All it takes is creativity and the right questions. Also, the creator can make a high-volume, discount piece—or design something so new and different that people will pay a premium for it.

Amid all this uncertainty, I see one pattern that remains the same. Since 1940, there's been a steadily growing movement toward health, fitness, and longevity that has driven the rise of many new sports and apparel brands. And even before COVID, people were embracing the outdoors in a big way. With those long-term trends in mind, our family business keeps looking for opportunities connected to getting folks moving and staying healthy. Because both things lead to better sex, better marriages, stronger families, and longer lives, it creates a virtuous cycle.

With all the hype around AI, some pundits have predicted that it will eventually do everything for us. Are we headed for a future like the one in the movie *WALL-E*, where everybody's overweight and sits around on floating lounge chairs all day? I don't think so.

My hunch is that the movement toward better health and fitness will continue, with Darwinism taking care of the naysayers—who will have fewer or no kids because they believe the world is going to hell. When in fact, nothing could be further from the truth.

Who knows? Maybe someday soon, our food will be a nutritionally balanced pill, and we'll all spend our entire lives fit and healthy, thanks to good decisions and medical advances. It's better than any number of alternatives. No matter how things play out, I only see growing demand for the athletic apparel and equipment that Amer sells.

Needless to say, I'm as fanatical as anyone about physical wellness. Typically, I spend half my day being proactive about my health. The way I see it, every hour is an investment in my longevity. Besides eating well and making time for FSHD therapy, I make a point of getting outside and enjoying myself. For example, Summer and I play tennis five days a week. In fact, I just got back from a game.

As the hours I devote to health keep growing, my time at the office is shrinking. And when I am doing something work-related, it's often passing knowledge to the next generation, whether that's mentoring my kids or sitting on a board where I can advise rather than make decisions.

In some ways, my life is becoming simpler than ever. Do I need to accomplish anything bigger? Perhaps the opposite is true.

One of my goals is to open a single Westbeach store on West Fourth Avenue in Vancouver by the end of 2025. I don't know what I'll do with it. Maybe I'll just be an old man hanging around there, making clothes, and serving coffee. No question, that sounds 100 percent fine to me.

PROLOGUE:
THE END OF THE SURF, SKATE, AND SNOWBOARD BUSINESS

The Final Days of Westbeach

The year was 1995. After sixteen years in the surf, skate, and snowboard markets, it had become clear that my company, Westbeach Snowboard, wasn't going to pay the mortgage or feed my family. There was too much product for too few snowboarders. Profits were nonexistent. Westbeach found itself taking bigger and bigger risks.

Finally, the inevitable happened. We had a $5 million order of snowboard jackets being manufactured in Asia, and we ran out of zippers. We told our suppliers we needed $30,000 worth of zippers on credit. They said no. We had extended ourselves repeatedly and had reached our limit. The goodwill of our suppliers had dried up.

We asked our bank. They also said no. The bank then put us in *special accounts*—a euphemism for impending bankruptcy.

This was a do-or-die situation. We needed money for zippers, and we needed it quickly. In the seasonal apparel market, if you're a month late in delivering your inventory, the consequences are dire.

A private equity (PE) firm called Mercantile Bancorp had been waiting on the sidelines. They quickly invested in Westbeach for 30 percent of our company, providing the capital we so badly needed to address the zipper crisis. Mercantile saw our value and believed a cash injection would allow us to flourish.

Even though we were in dire straits, giving up 30 percent of our company seemed unfair. My two partners and I had been working hard for years, always intent on maintaining our independence. Unfortunately, there was no alternative.

Mercantile suggested we form a board of directors made up of mentors. These mentors would have no vested interest in the company other than helping three inexperienced owners negotiate their way through the world of governance and oversight. A guy named Blair Mullen was Mercantile's operating partner inside Westbeach. Blair straightened out our accounting systems and streamlined our inventory procedures. From the very start, Blair did a good job, and I respected his work.

Not long after that, I was in Japan showing our line at Tokyo Levante, the office of our Japanese distributor. I was wrapping up there, getting ready to head to Norway, when a fax from Blair came through.

"I've decided to take over as CEO of the company," Blair's fax advised.

I was in shock. Even though I didn't hold the title, I had always considered myself the unofficial CEO of Westbeach. I'd founded the company, and I believed I drove the outcome of most key decisions. I hadn't had a boss in ten years! The whole scenario was the polar opposite of what I'd wanted to achieve by going into business for myself.

Team of One

I knew myself well enough to know that in crisis or survival situations, I often acted like a *Team of One*, taking everything on because I couldn't trust others to do what I thought was right. It seemed like Westbeach had always been in crisis.

On the other hand, Mercantile had also made many weak areas stronger, and fixed things that, due to my inexperience, I hadn't even recognized as problems.

As three owners, we each wanted to use our third of the budget to make our own areas work effectively. But mediocrity is inevitable when there is not one final decision-maker to manage priorities, differentiate the company, and take advantage of a changing marketplace. Perhaps my getting out of the way and accepting Blair as CEO was best for Westbeach.

Here we were, fifteen years after I started Westbeach, and ten years after partnering as a trio. We had a wholesale business with a few vertical retail stores, a board of directors, and an experienced CEO, but we still weren't turning a profit. (By "vertical retail" I mean we owned retail stores and essentially sold to ourselves, eliminating the middleman-wholesaler. Consequentially, a vertical retailer is able to create double the profits compared to other apparel companies that use a wholesale model.) Year after year, our mixed vertical and wholesale model just wasn't working. After we'd covered our expenses, there was never anything left to move us to the next level.

The Snowboard Scene

Meanwhile, the snowboard market was about to hit its first major obstacle.

In 1995, the snowboard business was robust, particularly in Japan. But, by 1996, both the Japanese yen and their snowboard market began to falter. Japan represented 30 percent of our global sales. I was concerned. We still had our lease obligations, wages, and operating and various other costs; if 30 percent of our sales went away, our company would collapse.

Within a few years, the snowboard market, just like the surf and skate market before it, entered a widespread product commoditization phase. It was followed by many mergers and acquisitions. When consumers begin to see products as commodities, they no longer see the unique features of individual products and often make purchasing choices based on price alone. Companies must merge with or acquire competitors to prevent endless price dropping. The only two public companies were Ride Snowboards (where my brother was VP of brand) and Morrow Snowboards. Both companies had been hit hard trying to save their brands. They limited backdoor sales through fake overseas companies to big Japanese trading houses.

As public companies, Ride and Morrow (who both made snowboards) wanted to acquire companies to replace lost Japanese sales. They were playing the public market quarterly analyst game and needed to show higher sales to maintain investor confidence. An easy solve was acquiring other snowboard apparel brands . . . brands such as Westbeach, which had been around since the beginning.

If we were going to get any money out of this business, we needed to sell. We'd already had talks with Morrow, but those discussions had failed when Morrow decided to make their own apparel line.

Fortunately for us, the Morrow clothing brand was not successful.

Negotiating with Morrow

As Westbeach was a proven brand in the global snowboard apparel market, Morrow came back to the table. Unbeknownst to Morrow, we were desperate. It was a Monday, and by that Friday we wouldn't be able to make payroll. We knew Morrow was operating without a chief financial officer (CFO). At this point, I'd owned and run Westbeach for almost eighteen years, earning an average of $40,000 per year.

On that Wednesday, Morrow bought Westbeach for $15 million, based purely on brand value. The value of the brand would be a lesson in what cannot be measured before someone else is willing to pay.

The sale of Westbeach to Morrow had come with specific strings attached—primarily the requirement for me to work for Morrow and to relocate to their headquarters in Salem, Oregon.

Because I love to learn, I was excited to observe what happened to a company's culture when it merged with another company.

In my tenure at Morrow, I'd had one good idea. It was a yoga graphic T-shirt that the Japanese snowboarders loved. From the inspiration of the T-shirt, the next Japanese snowboard contest started with a yoga warm-up—on snowboards.

Unfortunately, in 1997, my twelve-month obligation to Morrow lasted only eight months. Morrow had spent their last $15 million buying Westbeach. My job in future business development ended when I suggested the company pivot from snowboard hardware and apparel into mountain biking.

My Eighteen-Year MBA

I was officially unemployed. After Mercantile and the banks took their share, and after our original debts were covered, each partner took home about $1 million (or $800,000 after taxes). For as long as I could remember, I'd been grinding it out, working long hours, constantly travelling. Having this new financial cushion was an indescribable relief. For the first time in a very long time, I could breathe!

Westbeach had zero profit. Our two vertical retail stores made a million dollars a year while our international whole-sale business lost a million dollars in the same span of time. Inside of this was a lesson worth billions: the idea of a purely vertical retail model, a principle that would be key to my next business venture. Insights like this are why I've come to think of my Westbeach years as my "eighteen-year MBA." It was an education that would prove far more valuable than the $800,000 I walked away with.

Coming out of university, I knew nothing about the production of fabric, or how to open stores or form partnership agreements. I knew nothing about selling or collecting money. I was inexperienced in the business of business. I knew nothing of financing, deals, and transactions. I was also a terrible negotiator. In fact, in many ways, I wanted to be a phys-ed teacher, like my dad.

More than anything else, I wanted to help people achieve their full potential.

lululemon
and the
future of
technical
apparel

CHAPTER 1:
FROM CALIFORNIA TO CALGARY

Live life on the court not in the stands.

The American Dream

If I look back at the earliest parts of my life, there are certain themes that from day one shaped me and steered me toward the companies I developed. This is true for everyone, I'm sure, but for me, those themes were my grandparents' approach to business, my parents' tough financial circumstances, my dual Canadian-American citizenship (I was born in L.A. and raised in Alberta), and, perhaps most of all, my involvement in athletics.

My dad, Dennis Wilson, was Calgary's Athlete of the Year in 1952 when he was eighteen. He played both hockey and football—the two big sports in Calgary in those days. Dad joined the farm team for the Chicago Blackhawks. Unfortunately, they soon folded due to team finances. In 1954, he went to Brigham Young University (BYU) in Utah to play football.

My mom, Mary Ruth Noel, hailed from San Diego. She was a gymnast and became the first female lifeguard at the

Plunge Pool in Mission Beach, San Diego. When she was old enough to go to college, as the family story goes, her father, James Noel, was worried about Communist infiltration in California universities (this was the 1950s!), so he was eager for his daughter to go to university somewhere quieter. Like Utah.

So, there they were—my parents-to-be—probably the only two non-Mormons at BYU. She was nineteen, and he was twenty-one. Since I was born in April 1955, I can only imagine Mom and Dad had known each other for all of ten or eleven minutes before certain things happened.

My parents had a shotgun wedding in San Diego, Mom's hometown. From there they moved to Orange County, near a new development called Disneyland.

It didn't take long for our little family to grow. My sister Noel was born in 1957, and my brother Brett was born in 1960.

I'll offer a few memories to set the scene. Nuclear emergency drills were performed monthly at our elementary school. Despite the fears of a third world war, kids could roam freely. Neighbourhoods had a naturally occurring block watch from house to house and family to family.

All adults smoked and drank (my parents, in fact, both smoked and drank all through my mother's pregnancies). This was an era best depicted today by the show *Mad Men*, a show that so accurately reflects the culture of 1960s New York advertisers who were themselves creating the image of the ideal life at the time.

Money was often short in our house. My dad wasn't playing football anymore—he was working on a teaching degree. To make ends meet he also drove a UPS delivery truck from L.A. to San Diego and back most nights. This was in addition to attending classes during the day. Only a person in their mid-twenties can keep up a pace like that.

My mom, meanwhile, was the stay-at-home parent. She was made to drive a sewing machine! From early on, I learned about patterns, fabric, and clothing design through watching and helping her work.

As a young boy, I wasn't interested in sewing as a skill, because learning it properly was too time-consuming. But if I wanted to spend time with my mom, I had to spend it in the sewing room while she was working. The room was dominated by a large working table, with shelves on which she stored fabric and patterns. She had all these paper Butterick patterns with pictures on the front. Mom would lay the pattern flat, cut it out, pin it onto the fabric, and from there use it to guide the sewing and stitching.

I vividly remember watching my mom as she carefully adjusted the pattern to get full use of the fabric—without waste and without destroying the integrity of the garment.

With Westbeach and later with lululemon, I would see twenty to fifty layers of fabric cut in a stack with an industrial laser cutter, meaning that every square inch cost thousands of dollars. By implementing my mom's tricks, and by understanding the real basics of sewing and patterning, the production costs—expensive as they were—were kept to a minimum.

When my dad finished his teaching degree a few years later, he and my mom moved to Calgary. Calgary was Dad's hometown. He was happy to return to the place he knew best. My mom wanted to put distance between herself and her parents. My maternal grandmother, also named Mary, was a very dominant person, and my mom had a rebellious streak. A move to Canada was her way out from under her mother's control.

I was five when we relocated to Calgary and became landed immigrants.

We weren't wealthy, but we still had a good time growing

up in a suburban neighbourhood. As my sister, Noel, remembers, "Chip would organize games like prison tag or kick-the-can every night during the summer. Kids just gravitated to our house because of him."

Mom continued to stay at home, and Dad got a job teaching physical education and driving a taxi at night to make the mortgage payments.

James and Mary

Even after the move to Calgary, I returned most summers to California to visit my mother's parents. I didn't know it at the time, but my grandparents would both play key roles in my life as an entrepreneur.

My grandparents were both originally from the Midwest. When my grandpa moved to California, they kept in touch with one another. Eventually, he asked my grandma to come out to the coast and marry him. She accepted. They moved to San Diego, where they opened a furniture business. Their business specialized in selling furniture to, and then repurchasing it from, US Marines, in the area around Ocean Beach.

Part of the success of their business was due to my grandfather's personality. He'd always had a personal style that appealed to his community, and it wasn't long after he and my grandmother had moved to San Diego that he was serving as head of the Kiwanis Club and became deputy mayor. People loved to visit him and get caught up on all the local gossip.

My grandmother, meanwhile, did the *selling*. Grandma was a hard-nosed businesswoman through and through. She had a very strong personality; some people might even say she was overbearing, but I never thought so. She just knew what she wanted in life and was passionate about getting it. And even though she'd trained as a nurse, she'd also spent quite a bit of time closely studying the sales process.

In those days, Dale Carnegie's famous book *How to Win Friends and Influence People* was a popular reference for aspiring businesspeople. When I was older, my mom told me she thought that she would never have been born if the birth control pill had existed when my grandmother was a young woman.

This wasn't a comment on their relationship, it was just to say my grandmother was a fiercely independent, smart, determined woman. She likely would have put business first in her life had she grown up in different times.

Once their furniture business was well-established, my grandparents diversified their interests. They bought apartments throughout San Diego. My grandparents had also invested in mutual funds.

As a kid of nine or ten, my grandparents invested for me in the same funds in which they had their money. I remember watching and being excited as those stocks kept climbing.

And then, in August of 1966, there was a massive computer fraud of a multi-level marketing company, one of the very first of its kind. My grandparents were among the victims of the fraud. They lost their house and had to move into a trailer park east of San Diego, where the property taxes were much lower.

It was tough, but a great part about being an American is that frequently a big reward comes when you take a big risk. In interviews I've heard or read with Americans, even poor Americans accept income disparity for the ability to risk for a big reward. To rebuild some of what they'd lost, my grandmother took her born business skills into multi-level marketing. She was the perfect person for it.

My grandfather, meanwhile, spent a lot more time with me and my sister and brother whenever we visited them. He'd help us look for ski equipment and took us to the beach. He also took us to the hospital where he was getting chemotherapy treatments. He had been diagnosed with prostate cancer right around the time they'd lost their mutual funds.

In retrospect, I understand now he was spending all the time he could with us because Grandpa knew he had little time left. He died in 1967 at the age of sixty-five. He'd lived only 24,000 days.

Outside of the business they ran and their investments in mutual funds, my grandparents also provided a significant source of stability throughout my childhood. This was especially true as my parents' relationship became more and more strained.

While my grandfather was still living, I saw that he and my grandmother were two people who were in love and who enjoyed working together every day. There wasn't one thing they did separately. They were a great example in showing me that was the life I knew I wanted to have. Having a woman in my life who embodied the same partnership qualities as my grandmother would someday be my perfect match.

Hard Times in Calgary

In Calgary throughout the 1960s, times were tough for my parents. Money was still short much of the time. I don't think my mother had known what she was getting herself into when she agreed to move to Calgary.

For one thing, she'd had no idea how bitterly cold the winters would be. She'd grown up with the fresh fruits and vegetables for which California has always been famous. However, Alberta in the 1950s and '60s was solely a meat-and-potatoes kind of place. The complete lack of fresh produce appalled her and made her question the move.

My parents were in their early twenties when they'd met— the unplanned pregnancy had really almost forced them to come together. They tried to make it work, but they were never very good at communicating with each other.

Added to that shaky foundation were constant financial pressures and three young children. My dad once told me the most important thing on his mind on the day of his wedding was how to throw a football accurately. That put their relationship into perspective for me.

Despite the struggles of survival mode, we received a fantastic amount of love. My parents' theory of raising us was that by age six we should be able to safely take the bus downtown and back on our own.

We had a lot of freedom in our house since any spare time my parents had was mostly taken up with trying to earn a few extra dollars—the rule was to do what you wanted and make it to bed on your own time. But, because we were all competitive swimmers, we automatically knew we needed to get to bed early, so we could make 6 a.m. practise the next morning. This was one aspect of the self-sufficiency I learned early on.

Competitive Swimming

Noel, Brett, and I had all been swimming for as long as I could remember. My siblings and I had access to a swimming pool every summer as my mother had worked as a lifeguard in San Diego, and my dad had a summer director job at a Kiwanis camp for underprivileged kids. That was our introduction to swimming.

"Our whole family would get up every morning for swimming," says Noel. "Chip was pretty motivated. I think he was probably the most motivated. I did not really like swimming. I was very successful in it, but I would have much rather been hanging out with my friends. But Chip embraced the swimming and was exceptional at it, too."

It worked for my parents, too—given their relentless

schedules, it was good for them to find something occupied us. Our family life soon revolved around seven or eight practises a week and meets on the weekends. Everything was about swimming.

Swimming was also a great activity for us because it was affordable. All you needed was a bathing suit and a pair of goggles, and you were good to go. Despite that, I managed to find something I so desperately wanted, but couldn't afford—the perfect swimsuit. The only swimsuits available in Calgary at the time were made by Speedo, and they were all solid colours. In fact, when Speedo introduced simple stripes on their suits, it took the swimming scene by storm.

One day when I was eleven or twelve, I saw a suit at a swim meet that was totally different. The material was a colourful flower pattern. I wanted it immediately.

I asked the kid wearing it where he'd gotten the suit. "Texas," he replied.

I'd become used to not being able to afford the clothes I wanted, but I was determined to get that suit. My mom considered it, and I suggested to her that if I liked the style of the suit, then maybe other kids would like the style, too. If we ordered a bunch and sold them, I told her, then we could make a small profit and use the money to cover the cost of my suit.

We brought in the bathing suits, and they sold like crazy! We'd purchased the suits from the supplier for maybe thirteen dollars, then sold them for double that. They were something no one had ever seen before—something new. Since they weren't available in Canada, their exclusivity gave them an additional appeal. As I had negotiated with my mother, I got my own suit for free. It was a small, but powerful success.

That experience taught me about importing, shipping costs, and sales. Because I had been on a couple of age-group teams at the national level and was a good swimmer, I also noticed that others started to follow what I wore. I couldn't afford an on-deck tracksuit, so I wore torn, beat-up, loose jeans, and graphic T-shirts. That ensemble was emulated and soon became standard swim meet gear. Nike later realized the power of tastemaker athletes and changed the sports business model with sponsorships.

The 100–Metre Backstroke

I believe every person has ten moments or decisions in their life that stay with them and affect who they become. For me, one of these moments happened at a swim meet when I was ten. Although I had a naturally athletic build, I was a very mediocre swimmer overall. I hadn't done anything spectacular in my age-group.

Anyway, at this swim meet, just as I was getting ready for the 100-metre backstroke, my dad came over to me and said, "Chip, I've got this theory . . ."

It wasn't unusual to hear this—my dad had many theories about vitamins, nutrition, and athletics, long before the wellness movement became popular. My dad also believed pain was all in the mind. As such, the mind could learn to control that pain and harness it for beneficial training and competing.

In athletics in 1965, the prevailing theory of how to approach a competition or meet, was to save your energy until the end and make sure you looked good at the finish line. "Let's try something different," my dad said. "Why don't you just go full out from the start, instead of saving it up and looking good at the finish? If you collapse or start to drown, I'll come and get you right away, but instead of thinking it's a 100-metre race, think of it more like it's 25 metres. Just a one-length sprint and take it one length at a time and go for it."

I went with his theory and ended up breaking a Canadian record, finishing the race eight or nine seconds below my previous time. We had to do the race again the next day because the officials thought it had been a mistake with the clock, but I did it the same way again, and it worked just as well the second time.

This event changed the way I approached life. Since then, I've noticed that most people never give 100 percent in their business, or their commitments, or their relationships. They always leave a little in reserve, even for things that don't have a final sprint at the end. They're afraid that overexerting, taking risks, overcommitting, will make them fail. Since that race, I've been afraid I would fail because I didn't give something my all. This mindset—Dad's "poolside theory"—has served me well, and I can trace it back to that day.

Beyond that, it also set up my relationship with goals. Youth athletic records for swimming at that time were kept for ages 10 and under, 11–12, and 13–14. Having set the record while still in the youngest division, I knew exactly what the next record was and by what date I had to beat it. I didn't have the vocabulary for it at the time, but setting, attempting, succeeding, and even failing at setting these records built a pattern for me that drove my success later in life.

Discovering My "Act"

With three of us growing and swimming, we were also burning an astronomical number of calories. The practical side of this hit hard after my parents' inevitable divorce (I was thirteen at the time). Once the divorce was final, my dad basically had to fund *two* households on his small income as a phys-ed teacher.

I came home for lunch one day, and there was nothing in the fridge. My mom was away working one of her many odd jobs, but her family allowance cheque had come in the mail.

So, I forged her signature on the cheque, cashed it at Safeway, bought groceries, came home, and ate.

From this situation, I (or at least my subconscious child) learned that I couldn't count on anybody else in my life to take care of me, including those who loved me. I had to be self-sufficient if was to survive.

As I got older, my self-sufficiency appeared whenever I perceived myself to be in any situation where my survival was threatened. When I would find myself in tight spots in business or relationships, I would often shun everybody around me and think, "I'll fix this by myself, I can't count on anyone to help me." I came to the immature conclusion that there wasn't much point in asking others for help.

With my first company, Westbeach, I believed I could never go on vacation or take days off, and that I had to be in on every single move and decision. I would make a lot of mistakes trying to do it all on my own and not recognizing that people are capable and love to help someone who's passionate and hard-working.

Later in my life, through the Landmark Forum self-development course, I would learn how every person develops an "Act." An Act is learned early in life when a child faces a perceived moment of survival and develops a strategy to help them survive the situation. For the balance of a person's life, their Act—effective or not—subconsciously kicks in whenever the person perceives themselves to be in a threatened position.

Changing Circumstances

It's counterintuitive, but looking back, I think my parents' divorce was a turn of good luck for me and my siblings. Despite his roots as an Albertan (a province known for its oil business conservatism), my dad was very much a hippie at heart.

He wanted someone who would be a partner and talk with him about everything. My mom, on the other hand, wanted to take care of the house and wanted to defer most of the decision-making and leadership to her husband.

My parents just weren't suited to each other, but after they split, they both married people who turned out to be their perfect partners.

Remarriage also changed my parents' respective financial situations. My mom married an intellectual geologist named Frank Conrad. Our living situation changed dramatically. We moved from Lakeview to the upper-class neighbourhood of Mount Royal in Calgary. The neighbouring families were all well-off, but they also had a strong work ethic. I learned a lot from the parents of my new friends. And, I found those friends and their parents welcomed me with open arms.

My dad, meanwhile, married a woman named Cathy Lyness, who worked as a flight attendant with Air Canada. This worked out to be an amazing opportunity. As family members, my siblings and I were entitled to five free trips per year anywhere in the world, to be used until we were age twenty-five, if we were still in school.

Before I turned twenty-five, I would take the opportunity to travel the world. By the age of twenty-five, in 1980, I might have been the most well-travelled person of my age, anywhere.

The Purple Shirt

When I was maybe thirteen or fourteen, I went on a date with a girl who came from the small cow town of Stettler, Alberta. I had bought a very cool Jimi Hendrix–style purple shirt, a preview of what would become a lifelong love of design and fashion. But, when I went to meet her at her house, she looked at the shirt, and my adolescent brain interpreted her facial expression as, "Wow, *ugly*."

The two of us went to a party at a schoolmate's house, and it didn't get any better from there. It seemed everyone was making fun of my shirt. That had a profound effect on me—for the rest of my life, I never bought another purple shirt. As I aged, I had more bad experiences with many other shirt colours. Eventually, I would visit a store to buy a shirt and, although there were ten colours, I would only really have a choice between white and white—which is no choice at all. I believe we do this with cars, shoes, business processes, and even spouses.

We all have experiences in our past that cut us off from our future potential. This is something my personal development has helped me better understand. Our past experiences subconsciously confine what we believe is possible in life. If something didn't work when I was thirteen, it doesn't mean it won't work at another time in my life.

Imagine if I had been in a car accident at age thirty and suffered complete amnesia. With no memory of my past and $100 to buy a shirt, I would have free choice of all colours, including purple. The point is, later in life, once I became able to understand how to free myself from past experiences, I gained the ability to embrace a future with a variety of choices, leading to multiple new ideas. My past stopped confining and defining my future. This realization was life-changing for me.

First Forays into Mindfulness

The second instructive event from my youth was my introduction to mindfulness as a discipline.

This initially had more to do with my dad than it did for me. I would never say I am like Steve Jobs, but my dad was. Like Jobs, my dad had the weird diets, communes, yoga, gestalt psychology, and the like, down to an art form. He was always looking for the meaning of life, but was also determined not to find it—if he did, he was worried his life would no longer have a purpose.

By the early 1970s, my dad travelled to San Francisco and took an Erhard Seminar Training (EST) course, which was the precursor to the Landmark course. I remember my dad returning from the course and telling me he'd discovered the meaning of life. "It's living in the moment," he said.

At the time, I thought my father was a bit of a nutcase.

Just before my dad could legally retire from teaching, he phoned in permanently sick and moved to California to become an assistant gardener at the Esalen Institute. Esalen is a nonprofit retreat centre founded by a pair of Stanford graduates in the early 1960s. Numerous human potential practises—including meditation, yoga, and alternative medicine—have been explored at Esalen since its inception. During his time there, my dad even went into seclusion and did a lot of soul-searching. If you saw the last scene in the series finale of *Mad Men*, you saw Esalen.

Imagine me, at age sixteen, rolling my eyes, wondering why my dad was into all this weird stuff. Of course, I did not understand at that time how much mindfulness and Esalen-style teachings would become a big part of my own life.

Esalen seemed to have a new context for health and the health care system. For example, if a person had an illness in the kidneys, a doctor would usually prescribe a solution to fix the kidneys. At Esalen, however, they were asking, "Why did the kidney get sick in the first place?" This context would set me up for the foundation of lululemon's personal development in 1998.

Meanwhile, I reflected on the ridiculous number of lengths I swam each day while looking at nothing but a black line at the bottom of the pool. Using the lessons my dad had taught me, I coped with physical pain by taking my mind away, while my body took itself beyond its limit. In retrospect, this was Mindfulness 101. I now understand those twice-daily workouts taught me how to be *present*.

The runner's high is a sensation that occurs after thirty-five minutes of a sustained, high-rate heartbeat. The brain releases hormones which take the athlete into an energized mental and physical space. The sensation usually lasts for about four hours. The amazing thing about an athlete's high: the person's past disappears and becomes irrelevant.

During that high, as the past becomes blank, so too does the future. We can only think of the future based on what we know from our past. When we don't focus on the past, and the future is eliminated, all that is left is the present. The present is where all life really occurs. This was the origin of "The meaning of life may be living in the moment," which became a key part of lululemon's manifesto (more on that later). I have my eccentric father to thank for introducing me to it.

CHAPTER 2:
THE SEVENTIES

There is no performance without action.

Thank God for Swimming

In 1972, at the age of sixteen, I graduated from high school. I was able to graduate early because I had skipped the second grade. Even after skipping a grade, I was always the biggest kid in my class. But I was also a mediocre student. People seemed to expect more out of me socially than I could deliver. I remember a group of guys coming up behind me and saying, "Big like bull, dumb as a refrigerator." I now know that every child has their insecure moments, but it didn't feel like that then. My insecurity manifested as my inability to be social at school.

That's why I thank God for swimming. Fifty percent of the swimmers were girls, who became my absolute best friends—even surrogate family members. Through competition, we lived and travelled with each other for years. Some of the girls I swam with went on to become Olympic athletes. Our coach, Ted Thomas, became Canada's Olympic swimming coach.

What I knew of female drive and competitiveness came from these swimming friendships. One thing that struck me was the girls' constant complaints about their swim suits, of strap location and rashes that developed under their armpits from thousands of stroke rotations. The girls were always coming up with new ideas for strap designs, but there was never anyone at Speedo to whom to give these ideas.

When the time came to move to university, I had a couple of swimming scholarships to consider. These were critical because my parents had no money to contribute. By that point, I'd reached a turning point in my time as a swimmer. I was six foot three and about 220 pounds—150 percent the size of an average swimmer at that time. I learned that it meant I was a sprinter.

Competitive swimming had for a long time been mainly 50- and 100-metre events but was now changing to consist mostly of 200-metre and 400-metre events, especially in the lead-up to the 1976 Olympics. Without enough events for a sprinter being offered, I knew my competitive swimming career was ending.

There was also a big part of me that didn't want to be told what to do anymore, having spent much of my life in a highly structured training routine. I decided not to go with the scholarships.

University of Alberta

I went to the University of Alberta, in Edmonton, 200 miles away. Far enough away from my parents for independence, but not so far away that I couldn't get my laundry done and have a home-cooked meal every now and again.

Once I started at the university, I played football. I still swam, although the swimming was on my own terms now. At the varsity level, swimming and football were an unusual combination of sports. I'd go into the football season in

August weighing 240 pounds. Football season ended in November. By February, I would have to be trimmed down to 190 pounds to be ready for the swimming nationals. Once the nationals had finished, I'd have to lift weights and eat like crazy to bulk up to my football weight. But that's what you can do with your body when you're eighteen years old.

My major at university started off in science electives because I loved biology. For a time, I thought I might pursue a career as an ocean marine biologist at Scripps in San Diego. Unfortunately, it didn't take me long to realize there was no way I could afford to study at Scripps.

The Pipeline in Alaska

When I was close to the end of my second year at the University of Alberta, I realized that I had no passion for anything outside of athletics. I didn't know what I would do with the rest of my life. Then one day I was at the Edmonton Airport, coming back from Calgary, and I ran into the mother of a friend. We struck up a conversation.

"I'm going up to Alaska," she told me. "My husband is a project manager on one of the five sections of the Alaska oil pipeline. Too bad you're not American," she added, "or you could go up and work there if you were interested."

The Alaska pipeline was an 800-mile steel pipe through the heart of America's last untouched wilderness. It was one of the biggest and most expensive private enterprises in global history. It was also something I'd never thought of before, and, unbeknownst to my friend's mother, I *was* American, at least in the sense of my dual citizenship.

The day after my second year of university ended, I found myself on a plane headed for Alaska. I got to customs in Fairbanks, thought about it, and decided to tell the US border agent I was Canadian. The agent went through my bag, and it was all construction workwear, safety boots, and the like.

"I think you're coming here to work and to take an American's job, so I won't let you in," he said to me.

This was a problem. I had no money to fly back. All I had was my dual citizenship. So, I tried again, this time telling the agent I was coming into Alaska as an American.

"Great," the agent said. "Step across." I did as I was told and stepped over the line into American territory. "Report to your draft board first thing tomorrow morning," he added.

Oh God, I thought. This is precisely what I had been trying to avoid when I told the border agent I was Canadian. This was the mid-1970s, just after the end of the Vietnam War, and I did not understand where I might end up if I reported to the draft board. So, I never reported to the draft board.

A couple of weeks later, I was working on the pipeline. Much of it was hard labour in deep cold. The camp, consisting of about 200 to 800 men, was in the middle of nowhere, several hours east of Fairbanks. I often worked as a high-rigger, which meant climbing to the top of a crane to connect it to another crane in -30°C temperatures.

For my last year, I worked way out at a junction in the pipeline, monitoring a fan to make sure it didn't run out of gas. This task led to long, long days, with nothing much to do but read—I'll come back to that.

Life in the base camp was good, almost too good. Alaska, like Calgary, was going through an oil boom. That meant we had steak and snow crab nearly every night, movies to watch, and many other distractions—not all of them healthy. I worked with men mostly from the deep south; even today, if under the influence of a couple of beers, I have a decent Okie accent.

There was also a man in his fifties named Billy O'Callaghan, an unrepentant Irish alcoholic whose only goal was to eventually die in the arms of a sixteen-year-old at the Mustang Ranch in Las Vegas (this was an era when there was no political correctness). Billy kind of took me under his wing, and whenever I did something correctly—some task, repair, work, or whatever—Billy would say, "Fine as wine, partner, fine as wine."

Billy's motto, *fine as wine*, stuck with me after that and became something I mentally connected with quality craftsmanship.

I didn't plan on being there for two years. At first, I thought it would just be for the summer, then I'd go back to school come the fall. On the other hand, I'd only made $3.50 an hour in Calgary doing various odd jobs. While on the pipeline, I was making $13.50 an hour. I was also pulling eighteen-hour days, seven days a week, since there wasn't much else to do. Anything over eight hours was double-time. Triple-time on holidays and Sundays. My first three days I made $600 working a holiday weekend—which was more money than I would've made all summer back in Calgary.

Besides the money, there was another experience that would shape me in later life. In the base camp, I was surrounded by a lot of drugs and alcohol, and a lot of men going through hard phases in their lives. I didn't like the drinking and the drugs all that much, so I stayed away from them.

The Top One Hundred Novels

Around that same time, my mom sent me an article from the *New York Times*. (I believe the author was named Art Buchwald). The article drew connections between the human body and athletics, and how the brain was affected. There was research showing the brain improved from mental gymnastics in the same way the body improved from athletic conditioning—say, from swimming drills, for example.

You had to train the brain, Buchwald suggested, as you would train your muscles, for it to work at full capacity. Even as a nineteen-year-old, I understood this clearly. For 1975, this was radical thinking.

I could use my time in Alaska to not only earn money but to train my brain as well. So, I stopped smoking marijuana and brought my teenage drinking to an end. I set myself a goal of reading a novel a day. There was more than enough time in which to do it.

I started off with a list of the top one hundred books of all time that I had seen in a newspaper. This undertaking made me likely one of the best-read nineteen-year-olds in the world. Two books, in particular, stood out: *Catch-22* by Joseph Heller, a comedy about living in the moment, and *Atlas Shrugged*, by Ayn Rand.

(Full disclosure: I could not get through James Joyce's *Ulysses*. Also, as I hope becomes clear throughout this book, I wish I'd had a chance to read Sun Tzu's *Art of War* and Machiavelli's *The Prince* while in Alaska.)

Atlas Shrugged is about a lot of things, but to put it most simply, it tells the story of a few visionary innovators on a quest to become great people and to produce a great product. There's Dagny Taggart, the professional woman in her early thirties who keeps her family's railroad empire running (despite her brother's incompetence). There's Dagny's love interest, industrialist Hank Rearden, who invents a new metal alloy stronger than steel, and who must overcome the schemes of politicians and relatives who, unable to create greatness of their own, suck the life out of Hank.

Then there's John Galt, the mysterious engineer and philosopher who remains mostly unidentified through much of the story. The question "Who is John Galt?" is a major recurring theme in *Atlas Shrugged* and is a phrase that has since become a cultural touchstone of its own.

Atlas Shrugged was my first major introduction to the idea of elevating the world from mediocrity to greatness through individual creativity, dedication, and vision. I did not understand then what kind of a theme this would be for me in the years to come.

Atlas Shrugged also brought into focus the many inefficiencies of the unionized labour system. I had a union job on the pipeline—which was exactly why I had so much time to read. But there were times in Alaska when I saw a simple task being performed by three people because the union required one guy to drive a machine, a different guy to flip a switch, and a third guy to make sure the machine didn't run out of gas.

There was no room for innovation or individuality. I saw socialism at its worst. I saw union bosses ensuring work was mediocre, so the company could hire more people, so the union could collect more dues. I saw an underside of lazy people who would rather strike than work. And then there were the people who wanted others to create, invent, and risk, and still pay the union workers untold amounts for mediocre work.

This was a valuable lesson as a young man because finding out what I wanted in life was sometimes distinguished by finding out what I *didn't* want—another concept I wouldn't fully understand for several more years.

At any rate, I was saving money, and I was focused on training and developing my brain. It occurred to me to start laying out some goals for the years to come, knowing I would not stay in Alaska forever.

For one thing, I recognized that my work on the pipeline was me trading my life for money. I was working eighteen-hour days, not meeting any girls, not experiencing the things my friends were doing, and not playing sports. I wasn't living in a city—I was in a camp with two hundred other men, getting up in the morning in sub zero weather and going to work and back, day in and day out.

Swimming had given me a decade of goal-setting experience. For each age group, there was a definable record time I had to beat, and I had to beat it by my birthday, before moving into the next age group.

Looking further into the future, I set the goal of owning my own house by twenty, running my own business by age thirty, and being retired by forty (meaning I would be 100 percent in control of my whole life). Running my own business was in my blood because I was creative, stubborn, stupid, and unstoppable. At the very least it would mean I wasn't trading my life for money on someone else's terms.

This might seem like the daydreams of a nineteen-year-old working in the middle of nowhere, making good money for the first time in his life, but to me, my goals were a serious, authentic way of envisioning the years to come.

Back to Civilization

I left the pipeline almost eighteen months after I'd arrived, and by then I'd made about $150,000 (over $600,000 in today's money).[1] With the opportunity to earn that kind of money, it's natural to wonder why I didn't stay in Alaska longer.

The reality is, I was grinding my teeth. Plus, the longer I stayed on the pipeline, the longer it would take me to reintegrate into society. I had to learn not to swear with every second word, and I didn't know how to have a conversation without bringing up some pipeline story.

I recognized it took many—if not most—other people to work until they were forty to earn a nest egg like the one I had. If I could start off at nineteen or twenty with that amount of money, what could my life be like? I found that question

1. "Value of $200,000 in 1976," Inflation Calculator, Saving.org, accessed August 16, 2018, https://www.saving.org/inflation/inflation.php?amount =200,000&year=1976.

fascinating back then and still do now. If everybody in this world was given what I had and didn't have to work until they were forty to get it, would they later have the same successes, as I did? Was I really anyone special in this whole thing, or was I just lucky to have met that woman at the airport who'd turned me on to the job on the pipeline?

Meanwhile, I'd achieved one of my goals—I'd bought a house, sight unseen.

The house had three suites. Even though I had money in the bank, I took out a mortgage at 19 percent, not yet understanding how I should have paid that mortgage off with my money in the bank that was collecting 3 percent interest. My first lesson in cash flow. I was a homeowner, and I was only nineteen. All I needed to do now was find some tenants.

Leaving the pipeline camp was as big a day as I could imagine. It was like driving home from the hospital with your first child. I drove to Fairbanks and got on a plane to fly home. Most of the other men there would work eight weeks and then take two weeks off and go home for a visit, but I'd worked for eighteen months, often eighteen-hour days, with only a few days off. The only way I could keep myself motivated was knowing every hour I worked would mean I could stay two days in a bed-and-breakfast on Accra Beach in Barbados.

Back in Calgary, the first thing I did was to inspect my new house. I soon found myself looking at one of the ugliest, oldest buildings I'd ever seen—an original farmhouse now in the middle of the city. The house was on a hill and had great views of the surrounding city, but the views and a small stand of fruit trees (some of the only fruit trees in the city) were the only things the house had going for it.

I've always been a very nonmaterialistic person, but I also love quality. In 1976, it was not American quality that impressed me, but German or Japanese. On my return to Calgary, as soon as I'd realized the house I'd purchased was anything but quality, I bought a Mercedes-Benz as a present to myself. At the time, there were very few Mercedes in Canada, but those vehicles were the epitome of the quality with which I wanted to surround myself.

Now I found myself with these two possessions. Both were a lesson in business. My house was basically falling down, costing me massive amounts in cash flow just to keep it standing. And then, I had this beautiful car. Despite the high-quality nature of the car, any time one little thing went wrong with it, the dealership would have to fly in a piece from Germany, costing me hundreds and hundreds of dollars for some routine repair.

From then on, I only wanted to buy cars I knew were reliable, would seldom break down, and wouldn't cost much to run. A Honda Civic, for example. I also promised myself I would only buy houses I knew were built with solid craftsmanship. I would always make sure the windows were double-paned to keep winter heating expenses down.

A short-term tenant at my house was Frank Troughton, a new friend I'd made on my return to the university football team. Frank was twenty-one and newly divorced.

"Chip didn't really have a penchant for football," says Frank, "because as big and as strong as he was, he just wasn't mean enough to be a football player. He was stubborn, but also incredibly easygoing. He was a tall, blonde surfer who walked around Calgary in shorts, flip-flops, and no shirt once the temperature got above freezing. I always knew Chip was a little bit different. He was the entrepreneurial type, and I was sure he'd find his way in life."

Frank also has one especially funny recollection that sums up our life in that place.

1964 *Me in my natural habitat*

1961 *Father*

1959 *Mother*

1975 *Sitting in the pipeline*

DO ONE THING A DAY THAT SCARES YOU

1975 *Somewhere deep in the middle of nowhere, Alaska—see I did have hair!*

I was actually living at the house Chip had bought with the money he'd earned up on the pipeline. I was working security at a bar downtown during Stampede Rodeo Week. Well, I was a bit of a wild man back then, and I ended up getting into a confrontation with a couple of biker guys. I must have pissed them off good because they followed me back to Chip's place and let me know that they'd be back with a bunch of guys from their gang.

The bikers took off, and I ran upstairs to wake Chip up—it was around 3 a.m. by this point. I said: 'Hey, we have to get prepared. We're going to have a situation on our hands here.' I grabbed my shotgun and went downstairs to the porch. There was Chip walking around the house, stark naked, brandishing a golf club. This is how he would greet a motorcycle gang that was ready to unleash hell.

The situation was serious enough that a SWAT team was dispatched to the scene and, as luck would have it, those guys arrived at around the same time as the bikers. And there's Chip, still naked, a golf club in his hands, ready to go down swinging.

When I look back on my early life, I feel like the luckiest guy in the world. As things turned out, I lived in that house until 1985. Still, these events were just preparing me for the next phase of my life.

CHAPTER 3:
FINE AS WINE

On my tombstone I want it to say: "All used up." —Werner Erhard

Finishing University

As I moved through 1976 and finished my second year in business school, the faculty politely suggested that, perhaps, business school was not for me. I couldn't pass accounting.

By then, I was so tired of school I took the easiest courses I could just to finish quickly. Despite my struggles with accounting, I majored in economics and got near perfect marks with little effort. I was a creative business student, and economics is an art. It is a subject in which there is never a right answer, so I succeeded. Economics seemed a relatively easy way to bullshit my way through. I concluded that everyone should take the easiest courses they could because what comes easiest will ultimately be the most fulfilling in life.

Having transferred to the University of Calgary, I played football (a sport in which I was mediocre), wrestled (quite poorly), and swam (only on relay teams). In 1979, after a two-week stint with the local pro football team, I quit to learn how to distance run and to get my 250 pounds down to 210.

I graduated in 1979, seven years after I'd started university. I hadn't blown all my Alaska money just yet. There was one more thing I would spend a lot of money on.

Chip Wilson, Global Person

I still had five free airline tickets anywhere in the world each year. I took full advantage of the opportunity. Although the tickets were free, I spent a lot of money on the trips outside of airfare.

I was very fortunate to have seen as much of the world as I could by my early twenties. On one trip, I had a four-hour layover in Rio while on my way to Cape Town, South Africa. I got off the plane, walked around, and within an hour I had decided Cape Town could wait, maybe indefinitely. At that moment, Rio seemed like the most fantastic place in the world.

It helped, I suppose, that it was New Year's Eve. I knew nothing about places with names like Copacabana or Ipanema, but everywhere I looked the Brazilians were dressed up in their best. I loved the Latin flair of the culture and how everybody was so expressive, especially when I contrasted Rio against the conservatism of North America.

On another trip, I went to Barbados. I finished my last exam and got on a plane the next day. I told no one I was going. In all these travels, I learned how small the world was. Imagine getting on a plane and going anywhere.

It was 3:00 a.m. on my fourth day in Barbados, and I was at a disco called Alexandria's. After a few drinks, I turned around and saw someone that looked like my dad. I went up to the man, thinking that perhaps every person really did have a doppelganger, and asked, "Are you my dad?"

He replied, rather matter-of-factly, "Yes," then asked me if I wanted to go surfing the next day.

I laughed and politely declined. The last place that I had ever wanted to meet my dad's doppelganger was in a disco in the Caribbean, so we went our separate ways. The moment was surreal.

Toward the end of 1979, my university days were finished, and my free travel perks had come to an end. I had about $85,000 left in the bank and was thinking about what was next.

California Wrap Shorts

As with many other things in my life, the answer turned out to be in California.

In the fall of 1979, on a trip to visit my grandmother in San Diego, I noticed Ocean Pacific (OP) making men's surf shorts in corduroy for men to wear when not surfing. At the same time, I saw girls wearing wrap shorts that were tied on one side, then brought up underneath and tied again in the back. They came in bright, bold colours and patterns, often safari- or Hawaiian-printed fabrics.

From what I knew about sewing and tailoring—from watching my mother over the years—I noticed how simple, comfortable, and functional these shorts were.

Since I visited California annually, I knew this was a new style. I knew the critical mass of people and trends in California had a way of eventually influencing what people would wear everywhere else. I brought a pair of the shorts back to Calgary as a present to my then-girlfriend, Cindy Wilson (no relation).

I showed her the wrap shorts from California, and she loved them. So did her friends. This was the first positive sign of the demand for the shorts.

My initial thought was for us to make them ourselves. The pattern seemed simple enough, and Cindy and I had learned a thing or two about sewing from our mothers, such as making the first pattern from newsprint. It turned out I'd overestimated my abilities somewhat, and even though I sewed a few pairs after I'd cut the pattern, I don't think anyone would have wanted to wear them.

I reflected on my mom's hobby. I believed there had to be other great seamstresses like her that would love to make extra money. I put an ad in the newspaper and quickly got replies from perhaps a dozen women. This was an encouraging response, but I wanted to narrow the field further, so I could ensure high-quality work.

To do this, we cut bolts of fabric—all of it 100 percent cotton and brightly flowered or otherwise boldly patterned—and delivered the fabric to each seamstress who'd answered ads. I asked them to make ten of the wrap shorts. From there I narrowed it down to the five who did good work.

Of those five, one woman produced significantly more than the other four. Her name was Josephine Terratiano. Josephine, a wonderful Italian woman, was sharing the work with her relatives, who, like her, were all highly-skilled couture tailors. This became my own Italian connection.

As my mother, her husband, and my sister and brother had moved back to the States, and my dad spent more time at the Esalen Institute in Big Sur, the Terratianos became almost a second family to me.

"My mom was a seamstress, and my sisters were seamstresses," Josephine recalls, "but my only profession is sewing. I did all my sewing with all my heart. And Chip, he was lucky to find me!"

Josephine and her sisters made about 300 pairs of the shorts, and I branded them *Fine as Wine* as a nod to Billy

O'Callaghan, my old mentor on the pipeline. After Cindy and I sold the shorts to her friends, I took them to the major department stores in Calgary to see if they might be interested in selling them.

Nobody seemed to believe these shorts were viable or sellable on any level.

This was my first inventory problem. Lots of product and nowhere to sell, but I was confident if I could get past the store buyers, people would want the product. The idea was to get people living a kilometre above sea-level and a twelve-hour drive from the West Coast excited about Southern California-inspired surfwear. I couldn't do it by selling wholesale to big department stores. That meant I would have to figure out how to get out of this inventory mess myself.

The more I considered the problem, the more I came back to one of the most basic sales concepts I could imagine—a lemonade stand!

The plan was simple. A nice-looking wooden booth and a three-month summertime lease in downtown Calgary. That was my plan to sell my stock of shorts and the genesis of a sophisticated vertical retail business. Cindy would work the booth all week. We would both work on weekends.

Assessing Career Options

A few months after making 300 pairs of shorts and graduating from university, I'd received a letter from London Life Insurance, one of the biggest insurance companies in Canada. It was a wonderful letter, full of compliments. Apparently, these people knew who I was from my varsity sports.

"We have been following you and your esteemed athletic career at university, and we feel you'd be a great employee at London Life," they told me. Here was one option.

I called London Life, and they invited me for an interview. When I arrived, I noticed how everyone was very prim and proper. The Calgary formal look: a Prada suit with alligator cowboy boots. But anyone who knew me back then knew all I ever wore were shorts and sandals, even through the winter. That was how I dressed for the interview. I'd been so enamoured by their letter, I thought they knew me on some personal, intimate level—enough to know how I liked to dress.

In reality, London Life's initial correspondence with me was more of a form letter, made to sound intimate and personal. They didn't know me at all. I did not get the job at London Life.

I then applied for a job at Dome Petroleum, a Calgary-based oil and gas company. I wore a suit. With my economics degree in hand, Dome hired me on as a Landman. I remember getting dressed in a suit in front of the mirror and saying to myself, "Halloween, every day."

Working as a Landman meant negotiating mineral rights, exploration rights, and various business agreements. I worked on the thirtieth floor of the Dome Tower in downtown Calgary, and my salary was about $30,000 a year—good money for a boy of twenty-five. I was terrible at my job, and I apologize to anyone with whom I had to work.

I had one of the first female managers in the oil business, and she was great, but I wasn't the right putty out of which to make a decent employee. I was sent to many courses, but I couldn't pay attention because my own mind was too busy. My mind was muddled with fundamental questions of life. Would I ever get married? Could I get a date for Friday night? Would I have enough money to retire? Would I ever have children? Could I pay for a family? What would happen if I got sick? Etc.

These were not courses that developed my maturity. I

couldn't pile on work development courses until I had myself figured out.

Shortly after I started at Dome, I met a guy named Scott Sibley, who had just come to Dome through a merger. We'd both been at the University of Alberta at the same time. Some of Scott's closest friends had been on the football team with me. We figured we must have been at dozens of house parties together (as I recall, Scott would have a cocktail in his hand and a girl on his arm, while I would have a litre of milk in mine and no girl), but we'd never formally met.

As much as I knew my job at Dome was a good one, I knew I was looking at the same trap I'd experienced on the pipeline in Alaska—trading my life for money. The goal of working for myself by age thirty gave me a tangible sense of something to work toward, particularly with Fine as Wine (now renamed Westbeach) just getting off the ground.

The name, *Westbeach*, was derived from my subconscious need to get back to the West Coast. My childhood on Ocean Beach in San Diego had imprinted a feeling in me that I was trying to recreate in the prairie city of Calgary.

The Triathlon

Throughout the same period, in the spring and summer of 1980, I had become interested in triathlons.

There were a few ways I'd come across the idea of doing a triathlon. As a competitive swimmer, the 2.4-mile swim was easy, since that was the distance swimmers swam to warm up for a workout. I'd also recently taken up cycling, as I found the act of pulling up with foot cages on the pedals fixed the back injuries I'd sustained from playing football. So, I was already regularly doing two of the three main exercises that compose a triathlon.

I was also looking for a new physical challenge. Through

swimming I'd come to believe my mind had ultimate power over my body—but what about something I hadn't tried? Something like the Ironman? The first Ironman was held in Hawaii in 1978. Since so few people had done it, there was really no context, no collective understanding of what it demanded. I may as well have said I wanted to run across the Gobi Desert.

However, I believed if I could do an Ironman at fifty pounds heavier than average, I could train my brain to believe that anything is possible. Knowing you can achieve what seems impossible is one of the most significant things someone can derive from athletic activity.

No one had figured out how to make clothing for triathletes. The average time to complete a short triathlon was a couple of hours. For the Ironman, it was about nine to ten hours, or thirteen hours in my case. Either way, it was a lot of time. Transitioning out of salt water, if the seams inside an athlete's apparel were off a little bit, or if there was any rubbing or chafing, it would be a pain more painful than the race itself.

I spent a little time and money designing a Lycra garment with the seams moved away from the inner thighs and from under the arms. The result was a pair of shorts with a look, feel, and function that had never before existed. I was excited by the technical achievement of these shorts. This design appealed to me in a far more creative way than the wrap shorts we'd made for Westbeach since those wrap shorts didn't solve a functional problem of any kind.

Unfortunately, I was eight years ahead of the mainstream popularity of the triathlon movement. There just weren't enough people participating in the sport to make the demand worthwhile—not yet, anyway. I sold the shorts wholesale to a few cycling shops, but the experiment went no further.

Still, I couldn't ignore that deep-seated, creative satisfaction I'd felt from designing and producing a high-quality, technical garment. This was a passion that would drive me with Westbeach when we eventually moved on from surfing to skateboarding and then to snowboarding gear, and it would move to the forefront with lululemon, still two decades away.

The First Season in Business

At last, Cindy and I opened our booth when spring arrived. It didn't take long to see how high the demand was. The incredible thing about the first season at the booth was seeing how people actually wanted to buy our product. It excited them.

Fortunately, the Dome Oil Tower was across the street from our booth. At the end of the day, I would collect the cash, go buy fabric and take it to the other end of the city to the seamstresses and tailors. I would then go for a ninety-minute swim, eat all I could, and go to bed. In the morning, I would wake up early and go for a two-hour bike ride, then go to the other side of the city to pick up finished goods from Josephine and deliver them to the store. I would then skateboard into work in my suit and run a 10k at lunch.

Those days of starting a business and training for a triathlon were wonderful and energizing. I loved it all.

CHAPTER 4:
LESSONS LEARNED

The founder of Spotify says, in his experience, every company has three near-death experiences before a successful platform for success is created.

Discovering Vertical Retail

Before our first season, many people told me I was making a huge mistake by opening my own lemonade-stand-store—as modest as it was—in the outdoor 8th Avenue Mall. I kept hearing that the clothing business was tough. But, to me, it seemed simple. I bought the fabric, I oversaw the production of the garments, I brought them to the booth, and when Cindy wasn't available, I did the selling myself.

What I didn't realize at the time is that I was inventing vertical retailing.

Because I had my own stores, my margins (something about which I was just learning) must have been huge, but there was no vertical model with which to compare it. The whole process seemed so simple. I got paid every day instead of waiting for wholesale payments to come sixty days after shipping.

However, I still had a wide variety of costs to deal with on my own. The booth and the labour, for starters, but also the production.

My economics degree finally came to some use. I knew a profitable business would need critical mass and economy-of-scale production. Unless I could make a minimum of 500 to 2,000 units of a style at a time, I couldn't get the production price low enough to resell and make a profit. It didn't matter if I made any money because I knew I was in it for the long-run. I needed to learn everything about business I didn't yet know. In life, there's no performance without action.

The Bank Is in a Lot of Trouble

In 1980, at the end of our first summer, Cindy went off to university (she was studying architecture at the University of British Columbia), and I closed the booth for winter and planned for the next season. We'd made a little money, about $5,500, that season.

I needed to buy about $20,000 of fabric for next season's production. I was continuing to loan money from my oil job to Westbeach, and I knew that if I spent all my money on fabric, it would leave me unable to pay our sewing costs—one of Westbeach's first production challenges.

In search of a solution, I went to Josephine Terratiano and asked her to do the sewing over the winter, with a promise to pay her come the following summer once that inventory sold. This was a big thing to ask. It hinged on authenticity, trust, and the sense of family I'd developed with Josephine—the personal aspects of a business relationship that can't always be captured by formal agreements.

However, it was also advantageous for Josephine because I could purchase double the fabric and she got to sew twice as much as I otherwise would've been able to buy, which meant she was due twice as much money when the time came to pay her. Ultimately, it was beneficial for both parties.

Meanwhile, as we moved through fall and into winter, I continued at Dome. Here I was sitting up in the Dome Tower on the thirtieth floor, working on multimillion-dollar contracts, with the little Westbeach booth closed for the winter. Dome was a good job, but I stayed mindful of my goal to leave the company and be working for myself by age thirty, and the longer-range goal of retiring by forty.

Suddenly, in a flash, I saw my future life if I stayed at Dome. I would become a VP, I would be married, move to the suburbs, have a couple of kids, retire at sixty, become a serious cyclist, and then die. I said to myself, "Great, Chip, that's one life, and there is no point in living it again. Let's live a new life." I believed I had just gained 15,000 days of life.

My mother, having been a child of the Depression, was anxious. "When Chip went into business for himself, I was scared," she says. "I mean, I was scared for him because I didn't know where it would lead, but it taught me a lot of things. Going from the petroleum industry into the clothing business is a huge hurdle."

My dad puts it more bluntly: "I think Chip was kind of bored at Dome. I think he knew it wasn't the direction he wanted to go."

With Westbeach, I was always learning and challenged because I was encountering a brand-new situation every day of my life. I never knew what would happen next or what I would learn. Whereas, with being in business for someone else (in my case, Dome), there was always that fixed progression through the ranks, through the years, until you reach a prescribed end.

Dome Petroleum ended up as the largest bankruptcy in Canadian history. It was a company built on a deck of cards. I was a fortunate beneficiary as I spent two-and-a-half years with Dome when the company was in exponential growth and two-and-a-half years when the company was in bankruptcy, working under bank protection.

I promised myself I never wanted to owe banks money and be under their control. However, I loved a quote that came from the circumstances: "If you owe the bank $2 million and you can't pay up, you are in a lot of trouble. If you owe the bank $20 billion and you can't pay up, the bank is in a lot of trouble."

The Second Season in Business

As we moved into the spring of 1981, Westbeach underwent a small expansion. I added another lemonade-stand booth in Calgary and an outlet in Edmonton. The Edmonton location was a ski shop (this was the advent of the pop-up store concept we would later perfect at lululemon). The ski shop closed during summertime, which made it ideal for a seasonal retail venture like Westbeach.

That summer, having a booth only allowed customers to buy our stuff, not try it on. If we were going to continue to grow, we would need a store with change rooms. The demand was there. Westbeach was growing. We hadn't yet reached own critical production mass, but I had no doubt we had created something that didn't otherwise exist.

My partner, however, did not share this belief.

As the summer of 1981 ended, I said goodbye to Cindy as she headed back to school. We were about to embark on another year of a long-distance relationship. In those days, there was no email or internet to keep us connected. Long-distance phone calls were expensive, which made you constantly consider how much time you could afford to talk, and snail mail, even then, seemed slow and archaic.

The conditions were there for Cindy and me to grow in different directions, and we ended both our personal and business relationships. Separating the business part was messy; Cindy had not been involved in the accounting and didn't understand that Westbeach was worth negative $20,000 due to a personal loan I had provided.

The Third Season in Business

Despite the painful breakup with Cindy, my faith in the demand for Westbeach remained unshaken. I still believed I could be the best in the world at something. I was seeing a West Coast way of life manifesting itself into an athletic style far different from that of Europe or the East Coast. This style could be described as the *hoodie look* and is the genesis of the apparel worn by Silicon Valley techies. Still, the term *lifestyle clothing* had not yet been coined. Neither had the word *extreme* in the context of describing extreme sports.

Then, in the summer of 1982, I finally moved Westbeach into an actual storefront. The shop was formerly a 1970s upscale hippie store called The Strawberry Experiment, a well-known downtown Calgary retail location forty feet from where my booth had been. The previous store owner had poured a lot of money into the place, adding a glass floor over a fish tank, strobe lights, and shag carpeting—the works. I worked hard to enhance the unique, retro vibe of the place, to give customers a feeling they wouldn't get in other clothing stores.

On a trip to Mexico City, I had gone into a discount store that sold beautiful clothing. I bought $5,000 worth of clothing, brought it back to Calgary, and it sold out immediately. I went back again and bought $15,000 worth and turned it around with the same results. When I went back a third time, the store had shut down. Little did I know at the time, but I was buying Guess clothing when the brand was near its genesis and had huge brand pull. Guess was unavailable in Canada or the US, and women shoppers knew something I didn't. It was a great driver of people into our fledgling store.

I also hired two women, Kathy and Cathy, to cover the sales and management of the store. I'd met Kathy and Cathy when they were working at Calgary's first cappuccino café, a place called Bagels & Buns. It was on 17th Avenue, below the spot where my dad's family had lived in the 1940s.

I would go to this café every Saturday and Sunday to read newspapers and get the only cappuccino in town. As I watched the efficiency of Kathy and Cathy behind the counter, they struck me as some of the most amazing workers I'd ever seen. Highly responsible, smart, motivated, and great with customers.

Kathy and Cathy were exactly the people I wanted in Westbeach's new store. As a learning experience, hiring them gave me my first brush with interviewing, training, and developing employees. I had no training myself, and I could only pass on the little I knew of my business philosophy. There were no books to read from which to learn how to do vertical retailing. Wholesale was a much "safer" option to address overhead and many other operating costs.

One of these wholesale deals was with Scott Sibley, the guy I'd become friends with during my first few months at Dome. A year or so earlier, Scott had left Dome to start a business in Vancouver with a man named Richard Mellon.

"I followed my passion and headed out to the West Coast to get into the sailboat business," Scott explains.

Unfortunately for Scott and Richard, the small sailboat business at the time was going through a downturn. The market for parts was drying up. "To get some cash rolling through the company," says Scott, "we looked at adding soft goods. That was where Chip came in. We arranged it so he would send us a bunch of inventory—shorts and T-shirts—on consignment. With this new focus of soft goods, we changed the name of the store to California BC."

There was a huge demand for Westbeach apparel in Vancouver, and soon, California BC became my biggest wholesale customer.

The Shift in Men's Apparel

In 1982, there was about to be a major shift in men's apparel. This would take Westbeach to the next level. Standard men's shorts were tight, with a short inseam—no more than three inches. If you had a dime in the pocket of those shorts, someone could read the date through the fabric.

Meanwhile, I'd been making baggy shorts for myself, with a nine- or ten-inch inseam. For a man of my size, I preferred semi-loose, longer shorts, of the kind I'd seen on businessmen in Bermuda during my global travel. I'd also seen how Australian surf-inspired shorts and hoodies were emerging as casual clothing in California.

Then, by the early eighties, Quiksilver (who were making surfwear for actual surfers) made shorts with a small waist and a large bum and thigh ratio, which mirrored the physical build surfers tended to have from squatting. This was functional apparel, built for an athletic requirement.

Because shorts designed specifically for an athletic body looked so good, girls everywhere wanted their boyfriends to wear the same shorts. As with other trends, I sensed what was happening on the West Coast would make its way to the rest of the world. There was an opportunity here for me if I could figure out how to take advantage of it.

My first attempt came when I was visiting the Quiksilver warehouse in California. The general manager showed me some unsellable inventory of men's pants they'd brought in from Australia. The pants were made with wild patterned fabric that was popular in Australia, but for which Americans were too conservative.

I offered to buy a thousand pants for a dollar apiece. The Quiksilver GM accepted this offer, happy enough just to get rid of the pants. I shipped the pants back to Canada and had them cut into long shorts, then priced them at $45 each. They had the look of the surf shorts I thought would soon take over. Sure enough, the shorts sold out in a week.

Reversible Shorts

The fast-selling Quiksilver pants-turned-shorts proved that a market existed for long, colourful shorts. I created a new design by adopting Quiksilver's fit, which included a very low rise in the front and a high rise in the back. The low front rise meant the fabric wouldn't double over when crouching and the high back meant no plumber's butt. It was a massive innovation in athletic apparel. These modifications worked perfectly, but the next hurdle was finding Hawaiian-type patterned fabric to offset the old look of solid colours. I couldn't afford to buy the right fabric, not in the 2,000- or 3,000-metre volumes I needed to make money. If I couldn't buy the fabric, I had to think of an alternative.

As I considered the problem, I thought about my mother. Along with all the other sewing she did, she'd also always been good at quilting. This, I realized, was the solution. I went around to all the discount fabric stores, bought up all the discounted, brightly-coloured end rolls of fabric I could find, cut them into squares, and had the seamstress quilt them together.

"When Chip was a kid he used to help me put my quilts together, and he'd come into the sewing room, but I never thought those moments we had would turn into a career," my mother remembers.

The quilted fabrics gave me the crazy, bright look I wanted—but the shorts lacked stability since they were put together using multiple small pieces of material. The solution to this problem was to create a black cotton underlay.

As an unexpected side effect, the black underlay not only solved the stability problem, it also made the shorts reversible. You could have the wild patterns on one side, or you could turn them inside-out and have a pair of plain black shorts, all in one garment. This thinking was the genesis of how I looked at all future designs. I discovered that when a consumer understood a garment was reversible, they subconsciously recognized them as two-for-one and halved the price in their mind.

Finally, I designed the shorts to be big enough to fit me. From a functional, technical standpoint, I hated the skin-tightness of the men's shorts in style at the time. I wanted something in which I could move much more freely. I wanted to create an anti-ball-crushing garment (I perfected this with lululemon's menswear).

As Josephine Terratiano says, in her heavy Italian accent, "Every time Chip came here, he had so many crazy ideas. He kept saying, 'Josephine, I have to have something different because young people, they go crazy and they spend money.' We used to make reversible shorts, $100 each. He said, 'Maybe some people they cannot buy these shorts 'cause they can't spend money but the young people, they go crazy.'"

Still, I knew that few men in Calgary, as conservative as they were, would buy wildly coloured *surf shorts*, so I rebranded them as *BBQ shorts*. I felt confident the regular guy just needed the right excuse to buy something that was usually out of his comfort zone. From this lesson, I learned that the naming of a product is a critical piece of sales success.

And that summer of 1982, people *did* go crazy for this new line of barbecue shorts.

These long, loose, anti-ball-crushing-fit shorts gave all men a clothing option they'd never had before. People were buying the shorts as quickly as I could make them, often four or five pairs at a time. They were, I realized, purchasing the shorts not just for themselves, but to send to friends and relatives all over the world, who couldn't get them anywhere else.

At last, I was the best in the world at something.

CHAPTER 5:
THE SHIFT

The best way to predict the future is to make it yourself. —Peter Diamandis

Skateboarding

Westbeach's original customers had been women interested in the wrap shorts. I'd expanded the women's styles, but my female customers had been overtaken by twenty-five- to forty-year-old men demanding the reversible barbecue shorts.

There was about to be another shift.

I had begun to experience how the Westbeach store was virtually empty during the day. Lunch hour would be busy when business people came, but otherwise, little happened … until 3:30 p.m. every day, when the store filled up with kids. Young boys, mostly between twelve and sixteen. They weren't just coming in to look. They were buying.

Barbecue shorts had turned into skateboard shorts.

Back in the mid-seventies, skateboarding had experienced an explosion in popularity. As with surfing, the skateboarding boom traced its roots to southern California. Some of this history is portrayed in the 2005 film *Lords of Dogtown*, based on real-life skateboard figures Stacy Peralta, Jay Adams, and Tony Alva.

By the mid-eighties, public skateparks had appeared all over North America. This coincided with skaters building their own ramps in their backyards and using whatever public spaces (steps, railings, and numerous other things) they could find. At the time, smaller skateboard companies, owned by skaters themselves, were cropping up and on the leading edge of this dynamic new trend.

As with surfing, the unique physical demands and range of motion in skateboarding required baggy, loose-fitting garments—better yet if they hung long enough to cover and protect the knees. Of course, the low front rise and high back rise worked the same for skate as it did for surf. It was bringing those boys into my store.

It did not take me long to realize that this was my new customer base. I adjusted the store to match. I bought a piranha named Jake, put him in the fish tank, and fed him every day at 3:30 p.m. Jake was aggressive and grew quickly. I also bought a Commodore 64. You couldn't do much with it—input an address (which was useful as a mailing database for me) and execute a few simple commands—but it was something the kids loved and gravitated toward as soon as they came in the store.

As Westbeach was the only surf and skate store operating in Canada, to supplement my own inventory, I became the distributor or licensee of surf and skate brands from the US. This included apparel made by Gordon & Smith, Santa Cruz, Stüssy, and Billabong, among others.

Outside the store, I took measures to ensure I had a close connection with the skateboarding scene. There were not yet any public skateparks in Calgary, so I invited the local skateboarders to build a ramp in the backyard of my ramshackle house.

The ramp went up quickly, and just as quickly got lots of use. It got so much use—at all hours, no less—that I finally chained it at night so I could sleep and sent out mailers with its hours of operation (this is where the address database in the Commodore 64 came in handy).

All these efforts to position Westbeach and myself at the front of the skateboarding scene were working. Westbeach made around $90,000 in 1983, exponentially more than its first few seasons.

Still, of that $90,000, perhaps $30,000 went into labour and production, and another $30,000 went into wages and leases. Financially, the brand was not yet at a critical mass, especially since I was mainly just selling in my own stores. To maintain its position at the front of the market, Westbeach would need to grow and evolve further. At some point, competitors and imitators were bound to appear.

On Integrity

The year 1983 was also marked by two important lessons in integrity. The first had to do with a car. As a young entrepreneur, I was trying to make ends meet wherever I could. I got rid of my Mercedes and replaced it with a used Volkswagen station wagon.

The station wagon would've been the perfect vehicle for what I needed, but it soon became apparent I had been sold a lemon. Exhaust fumes were coming up into the car. I either had to always drive with the windows down—not ideal in Calgary winters—or suffer a terrible headache. I realized I had to get rid of the car. So, I sold it. And I said nothing about the exhaust fumes to the man who bought it.

A week or two later the man called me. He said I'd known about the problem when I sold him the car, but I hadn't told him and had let him buy it anyway. He said I wasn't a very good person. It hurt me, but he was right. I didn't take the car back or refund him his money.

Part of this was because I was in survival mode with my business. But, part of it was because I justified my actions—somebody had done it to me (the person from who I'd originally bought the car), so I turned around and did it to somebody else. After the man on the phone told me I wasn't a very good person, I decided I never again wanted to be in a position where someone could say that about me or call my integrity into question.

This leads me to the second lesson. Not long after that incident with the car, I was in the Westbeach store, and I saw $200 in twenties on the ground. I picked it up, put it in my pocket, and looked around. There was nobody in my store just then, and $200 was a lot of money.

A little while later, I was sitting with the owner of an outdoor restaurant next door to Westbeach. During our conversation, a young woman came up to us, in semi-panic-mode, and told us she'd lost $200 somewhere around here. I asked her what denominations the money was in. She told me it was in twenty-dollar-bills. So, I pulled the $200 out of my pocket and gave it back to her.

She was relieved to have her money back. Maybe that was her month's rent. Then she went on her way. It felt good to help her out, but what was important to me at that moment was looking in the restaurant owner's eyes and knowing he saw in me a person of integrity—a person he could trust.

Those were two of the great teachings of my life.

Smoking in the Store

Another lesson I learned in the early days of Westbeach was in brand-building. I decided I would let no one into the store who was smoking.

You must understand how radical this was in the early '80s. For most people, it was like telling them not to breathe oxygen. Shoppers would scream and yell and swear and promise they would never bring their business to me.

I was determined to stand my ground. Even with the little evidence we had then, I felt sure smoking was making people sick. It seemed filthy and was not something I wanted to have associated with the youth and athleticism of my brand.

I could tell that by making enemies of the people I *didn't* want to wear my product, that it created a stronger group of loyalists who wanted to back a brand that stood for their health and a better future. This idea would be the foundational genesis of how to build a West Coast brand.

The Ironman

As Westbeach transitioned to a skating brand, I was still training intensively. My training was of a deeply personal nature. I'd always been a one-girl guy, and when Cindy broke off our relationship (and cleaned out the joint Westbeach account), I was devastated. My focused athletic activity and daily runner's high gave me an escape from all those feelings of heartbreak. To suppress my misery, I decided to do the Ironman.

My training also confirmed for me something I'd learned a couple of years earlier—my true passion was athletic clothing and technical apparel. Our clothing at Westbeach was flying off the shelves, which was terrific, but I still felt somewhat unfulfilled. I felt the Westbeach clothing was more about fashion than performing a specific function.

The 1983 Ironman was held on October 22 in Kailua-Kona. There was no prequalifying for the Ironman in 1983. For most people, it was their first time at an event of this length.

I was a fire hydrant in a race of greyhounds that year (a few years later, I would win the Clydesdale division of the Vancouver Triathlon). Later, I would joke about having had the opportunity to meet everyone on the Ironman—during the swim I'd been one the first out of the water, then everyone said hello as they passed me through the bike ride. I met many of those who had passed me while I was on the run because I ate ferociously on the bike ride. Many runners fell over from lack of nutrition.

After I crossed the finish line, I got a milkshake then went for a massage. At that moment, I swore I'd never do something like the Ironman again. I would run 10ks, and I would take up squash and mountain biking, but I knew my body wasn't meant for long distance.

CHAPTER 6:
THE NEXT LEVEL

Desperation creates brilliance.

Farewell to Dome

On April 25, 1985—my thirtieth birthday—I accomplished a goal I'd set for myself several years earlier. I quit my job at Dome Petroleum. From here on out, I intended to only work for myself. That left one more goal to achieve: retirement by age forty.

If retirement by age forty was going to happen, I would need to take Westbeach to the next level. Over the last year, the evolution from surf to skateboard had only become more pronounced. It was obvious to me that skateboarding, like surfing, would be a billion-dollar industry over the next five years. What was less clear was what I needed to do to capitalize on that evolution.

One of my main challenges was still producing five hundred to two thousand of each style to bring my costs down to make a profit. I was doing small wholesale consignments at various locations across North America, including Hamill's Surf Shop in San Diego, and Scott Sibley and Richard

Mellon's store in Vancouver, but I still couldn't achieve the right volume for anything bigger.

An example of this scaling challenge came at a trade show I attended in Singapore in 1986. Buyers from a big Japanese department store came by my booth and knew my reversible, long, quilted shorts were a product differentiator. But, from talking to me, these buyers knew I couldn't deliver what they wanted, namely product volume in the millions. We could not work out a deal, so instead, those same buyers went back to Japan and immediately trademarked the name Westbeach. The ramifications of not controlling my trade name would show up again soon.

Partnering with Scott and Richard

I began to consider partnering. If I didn't partner, once the skateboarding trend broke into the mainstream, someone with more money and more expertise would run me over. As it happened, Scott and Richard had been placing increasingly large orders of clothing to put in their store. By the summer of 1985, the three of us talked about joining forces.

In a partnership, an aspiring entrepreneur can learn how a different combination of skill sets need to come together to make the business work. You need a designer/creative and visionary, you need someone with a good sense of structure and accounting, and you need someone who's a people person, a genuine lover of people, to handle sales. It's almost impossible to find all these skills in one person.

This blend of expertise was something I saw in a partnership with Scott and Richard. Scott was gifted at sales and people. Richard was creative at heart, but he was also much older than our target demographic, which by default saw him handle the books and the business end of things. I was the manufacturer, product developer, and designer.

As we got the partnership discussions underway, I quickly learned how many aspects of expanding a business were beyond my experience. Richard knew about payables, receivables, and how to invoice properly. I didn't understand payment terms and financing.

Previously if someone sent me an invoice, I'd pay them in five days, even though I had thirty days before it was due. Had I been doing things the way Richard did, I could have used the money in the twenty-five days between the date I paid the invoice and the date it was due. Richard also knew a lot about setting up warehouses and shipping channels. I would never have known how to do this on my own.

They'd both recognized the clothing I supplied had more momentum and better profit than sailing equipment. They carried Westbeach clothing, and the other labels I distributed. By partnering, they could avoid my markup. Together, we thought we could position ourselves to be the leaders of the coming surfing and skateboarding trend.

In September 1985, I sold 66 percent of my business to Richard and Scott, making our merger official. Westbeach was now, truly, a West Coast company. Initially, our company grew quickly, which included changes in the way it was modelled.

"It started growing from a vertical retail model to a wholesale model," Scott remembers. "Whereas Chip's focus was on going to California to fill his own stores full of stuff, our new focus became importing and wholesaling into Canadian stores. Surfwear was growing like crazy."

Later that fall, we attended our first apparel industry trade show together in Montreal. During the eighties, booths at East Coast sporting goods conventions were weird. Company booths were run and manned by male sales reps in suits and ties, smoking cigarettes. All the clothes they were selling would smell like smoke. This was the common culture of East Coast business, and it was not how I wanted to operate. I detested unhealthy people in suits selling athletic products. It all seemed so fake.

We showed up at our first trade show in a Volkswagen convertible with surfboards, skateboards, shorts, T-shirts, and flip-flops. We played speed metal and had fun while we talked business. We had a brand and a culture and a way of marketing that nobody else did. Right away, the sporting goods industry sat up and took notice.

For the next several years, trade shows a few times a year—not just in Montreal but in places like Japan, Las Vegas, and Munich—would be a fact of life. The purpose of attending these trade shows was to keep securing wholesale deals for our brand.

This was well before I understood the power of vertical retail. Since I was still trying to reach effective economy-of-scale production, even after the partnership was formalized, wholesale deals seemed the best way to increase production quantities quickly.

Although that first tradeshow was fun and felt good—a positive sign for the beginning of our partnership—I did not understand how financially constrained we were about to find ourselves. For starters, Westbeach was already in debt.

Debt and Credit

When I'd entered the partnership, it was critically important to me to be debt-free. I didn't want a bank telling me how to run my business. I took the last of my nest egg and paid off everything I owed before I entered the partnership with Richard and Scott.

I didn't realize my two new partners were coming to the table with debts from their earlier business, Windlift Design.

That debt came with them. Right off the bat, the company owed money, with interest, to my new partner Richard.

The trouble wasn't just the payments and the lack of capital for growing the business—it was the drain on mental energy caused by the debt. I felt like 40 to 50 percent of our conversations revolved around money, where we could get it, and how we could operate without it. I wondered how much more creative we could have been if we'd been able to take our focus away from soul-crushing conversations.

Westbeach would continue to struggle with being in the red for the next several years. One way to address our money concerns was to secure a line of credit. Credit would play a significant role in how we operated, particularly with the California companies whose wares we were licensed to sell in Canada.

Unfortunately, this debt would define much of our time at Westbeach for the next ten years. We were always fighting the clock and near the end of our line of credit.

Testing Toronto

Meanwhile, we were also attempting to build a broader geographical presence. The Westbeach flagship store was in Vancouver, but I relocated to Toronto from Calgary. We thought we'd need a solid foothold out east since that's where 70 percent of the population lived.

To cover my own costs, I kept my house in Calgary, using it entirely as an income property, while I lived in *the dungeon of doom*—the unfinished dank basement of the Toronto store—to save money. The Beach was a highly incestuous neighbourhood, but the community took me under its wing, and I loved everyone I met.

Quickly, it became apparent that the vast majority of sales at our Toronto store were to the neighbourhood's emerging beach volleyball scene. With our struggles to find financing, we couldn't pursue the growth we'd intended for our East Coast presence.

We felt continuous pressure to adopt a wholesale model. As Scott says, "In the early days, it was recognized that if you wanted your company to get bigger, you've got to go wholesale. You can't go to the bank and finance retail. The banks hated retail because there was no proof of vertical retailing." I imagine early e-commerce companies had the same issue.

"With unlimited money, you could open up a bunch of retail stores," Scott adds, "but even then, it's riskier to do so. It worked well for lululemon, which is why it went the way it did. He grew it like that and was accepted by banks because lululemon proved the vertical model could make more money with less risk. But in the Westbeach days, we didn't have access to the resources that would make the vertical retail model possible."

By 1987, we knew it didn't make sense for me to stay in Toronto. My being there wasn't working for Westbeach, kind of like a strained long-distance relationship. We sold the Westbeach retail location to a Toronto beach volley designer named Fred Koops, who would go on to found Overkill.

Discovering Vancouver

From Toronto, I moved to Vancouver to live with Scott and Richard. They were living in a run-down five-suite mansion on Point Grey Road. The street runs along the beaches on the south side of English Bay and has since become one of the most expensive housing markets in the world.

While living there, I would wake up every morning to see a blue sky, freighters moving on the ocean, and snow-capped mountains I could almost touch. You could surf, ski, and sail, all in the same day. It was—and is—spectacular.

One morning, while waking up to that view, I made a goal to own a house on the beach in Vancouver by the age of fifty.

Despite the Westbeach partnership's many early challenges, I was in love with Vancouver already, and relocating there was one of the best moves I ever made, both professionally and personally.

We had stores in Calgary and Toronto. Stores in Seattle, Innsbruck, and Whistler would follow a few years later. Each store had three or four people working in it, and each store made a little over a million dollars a year. This was good revenue, but never enough to lift us out of debt created by the cash-flow-poor wholesaling model.

A Married Life

Most of my friends had been married for almost ten years. The seventies were a different era—most people got married before age twenty-four. My married friends had all had kids shortly after tying the knot. There I was, in my early thirties, still single, and living a different lifestyle. I'd started to subconsciously feel like I was missing out on the family aspect of life.

Finally, at thirty-three, I met and married a wonderful woman with whom I was meant to have two beautiful boys.

The New Flagship Store

Around that same time, a much bigger retail location became available just across the street from Westbeach's first store on West 4th Avenue. It was a financial stretch for Scott, Richard, and me to make the move, but with the extra space came a lot of opportunity.

Thinking back to the big skateboard ramp at my house in Calgary, I realized we could install the same in our store. It would only strengthen our position at the forefront of skateboarding culture in Canada. Almost right away, the ramp became an integral part of the culture of the store.

Having the ramp at the bigger West 4th store helped Westbeach become the biggest distributor of skateboards in Canada. This was not something I'd ever foreseen when I'd sold wrap shorts from a booth on the 8th Avenue Mall, but I'd paid attention to the trends, to what was coming a few years down the line, and as a result, this was how we'd evolved.

West 4th was a perfect location for selling skateboards because Kitsilano had a surfing community. Skateboarding gave surfers a way to surf on land, so to speak, all year round.

It was easy for Westbeach, then, because for the most part, skate was the same customer as surf. We prepared and filled orders in the basement of that pink house and shipped them all over Canada.

Our position at the front of Canada's skateboard scene stayed unchallenged until Powell Peralta—a company founded by George Powell and Stacy Peralta of *Lords of Dogtown* fame—came in with their enormously successful Bones Brigade branding. The Bones Brigade was a professional skateboarding team, formed in 1978, featuring the likes of Tony Hawk. After their popularity hit its peak in 1988, if there wasn't a skull-and-crossbones on your skateboards, you just couldn't sell them.

We quickly lost our hard-good skateboard business to Powell Peralta, as did other competitors, but it was good while it lasted.

Taking Vertical Further

Having the bigger location on West 4th also allowed us to bring Westbeach's production fully in-house. This was all part of an even larger vertical retail model I had imagined. I questioned why we shouldn't take vertical top to bottom.

There was no roadmap and no one from whom to learn. Intuitively, I'd come to understand how big an economic advantage we could have if we could make vertical retail and in-house production work. We would miss all the middleman markups and supply a better-quality product at a better price. This thought became my mantra as my business acumen developed.

I knew we had to achieve economy-of-scale production. Instead of making 400 units of a particular item, we had to increase production to 2,000 or more. That required buying all our own fabric, trim, zippers, snaps (sometimes not covering these costs upfront, and learning from those mistakes), learning how to inventory it all, and bringing in payroll and labour to make it all happen.

This was learning by doing, and it gave me a deep—if not formal—sense of how manufacturing and production work for a brand. To this day, that unique experience has given me the ability to walk into a retail store and within about fifteen seconds, sense what kind of sales, volume, and turnover the store is doing, and how happy the employees are. It's almost second nature for me, but the insight was hard-earned over my years at Westbeach.

Even after we'd centred Westbeach in Vancouver, I kept using Josephine Terratiano as a producer, but ultimately, we had to reconsider production. Vancouver had a large Asian immigrant community, which meant access to a high number of skilled, low-cost seamstresses and tailors, plus better connections with factories overseas.

Breaking the production relationship with Josephine was hard. She'd become like a mother. I've never been very good at keeping up relationships, and I'm not the best communicator, but I never forget people either.

Years later, after my personal fortunes had changed, I sent Josephine a shoebox with $10,000 cash in it and two first-class tickets to Italy. I didn't say who it was from—and apparently, I didn't need to. Not long after I'd sent her the shoebox, I "anonymously" received a tin of the same homemade biscotti I'd loved eating at Josephine's house many years before.

CHAPTER 7:
THE RISE OF SNOWBOARDING

Children are the orgasm of life. Just like you did not know what an orgasm was before you had one, nature does not let you know how great children are until you have them.

Becoming a Father

After I'd sold my house in Calgary, my wife and I used the money from that sale to buy, with a partner, a large three-suite house in Kitsilano.

Our first child, John James (JJ) Wilson, was born in 1988 at St. Paul's Hospital in downtown Vancouver. I can't imagine the experience of becoming a parent is much different for anyone else than it was for me. It was completely life-altering, but some of it came naturally. Despite their financial challenges, my parents had been very good to me, my sister, and my brother. They'd set examples that had prepared me to love this moment.

Having JJ also made me realize I couldn't take the same risks for myself anymore. I had to think about my family, provide for and take care of them. It was on me to make sure there was food in the fridge, clothes on everyone's back, and the mortgage was paid.

It might seem like this meant being around my family *more*, but, in practice, I was around *less*. I poured myself into my business, knowing this was the means of securing my family's future. Then, just a few months after JJ was born, we received the great news that we had a second son, Brett, on the way.

There was room for improvement in many areas of my life, but this wasn't a bad time. I was very happy to be a father. Real estate was on the rise in Vancouver, so the house we'd bought was gaining value, which alleviated some of the financial pressure.

Westbeach was at least breaking even. The three partners—Scott, Richard, and me—had agreed to increase the salaries we got from the company, from about $30,000 each to $60,000, mainly so Scott and Richard could prove enough income to pay mortgages and buy houses.

Continued Struggles

The partnership dynamic between Scott, Richard, and me was okay, but we were three partners with no CEO. That meant three, often separate, visions and three leadership styles. Westbeach was a *good* company, but not a *great* company, and for the moment, the three of us had no concept of what great was. For a long time, we'd believed our business would "get better next year," and that we'd finally surpass that break-even point.

At the same time, I'd realized we were at a crossroads. Although still popular and widespread, I felt skateboarding as a consumer trend would peak and decline, just like surfing had.

We knew our four vertical stores made a profit, and our

wholesale was a losing proposition, but we were stuck. We needed the wholesale orders to have economy-of-scale production, but wholesale sucked up so much free cash while we were waiting for payments, we weren't able to shift over to opening more stores.

We couldn't lower our prices in our stores because we had to support the pricing we gave our wholesalers. This foreshadowed the dilemma of future wholesalers who would fail because vertical businesses could perform so much better without middlemen.

We brought in a man named Marco Allinott as a minor partner to assist with retail operations.

Marco was a great guy. He was super diligent and very smart. His job was to run our stores, and, as such, he was closely involved with our customers and seeing what they saw at the retail level. Quickly after coming aboard, Marco proposed tripling the store inventory, so customers would buy six times more. We discovered that customers would return more often because they could almost always find a new or different item. It was a stretch, but we made it work, and sure enough, sales began to pop.

I would use this same strategy later when I was setting up lululemon stores.

Dropping American Brands

We decided to drop the American brands we'd been carrying since the formation of our partnership.

This idea was Richard's, and it was a great one. American brands were sucking up cash flow, and Westbeach clothing had better profit than they did. American brands had super marketing power behind them, and for a long time, they helped to get kids into our stores so we could sell them Westbeach-branded clothing.

Carrying these brands had given Westbeach a certain amount of validity. But the import costs, high to begin with, had become even more prohibitive, especially with the American dollar 30 percent higher than ours.

At the same time, we'd become better and better at our own manufacturing. We were making our products in Canada. Since we didn't have to pay import duty on our stuff, we invested that money in quality. We had something special—a very distinct product, at a better price, and a higher quality than the better-known American brands.

I also had an idea that changed the way we approached the athletic market. I knew hard goods, like surfboards and skateboards, gave us validity, but it was obvious all the profit was in clothing. I could see the "extreme" athletic market was 95 percent men, and the owners of sporting goods stores were 100 percent men.

Men were more engineering driven, and the men who owned sports stores did it because they loved hard goods. Clothing was an add-on they did not understand, and so, it was a small percentage of what they carried. I understood it in the opposite way. We carried just enough hard goods to be authentic, but we rearranged our store to be 10 percent hard goods and 90 percent apparel.

Still, dropping American brands and focusing on our own improved in-house production wasn't enough. If we were going to survive, we needed to evolve. We needed to get ahead of the next trend. And that next trend, I believed, was snowboarding.

The Rise of Snowboarding

My ability to predict the rise of snowboarding came from a few different sources.

One source was a man named Ken Achenbach, described

by *Transworld Skateboarding* as "the father of Canadian snowboarding."[2] Back in the early '80s, Ken had founded The Snoboard Shop in Calgary, where he acted as the Canadian distributor for Burton and Sims snowboards. He also experimented with selling skateboard decks, which made him a competitor in Westbeach's early days.

I'd been intrigued by the snowboarding scene, but the market was tiny. Through my failures with triathlon clothing in 1980 and beach volleyball in 1986, I'd learned there was no point doing anything until there were enough customers to make it worthwhile, and in 1983 and 1984, snowboarding just wasn't at that point.

It didn't help that snowboarding was banned in most ski resorts back then. In Canada, the only place you could snowboard was at Sunshine Village in Banff, Alberta. Snowboarding was *scary* for older skiers.

Skiers couldn't understand this obscure sport. It looked dangerous to them, sort of the way an older person looked at skateboarders coasting down the sidewalk. Many people skiing the mountains in the '80s were people who could afford it—grey-haired, conservative, fifty-somethings. They did not want to see something new take over their mountains.

Personally, I'd been snowboarding since 1983, and I loved it. Every Christmas, a group of friends and I would charter a helicopter to take us up to the peak in Canmore, Alberta, then we would snowboard down the powder-rich slopes. I understood the attraction of the sport.

My brother Brett also inspired me to give snowboarding more serious consideration. After moving to Colorado several years before, Brett had pursued an entrepreneurial career of his own. As I'd founded Westbeach, Brett had founded the

2. Hondo, "Fathers of Snowboarding: Ken Achenbach," *Transworld Snowboarding*, June 17, 2013, https://snowboarding.transworld.net/photos/fathers-of-snowboarding-ken-achenbach/.

original snowboard clothing company, called Wave Rave, in Boulder, Colorado, in 1986. Brett immediately connected himself with the Red Hot Chili Peppers at an early snowboard event. (I would go on to have the Chili Peppers at my wife's fortieth birthday party in our backyard in 2013—an unbelievable experience!)

"Chip and I intersected at a lot of trade shows," says Brett. "We'd typically meet up in Europe and in Japan. We were essentially competitors, but I don't think either of us felt like we were stomping on each other's territory because the market was so big."

Brett had come up for my wedding in August 1988, and, as he recalls, "I brought my snowboard and gear because you could go up to the glacier at Whistler and snowboard in the summer. That's when I told Chip, 'Look, this snowboarding thing is going to take off. You guys should definitely start making outerwear.'"

Meanwhile, more skiing locations were opening to snowboarding, as resorts realized it was time to think seriously about the additional revenue snowboarding could generate. As I'd seen with surfwear and skateboarding, trends that could move into the *street*—aka the mainstream—were where I wanted to put my efforts.

A trend's move into the street presented the opportunity to do a lot of business. For instance, if I'd just sold surf shorts to the world's 4,000 or so surfers (or slightly larger number of hard-core skateboarders), there would have been no business in that—not on any profitable scale. But, I'd been able to sell sport-inspired streetwear to people who wanted to emulate the sports they admired, if not actually participate in them.

These fringe customers who wanted to look the part were called "posers." The posers' purchasing power allowed core companies to produce enough quantity to bring prices down and quickly increase production volume.

There wasn't a lot of technology in surf or skate apparel. After my earlier experiments with triathlon gear, the idea of technical, functional apparel was still evolving in my brain. As snowboarding took hold, I saw how essential it was for people to have the right gear. Variable conditions on a big mountain can kill you if you're not dressed correctly.

By 1988, I believed it was the right time to get into snowboarding. My brother's Wave Rave snowboard clothing was amazing, and I could sense snowboarding would hit its critical mass in five years.

I went to my partners and the rest of the staff at Westbeach and told them my idea. Westbeach would refocus as a snowboard apparel company. There was little interest. (I would later have the same thing happen at lululemon when I proposed mindfulness, technical streetwear, and owning our own manufacturing).

"Around 1988, there was a big change in Westbeach," Scott Sibley remembers. "This change was something I have to give Chip credit for. He got us out of surfing before its decline and into skateboarding on its upswing, and back out, and into snowboarding right at its beginning.

"We were all partially resistant to make the jump into snowboarding. Sometimes Chip seemed to abandon ideas that still had legs, but I trusted his instincts. There were many people in the company—newer, younger people—that didn't trust him at all. I think this was frustrating for him. It's difficult not calling your own shots and having to work with the opinions of the twenty or so people that worked for Westbeach at that time."

Despite the resistance, I stuck to my instincts and pushed hard to bring the rest of the company around. I saw snowboarding as a winter sport, something that, unlike surfing or skateboarding, we didn't have to become California posers to do. With the summer Whistler glacier as the global hub for snowboarders, I knew that Vancouver was the perfect location to be the best in the world in snowboarding. In addition, we would be solidly authentic. That was very important.

Skateboarding now had 400 competitors and was becoming a commodity product. My instincts told me it was a market that would soon be in decline, which meant we had to do something. Because I had the power to do so, I renamed the company from Westbeach Surf to Westbeach Snowboard. I knew this would, in effect, force naysayers in the company to get on board (no pun intended) or leave.

To prepare for the upcoming winter season, we designed a line of loose-fitting outerwear. We made perhaps 400 pairs of overall-style pants, 800 non-overall pants, 1,000 pullover tops (pullovers were massively popular in the '80s), and other assorted items, including branded T-shirts.

The garments had no stretch, and there was nothing initially technical about them, but the anti-ski looseness of our garments allowed layering and breathability.

We didn't have the means to make this apparel in-house, so we outsourced it to garment manufacturers in Vancouver. We made the first line as cheaply as we could, which made it affordable to the fourteen-year-olds who made up the biggest snowboard demographic.

The immediate effect of rebranding was a tripling of our business. We had surf and skate apparel to sell in the spring/ summer, but for the first time, we also had a line of products to sell through the eight months of fall/winter. Westbeach was one of three companies in the world specifically making snowboard apparel.

"We kind of went all-in on snowboarding," says Scott, "and, of course, that made our company just skyrocket. We went over to ISPO, the largest sporting goods trade show in the world, held in Germany. We were the first to introduce this new sport—snowboarding—and because there was a three-year snow-drought there, we seemed crazy. But, the success this brought us was that we were now cemented as the very early players in the snowboard industry.

"As snowboarding grew," Scott adds, "we rode that growth."

CHAPTER 8:
HARD TIMES

To create the next best thing, you might have to leave something that is already working behind.

Near Bankruptcy

We'd recently visited bankruptcy lawyers to understand how the process worked. Unfortunately, we felt Westbeach was on the verge of collapse. We had been in snowboarding for only a short time, but like surf and skate before it, product supply was overtaking demand and prices were dropping.

I wanted to get out before snowboarding became a commodity business. Sports stores now had negotiating power and were making the brands pay more of their shipping, warehousing, and marketing costs. We couldn't continue to fund the wholesale model, and financial pressure was closing in on all sides.

My partner, Richard, also wanted to settle down, focus on his home, and build a family. He wanted to work shorter days, maybe six or eight hours, whereas I wanted to work double that, at least. Richard and I were not working well together. A huge part of that was our inability to communicate effectively. In survival mode, I defaulted to a command-and-control, Team of One style of operating, while Richard reverted to deception, and Scott reverted to being non-committal.

We all had our Acts in full bloom.

A Landmark Moment

For as long as I'd known him, Richard had been taking classes and courses in transformational development. My perception was that the lessons he learned were mostly fleeting, but in early 1990 he came into work super-excited about a weekend workshop he'd taken—the Landmark Forum. I found out this was a business that had evolved massively since its original inception as EST.

Over the next couple of weeks, both Scott and I noticed a massive improvement in Richard's state of mind and integrity. Richard attributed it all to his experience at Landmark and asked us to take the course ourselves. We all wanted to improve things at Westbeach, that much was clear, so Scott and I signed up to do the course together.

To illustrate more about Landmark, I'll give you an example from when I took the course. There was a woman who was about forty years old and had been raised in a union family. She told us how her father came home every day and complained about the union bosses, how the workers like him did all the work, while the bosses got all the money.

This had formed the story and the context for how this woman had viewed her life since her childhood. She told us how she'd gone to university, entered the workplace, got a good job, and a promotion. She'd reached a point where she was making $100,000 a year in a leadership position, but she was still haunted by her father's attitude.

Her father had hated management, leaders, bosses—

anyone making $100,000 a year who he'd call a corpo-
rate bum. So, subconsciously this woman found she was
constantly undermining herself. She would succeed, get to a job
of $100,000 a year, then quit because she just couldn't handle
being the person her father had always hated.

At Landmark, this woman was introduced to the possibility of imagining amnesia. What if she had no memory of her
past, of anything her father had said about bosses and management? If that was the case, this woman, with all her knowledge, ability, and education, could and would feel powerful to
go beyond her father's barrier.

The only person who'd been undermining her was her, and
she was doing so based on a disempowering story she'd told
herself. If free from her story of her father, there was nothing
she couldn't do.

The extent to which my past was exerting control over my
present was revealed to me during the course. I realized that
I constantly constructed stories based on past experiences to
make sense of my interpretation of other people's actions and
behaviours. What I had failed to recognize was the fictional
nature of the stories themselves. Even as I'm writing this book,
I am considering what stories I have created and what stories
are fact.

I began to understand that what were just my best guesses
had become facts in my mind. I based the course of my life on
these guesses, believing them to be absolute truths. As stories
accumulated over the years, they constrained me more and
more.

The Landmark Forum was a huge awakening. I thought of
all the things my dad had said, based on his visits to EST and
the Esalen Institute in the '70s, that I had dismissed without
even considering. I heard for the first time what he'd been
trying to tell me.

The course was transformational because it opened up 70 percent of my brain that was clogged with unnecessary thoughts. The Landmark course was really no different than shutting down a slow hard drive to clean viruses and rearrange information.

I also got clear I was going to die, and I was tired of a "fine" life. I wanted an "extraordinary" life.

The viruses in my brain were:

1. Managing lies I have told, so I don't get caught.
2. Repetitive complaining.
3. Not taking responsibility for my actions (i.e. selling a lemon of a car).
4. Acting inauthentic so I "looked good" to others (pretending to be what I was not).
5. Spending brain power doing what parents, friends, or society think I "should" do.
6. Consistently using the words "wish," "should," or "try," and skirting responsibility instead of taking action.
7. Creating excuses for not doing what I say I will do (like showing up on time).
8. Letting my past experiences limit my future choices (i.e. my purple shirt experience).
9. Not forgiving people for what I think they have done to me.

In my observation of thousands of people who have taken the Landmark Forum, the number one issue inhibiting people from living an extraordinary life is their inability to forgive their parents for the lousy job they did raising them. Mostly I experienced that people's interpretation of what occurred in their childhood and what actually happened was not the same. I have a theory that nature creates this weird human condition to cause friction to get adult children out of the house.

The course opened my life to a bigger purpose. In the words of Werner Erhard—the man who founded EST— I learned what "making a difference in the world" meant. Landmark helped me understand my life could be less about me, and more about inspiring people to know their own magnificence. As you might imagine, my context for living in the world changed dramatically.

Since we'd all taken the course, Richard, Scott, and I suddenly had a powerful new language to help us communicate with one another. The Landmark concepts gave us a common language and understanding of what we wanted for our lives and our business.

I became committed to doing and completing everything that came out of my mouth. I wanted people to count on me. If I said I would do something, I had to do it, do it on time, and do it in a quality manner. If something went wrong, either I could blame other people for the problem, or I could take responsibility for it. Only when I took responsibility would I have the means to fix the problem.

Looking at the past, I saw that my youth was a regimented life of eight swimming practices a week for seventeen years. When I quit swimming, I remember saying to myself, "I am never showing up on time, anywhere, for the rest of my life." For instance, I would tell people I would come to dinner at 7:00 p.m. or meet someone at 10:00 a.m., but I had no internal commitment to do what I had agreed to. I was always late. About three years later I noticed no one was calling me and my friends had all but disappeared.

I had learned that I had depleted my integrity, no one could count on me, and consequently, people stopped asking me to make plans with them. When I got clear that I was responsible, I also knew I could take action. I talked to all my former friends, apologized, and said I understood I had messed up and caused them upset. I then asked what I could do to put myself back in integrity with them. The answers were mostly muted, so I just committed to showing up on time. It took me three years to re-establish my reputation as someone who could be counted on.

"To this very day, I will say Landmark saved Westbeach," says Scott. "Suddenly, regardless of whether you like somebody or not, you recognize you're on the same team, and you start working together. Landmark helped us to communicate, and to redirect our focus from our problems to solutions."

We asked other people at Westbeach to attend the Landmark Forum. This was a hard thing to ask, because Westbeach, by this point, was a *mature* company, meaning it was difficult to alter the culture and sense of identity that had formed. Employees who'd been around for a while weren't interested in improving themselves. We found our employees were more interested in spending $500 on a jacket than exponentially developing their brains.

To an outsider, Landmark wasn't tangible. It wasn't something they could touch, and, in fairness, it seemed a little cultish to people who hadn't taken the course. We couldn't afford to send our employees, either, so if they attended the Forum, they would have to pay for it out-of-pocket. In the 2000s Oprah had a Vancouver man called Eckhart Tolle come to the show to discuss the book *The Power of Now*. I have often theorized that Mr. Tolle attended the Landmark Forum, and then wrote a book about the course.

Still, it gave me the idea of working the Forum into the very beginning stages of a company, before that closed-minded maturity could set in, and before employees would be happy with mediocre lives and a mediocre company that was just "fine." And this was exactly what I would do with lululemon. Ultimately, Landmark helped us work together to set Westbeach up to be sold.

If we hadn't done the course, we would have self-destructed, and I would never have had the money I used to start lululemon.

Divorce

All my working and business travel led my wife and me to divorce. Sadly, for almost four years, I felt like I saw my children very little. The reality was that I saw my boys more than most fathers did because I had to schedule and prioritize my time. I had to travel, out of necessity, for the business I was in—I had to make money to afford alimony and child support and to keep both households afloat.

The boys were too young to understand what was going on. Within a few years, they figured out their family was different. It seemed to cause a lot of confusion. JJ especially had difficulty with the transition as he always wanted the family to be together.

I don't think there's any such thing as an easy separation or divorce—some go slightly better than others. After my ex-wife and I did the Landmark course we had the communication tools to put the past behind us and make our boys our number one priority.

1989 *Me & my brother Brett in the Caribbean*

1985 *Our first logo, created by my partner Richard Mellon*

1981 *Anne Wilson, my grandmother, standing with me in my first Westbeach store, Calgary*

WESTBEACH

1993 *In Vancouver with Brett & JJ*

1984 *Cut and paste ads, to mimic
The Sex Pistols album*

1992 *Doing an ad for under 49¢*

**DO
IT
NOW**

1992 *Brett & JJ at my desk at Westbeach*

YOUR OUTLOOK ON LIFE IS A DIRECT REFLECTION OF HOW MUCH YOU LIKE YOURSELF

1993 *Karaoke in Japan with Kano Yamanaka & Scott Sibley*

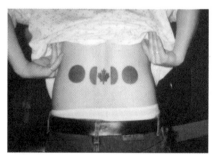

1989 *The first corporate logo tattoo I'd ever seen*

1994 *Me at our office in Japan*

1988 *Catalogue shoot (me in the middle)*

1991 *The Westbeach Snowboard Classic, Whistler, BC*

CHAPTER 9:
THE BUSINESS OF SNOWBOARDING

"The two most important days of your life are the day you are born and the day you find out why." —Mark Twain

Snowboarding Success

"The period between 1990 and 1995 was when the real fun started," says Scott Sibley. "We were major players. We built a distribution team and produced our own apparel. We had major lines of production. We had distribution networks in Europe and in Japan."

As our brand grew, so did the requirements on our in-house production (we could never produce snowboard apparel in-house, but we still produced our surf and skate wear). To help with this growth, I put an ad in the paper for a production manager.

One person who responded to the ad was a young guy named Frankie Hon, who had just arrived in Canada from Hong Kong. Frankie's experience was in distribution, not production management, but from the moment I met him, I could tell how smart and committed he was. I gave Frankie the job.

"My family immigrated to Canada in 1990, and I started looking for a job," Frankie remembers. "Chip interviewed me and offered me a job with Westbeach. The position had no title, but the intent was to coordinate with the existing production team. I was very impressed that he offered a job to a newcomer like me who had no Canadian experience."

Frankie was with Westbeach for two years. Then, Frankie met and married a woman named Elky, a fellow Chinese immigrant living in Vancouver. The two set up their own Vancouver-based garment factory. Frankie and Elky took much of our production team with them—but that was okay because our relationship was very strong.

"With Chip's encouragement, I started my own business in Canada," says Frankie.

A few years later, Frankie and Elky would start a larger manufacturing business, Charter Link Ltd., in Hong Kong. They would be a vital partner for me in the early days of lululemon, thanks to the personal relationship we'd begun at Westbeach.

Growing our in-house production, then eventually taking it externally, were just two aspects of the growth Westbeach was experiencing through the crazy early '90s. Even though financing was an ongoing challenge, the demand was massive, and the market was forgiving. My partners and I had to put into practice everything we'd developed over the previous five years—including our commitment to integrity and communication.

Advertising to Distributors

There were a few things we did differently or did for the first time, to put ourselves at the head of the snowboarding movement. One idea I had was to put ads in *Transworld Skateboarding*.

Transworld Skateboarding, established in 1983, was the worldwide go-to bible for surf, skate, and snowboard news. But there was an important distinction that should be pointed out—the ad I put in *Transworld Skateboarding* was not targeted toward customers; it was targeted to international distributors in order to exponentially grow sales and manufacturing quantities.

Previously, when our focus was surf and skateboard, we'd never advertised. We didn't need to. I was first in the surf and skate business in Canada, and throughout the early '80s, I'd received a lot of newspaper attention and editorials because I was the only adult who understood the youth market. This meant I never had to spend money on advertising.

It also actually helped us *not* to advertise, since there was an underground authenticity to surfing and skateboarding. Traditional advertising would have only taken away from that.

Building on Letters of Credit

We continued to operate on letters of credit, as we still didn't have enough money to afford upfront costs. Under this system, a distributor in Japan (or multiple distributors in Europe) would receive a sample line of Westbeach products. The distributors could show the sample line to potential customers.

Once orders were placed, the distributors would give us the orders with an accompanying letter of credit. We would then transfer that letter of credit over to our manufacturers in Asia. The manufacturers would ship the product orders directly to the distributors in Europe or Japan. From that profit, we could make the clothing for Canadian stores that would pay sixty days after delivery.

That was how Westbeach, once it rebranded as a snowboard apparel company, was built on virtually no money.

The key to this whole process was reaching the right distributors, and that was to whom the *Transworld Skateboarding* ads were targeted, not consumers. I wanted to let the skateboard world know we were the first and most original of companies in the new snowboarding industry.

If prospective distributors in Japan and Europe were looking for an authentic brand to sell in their markets, the *Transworld Skateboarding* ad would point them to Westbeach. This advertisement was an investment, a plan to make us look bigger than we were. And it worked.

Big Air Contest

I'd also considered other ways to promote the Westbeach brand, with the specific goal of break-even marketing. I thought a lot about what kind of event would attract people from around the world to snowboarding, and what occurred to me was a *big air contest.*

At the same time, Whistler Blackcomb had been trying to figure out how to make their season longer—how to make April as strong as other months. They'd planned a big ski festival (with a small snowboard component) to happen during one of the last weeks in April. I incorporated my idea with Whistler Blackcomb's festival plan. Westbeach, as always, was short on money, and we had to put $50,000 into the event to make it happen.

The first Westbeach Big Air contest, held in April 1991, was a total extravaganza. Over the next few years, it developed into a nighttime event at the base of Whistler

Mountain. There were amazing snowboarders performing tricks and stunts, jumping over huge gaps, and going through hula-hoops of fire. Down at the bottom of the hill, we had cheerleaders under the big air jump and beautiful women in hot tubs if the riders wanted to join. The crowd was huge, 10,000 people, and the vibe was crazy!

At one point, I had $5,000 cash which I rolled in toilet paper and fired out of a slingshot into the crowd. The wind hit at just that moment and blew all the money back at me. That didn't stop a mob of people from overwhelming my position to get at it. On-site security didn't stand a chance. That Westbeach Classic Big Air was a gigantic success and strongly contributed to Westbeach's unique brand identity.

After we ran Big Air for two years, Kokanee Brewing paid us to rename the event—Kokanee Westbeach Big Air. From then on, Kokanee ran the event and covered all the expenses, paying us $50,000. I've always loved developing marketing ideas that generated revenue.

Sponsoring Snowboarders

The majority of snowboard marketing at other companies was done by sponsoring athletes. Many of these athletes were kids, really, between fourteen and eighteen years old, at the top of their game in a sport that hadn't existed before. Big board manufacturers would pay a top snowboarder up to $1 million a year to use their branded boards at high-publicity events.

The board manufacturers (such as Morrow, Sims, Burton, and Ride) of the world could pay that kind of sponsorship money through the sheer volume they made selling products, mostly in Japan. Westbeach couldn't afford that, so we had to think of other innovative ways to market.

Rather than having two or three top snowboarders at $1

million each, I went to the individual mountains and found the half-dozen talented snowboarders just under the sponsorship level. These snowboarders were typically a little bit younger and friendlier than their more famous counterparts. They were also heroes of their community. They hadn't yet developed big attitudes or egos.

Our first team consisted of Kevin Young, Devun Walsh, Emanuel Krebs, Paul Culling, and Randy Friesen, all snow-boarders who would later become household names in the sport. Another one of our first team riders was a guy named Ross Rebagliati, who would win the first ever gold medal in snowboarding at the 1998 Olympics in Nagano. Famously—or infamously—Rebagliati tested positive for THC, had his win disqualified, then had that decision overturned by the IOC and his medal reinstated after they deemed marijuana not to be a banned substance.

As the relationship with our team evolved into a less for-mal, more economical kind of sponsorship, we gave our riders free clothes and arranged their travel. We would also arrange photography of our snowboarders at various events and locations, then put the pictures in *Transworld Skateboard-ing* to promote our riders' images for their big-paying board sponsors.

This *community branding* system worked out to be cheaper by millions of dollars—plus far more effective—than the marketing hoops our competitors were jumping through with their sponsorships.

I didn't want to "buy" the snowboarders on the Westbeach team. A strictly financial relationship felt inauthentic. When-ever I saw a sponsored athlete from Nike, my mind screamed "fraud" as I thought they were bought to promote the Nike brand without an authentic belief in the product.

For amateur athletes, the money was a godsend. I wanted to make technical clothing for the sport and have these young guys test it. This gave me an early taste of focus groups composed of my ideal customers, an important methodology I would later use with lululemon.

The First Focus Group

The first design group I put together consisted of our snowboard team, who were all fourteen- to sixteen-year-old boys. In all honesty, back then, my ego was looking for their stamp of approval. I knew that at thirty-two I looked like a grandpa and they might automatically reject whatever I showed them just because it was designed by an old man. I wanted them to test the products, tell me the clothing was awesome, then talk it up amongst their friends. I imagined these young guys acting as ambassadors and helping sell the line they'd tested. I was an inauthentic manipulator.

But, as the first focus group went forward, something happened that I didn't anticipate.

When I presented our riders with the clothes, they were not excited. They took one look at the line and, instead of telling me how impressed they were, their eyes told me they had different ideas. It was a hard thing to hear, but I knew it was crucial for me to understand this demographic, so I set about listening to what they genuinely wanted.

The snowboarders told me to make the apparel "fat," or oversized. Hip-hop-inspired, gun-hiding clothing was developing as an underground trend. These riders knew what they wanted, and they were clear in their advice. I was skeptical, but I took them at their word. I was astute enough to know I wasn't listening to teen music and I wanted to see the world through their eyes. I made the changes and redesigned everything to be "super fat."

Westbeach recreated snowboard clothing; the designs

were the polar opposite to those of competitors and definitely as far from tight ski gear as possible. I learned my lesson about the power of listening to my target market, even if their initial feedback wasn't what I'd wanted to hear.

By the following year, however, I seemed to have forgotten that lesson.

Next season, I brought out a similar oversized look and again presented it to the snowboarder focus group. Once again, I went into this expecting their thumbs up. Wrong again. What they were looking for this time around had changed completely. They told me to make the clothes slimmer again, and they asked for solid colours instead of colour blocks.

I thought I knew better. We'd had such success with the oversized look I didn't want to change it up so quickly. I was also convinced that solid colours were a mistake since it looked too plain. I ignored the kids and went with my own designs, unmodified. Once again, they knew best. If we had slimmed the size and offered solid colours, our line would have sold like crazy. I'd ignored our target audience at my own peril.

Another critical thing I learned at the time was a concept I've come to think of as—"If you have to say it, you ain't it." In branding and marketing terms, this concept refers to the inauthenticity that occurs when a company includes what they do or produce in their brand name. For example, Westbeach Snowboard, which was the formal name of our company, rings false. A brand identity should be strong enough, and so in tune with its core customers that it speaks for itself.

Our design team didn't want our apparel to say Westbeach Snowboard. They wanted the word snowboard out.

The Japanese Perspective on Snowboarding

Snowboarding was our entry point to becoming a truly global company. The Berlin Wall had fallen, and we saw our goods being sold in East Berlin. At the same time, orders were coming in from state-owned stores in the mountains north of Beijing.

But, it's impossible to talk about the rise of snowboard culture without mentioning Japan, as indicated in the prologue to this book. The Japanese snowboard market was fascinating. Japanese customers seemed to have no problem buying a snowboard, mounting it on top of their car, and never using it. Many customers in Japan simply wanted to *look* like they were snowboarders. It should be noted there actually is fantastic snowboarding in the mountains of Japan, but the appearance was often as important as the actual sport.

Soon, Japan became 30 percent of our business, as it was with all other snowboard companies. By the early 1990s, the yen had become a hugely powerful currency, because of the Japanese economy's incredible growth from the end of the Second World War to the end of the Cold War. Everywhere I looked, Japanese people seemed to be buying up as much Western culture as they could, from Pebble Beach Golf Course to buildings in New York to the snowboard scene.

Keeping Japan going was the trick. Part of this was finding the money to match the growth and demand, but another part was meeting Japanese quality standards. After Westbeach had been distributing in Japan for a year or two, I sat down with our Japanese partner and said, "How are things going, what do I need to know?"

"Oh, very good," he told me, "but we're burning 20 percent of everything that you give us."

This was obviously shocking for me to hear. "What do you

mean you're burning 20 percent of everything we're giving you?" I asked.

"We meticulously go through all the inventory you send," he explained. "If there's even a little thread out of place, we burn the item. We don't want to wreck the brand."

That was when I first understood the Japanese demand for quality and how it was exponentially greater than anything we look for in North America. When a Japanese person goes to buy a car, they'll spend two hours looking for the tiniest scratch on the body. The importance of the visual effect of the purchase is unbelievable.

For me, this was really an insight into what quality is, and how a particular culture evaluates it. This insight gave context to what it was to be committed to quality. If we could meet Japanese quality standards, we could meet quality standards anywhere.

The Ski Association

In 1991, I was invited to Banff to speak at a meeting of the Canadian Ski Association, an organization that consisted of ski and equipment reps and resort owners and operators. These people were the old guard of skiing. They were still afraid of snowboarding and did not understand what to make of it. In their view, skiing, as a sport, was on the verge of dying—and with it, their livelihoods.

While in the car on my way to the Rocky Mountains to give my talk, I heard a story on CBC Radio. It was a profile of the time when Sherlock Holmes creator Sir Arthur Conan Doyle moved from London to Switzerland. Doyle made this move because his wife had respiratory disease and needed the cleaner air of the Alps.

While Doyle was in Switzerland, he filed a few articles

for the *London Times*. One article he wrote was about how appalled the Swiss were by the new sport of downhill skiing because they thought their national sport of tobogganing was at risk.

I referred to the Doyle profile when I gave my talk in Canmore. "Look, winter sports are always evolving," I told them. "We have skiing, but, now, we also have snowboarding."

Knowing what I knew about the cyclical nature of trends, I also predicted skiing would make a comeback, perhaps in fifteen or twenty years' time. I said my own boys would look at me as old-fashioned, still using my snowboard while they hit the slopes on their skis. Sure enough, starting around 2010, skis began to mimic snowboard designs, and skiing was revitalized. Two of my five boys only ski.

Some of this perspective had come from our rebranding as a snowboard company. I thought back to how difficult it had been to enrol my partners—and the company itself—in snowboarding, even though it had turned out to be the right move. Whatever the next trend might be, it was reasonable to assume there would be just as much difficulty enrolling everyone in that new vision. Making bold moves with no provable outcome is scary to security-driven finance people.

Our communication had improved exponentially, and that improved communication led Scott, Richard, and me to align on the idea of selling Westbeach, sooner rather than later.

The rest, as the saying goes, is history—from the sale of Westbeach that I talked about in the prologue to the inception and beginning stages of lululemon. I had put in the 10,000 hours (at *least* that many) that author Malcolm Gladwell posits is the amount of time needed to master a discipline.

As my new venture got underway, I wondered—would my lessons with Westbeach in partnership, vertical retail, wholesale, and integrity be enough to prepare me for what was to come?

CHAPTER 10:
THE GENESIS OF LULULEMON

I am a designer and a creator. I believe the definition of a designer, or a creator is that they're never happy. The status quo is never enough. If the designer is happy then they are no longer striving for something better. Designers are almost always unhappy with what they've created which drives those around them crazy. I was never happy at lululemon as I knew there was always more to do. I could always make the company better and the process more efficient.

I was very clear that I was happy being unhappy. I could come across as unhappy because all I saw was possibility. I was unable to communicate to others the massive future I envisioned. I suspect this is what happens to someone like Elon Musk. Too many ideas and so little time.

The Poster on the Pole

Following the sale of Westbeach, I returned to Vancouver. It was 1998. I was enjoying more time with my sons, JJ and Brett; reconnecting with friends; and living by the beach in the most beautiful city in the world.

With all the time I'd spent keeping Westbeach afloat, I'd sacrificed a lot of time being a dad. The relocation of my position to Salem when we'd sold Westbeach had put a six-hour drive between me and my sons, which I did most weekends. "Our dad wasn't around very much, but he knows that," my son JJ recalls. "He tried to tell us, 'I'm doing this for the family. I'm not here today, but I will be tomorrow,' and just try to make something work for us. When you're five, six, seven, eight, nine, ten, you don't understand what that means."

As a lifelong entrepreneur, I knew that finding a mid- to high-level position in another company would be tricky, if not impossible. In my mind, an entrepreneur is too incompetent to work for anybody else. At forty-two, the money I'd made from the sale of Westbeach was too little to retire on, but it gave me some time to think about my next move.

I decided to take the Landmark Advanced course (a follow-up to the Landmark Forum I'd taken several years earlier) so I could review my life from an outside perspective. During the three-day course, I came to understand what I considered to be success in my life. The theme for any future venture would be "giving without the expectation of return." If I were ever to build a new company, my priority would be developing other people to be great.

I knew the only big job I wanted was to be the CEO of Nike. I was perfect for that role. No one understood athletics, shoes, sports psychology, sponsorship, and technical apparel like I did! Although at that point, the big future I saw for global athletics was mostly an unwritten script in my mind.

I even considered starting the next chapter of my life as a barista in a coffee shop—a job I could treat as a means of cash flow only—which would allow me to follow my curiosity wherever it led me.

With the money I'd made on the sale, I bought a reliable car and a house in the Vancouver beach neighbourhood of Kitsilano. I also made sure my sons were in the right school for their learning preferences.

Meanwhile, with an unknown future ahead of me, I had

my physical health to think about. From competitive swimming to football, from wrestling to triathlons, and from skateboarding and snowboarding to squash, I'd beat myself up. My back was a constant source of intense discomfort.

I was looking for a panacea for my pain when I saw a poster on a telephone pole advertising a form of exercise called yoga. A short time later, I found myself in Fiona Stang's yoga class, feeling an undeniable creative impulse once again.

The Yoga Class

Besides the instructor and me, there were five other people in the class—all females between the ages of eighteen and twenty-eight. I was forty-two and trying yoga for the first time. The class was taking place not in a dedicated studio, but at one end of a chilly, air-conditioned gym. Fitness machines were whirring just a few feet away as we rolled out our mats.

This was Kitsilano in 1998. "Kits" was Canada's version of San Francisco's Haight-Ashbury during the '70s. It was a mecca for the post-university, not-yet-married, athletic crowd. There were expansive views of the snow-capped North Shore mountains, multiple yacht clubs, long beaches, and hundreds of offshore islands. It had more athletic supply stores than any other place in the world. It was the origin of Greenpeace, organic foods, and an athletic lifestyle that was second-to-none.

At that time, yoga was a hippie concept in the same vein as meditation and the wellness communes that sprinkled the greater Vancouver area.

I was fortunate that the instructor, Fiona Stang, was very good. Fiona was poised, confident, smart, and approachable. She told me that she'd just moved to Vancouver from New York City, where she had been working in convertible bonds on Wall Street.

"I wanted the ocean and the mountains," Fiona told me. "My husband and I chose Vancouver, and here I am in this beautiful city teaching yoga. It's perfect."

I quickly learned that yoga required applying a level of concentration and awareness that left me with the same endorphin rush as the athletics of my past. It didn't come naturally to me; I'm a big guy and not blessed with an innate sense of balance, but I like to push myself in areas I haven't explored before.

I loved yoga from the first time I tried it.

New Creative Impulses

As I watched the class grow from six to thirty students in one month, I anticipated that yoga would be as strong a social-athletic movement as the surf-skate-snowboard business before it. I understood technical apparel, and I knew there was a much better solution than the sweaty, baggy, binding cotton the other students were wearing. In 1998, gym fashion was simply your worst throwaway clothes.

I knew a lot about sweating. For most of my life, I had three workouts a day, so I was sweaty most of the time. What I wore had to handle that. I wondered, "why shouldn't my clothing be unrestrictive and luxurious and save me time with cleaning and caring?" I knew that if I had to think about my clothing while I was competing, then the clothing was wrong. I always wanted to replace terrible athletic apparel. I wanted clothing that allowed for my mind to ease gracefully into the moment.

After my exposure to yoga, there was a brief period where I tried to ignore my creative impulses. I tried to ignore the urge to take a chance. If I stuck with the idea of being a barista, I could avoid years of uncertainty, stress, hard work, mounting responsibilities, and fiscal pressure. I could run from the way of life I'd been so glad to leave behind when we sold Westbeach.

No matter what I told myself, my creative urges intensified. I knew that I could spot athletic trends five to seven years before they emerged, and I knew that this was what was occurring for me now. I was also forty-two and mindful of the fact that my goal had been to retire at forty. I let my mind wander, and, rather than coming up with reasons not to start another business, I simply decided that if I started a new venture, I would approach it differently.

I'd started Westbeach with little capital and little experience. Now that I had a good amount of both, I could begin with a blank slate and create something in line with my beliefs. Many of these beliefs were formed by the many audiobooks I'd listened to on the six-hour return car rides from Vancouver to the Morrow offices in Salem. I'd listened to just about every audiobook I could find on business success, self-development, and the realization of human potential.

At my next yoga class, I talked to Fiona—my only expert on the subject at the time—about the clothing she and other yoga instructors and practitioners wore. Fiona told me instructors wore a particular line of dancewear. This line, however, only worked on the very fittest bodies, as the fabric was thin and pattern pieces were cut skinny to save money. When someone wearing the dancewear line bent over, the Lycra would stretch too far and become shiny—almost like a lightbulb. The thinness of the fabric resulted in transparency.

Transparency was the first issue that I wanted to solve. I believed that if I could solve the transparency problem, address camel-toe, and thicken the fabric to mask any imperfections, I could create a perfect athletic garment for women. If I could get a technical fabric that felt like cotton instead of plastic, then add properties to make it moisture-wicking and anti-stink, I could create the perfect pant. Nothing like this existed in the world.

With Westbeach, I had worked for two decades with teenage boys as a customer base. I would need a woman's input to properly develop the apparel I had in mind. I asked Fiona if she would be interested in a superior product at triple the price of the line she'd been wearing. She said yes. I explained to her that I was thinking about starting a yoga-apparel brand and that I wanted her to share her thoughts and feedback with me. She said yes again, and I took a big step toward putting my plans into action.

"Chip wanted to climb into my brain," says Fiona. "He wanted to know everything I could tell him about yoga. When he started talking about this company he was going to start, you should see the excitement in his face. That's how I feel about yoga."

Fiona's interest was inspiring, but there were still two other reasons to think carefully about embarking on another business venture—my sons JJ and Brett. I wanted to inspire my boys to find their own passions someday—what they could be the best in the world at—and how they could earn a good living while doing what they loved. I knew that retiring at forty-two and just sitting on an ever-diminishing pile of cash wouldn't convey these possibilities to my boys, especially as they approached adolescence.

I wondered if it would be possible to balance being a great dad with devoting my time and energy to getting a business off the ground. The answer, I realized, was that it was up to me. I made a choice to be engaged on both fronts—fatherhood and business. I felt it was imperative for JJ and Brett to be integrated into my new venture. After all the travelling I'd done with Westbeach, I was determined to never get on a plane again without having my family with me.

In JJ's words: "My memories of Dad's new venture started with Brett and me being brought into it. We were on a plane flying from Vancouver to San Diego to visit our grandma. Dad would always sit in the middle, sort of against his will because he was so big. Brett and I were little kids, but we were both drawing logos for lululemon. I'm not sure if any of those got adopted, but I think if you went through Dad's book of creativity you would see these squiggly lines, coming together to make a lululemon logo in some way. I think he's always tried to get us involved. His way of being a dad was to always educate us in what he was doing and how he was doing it."

The pieces were in place. All I needed now was to determine what my new venture would look like day to day.

CHAPTER 11:
THE WORLD IN 1998

Athletically induced endorphins are nature's stress-reducing drug.

No Athletic Clothing for Women

As of 1996, teenage girls had just broken into extreme sports, an area which had long been dominated by men. For decades before this, athletics and sweating were not known as feminine virtues. The "cool" girls regularly skipped phys-ed classes and smoked cigarettes. Of course, girls competed in Olympic events, although at much lower numbers than men. I was raised in the world of competitive swimming where girls made up 50 percent of the participants, but where there was also a high dropout rate when girls became women— curves made hydrodynamics challenging.

The first girls in non-Olympic sports entered through surfing, but most girls entered through snowboarding, as snowboarding was so much more accessible than surfing. The 1990s era of athletic girls coincided with the very Portland, Oregon, male grunge look, which went well with snowboarding fashion. As girls became women, the timing was right for them to express their sense of femininity through yoga.

Meanwhile, the World Wide Web was just being figured out (although e-commerce was still nonexistent). Boys were being coddled by their single mothers and girls were dominating education. Coke and Pepsi were marketed as the "American Dream," fast food was becoming a staple, and Americans were getting fat—but no one was acknowledging it.

In the world of apparel, most clothing shrunk after only a few wash-dry cycles—everyone used hot water and hot dryer settings. In this context, there was no athletic clothing for women, except for shrunken men's styles.

As I embarked on a new venture, I knew I was the only person in the world thinking of non-mountain technical apparel.

My ability to predict athletic trends was both a gift and a curse. I was designing items five years before public acceptance, so, naming the next trend, and getting it to stick, proved challenging. Back in 1995, I had coined the word *strech* (street-tech) to describe the intersection between streetwear and technical apparel, but the phonetics didn't work, and the term was never adopted. In 1996, I started calling the movement from office wear to street athletic clothing *streetnic* (street technical).

In 2014, the New York fashion media would eventually describe this intersection as *athleisure*, which is a term I don't like, even if I must acknowledge that it's here to stay. To me, athleisure denotes a non-athletic, smoking, diet coke-drinking woman in a shopping mall wearing an unflattering pink velour tracksuit. Too much leisure, too little athletics.

The Hedgehog Concept

A year earlier, during the six-hour drives to and from Oregon, while working for Morrow, I had listened to perhaps a hundred audiobooks. I loved the histories of the retail growth of Starbucks, Walmart, and General Electric. I listened to everything by Jim Collins.

From this listening, I concluded that four of the audiobooks summed up the other ninety-six. These main four comprised the philosophical, cultural, and people development ideas I wanted to use to form the basis of my new company. These audiobooks were:

1. *The Goal* by Eliyahu Goldratt[3]—a fun, fictional novel describing manufacturing bottlenecks, opportunities, and overall theory of constraints.
2. *The 7 Habits of Highly Effective People* by Stephen Covey.[4]
3. *The Psychology of Achievement* by Brian Tracy[5]—how to be a great citizen, parent, and goal-setter.
4. *Good to Great* by Jim Collins[6]—the concept is "good," the enemy is "great," and a "Level 5 leader" has trained a replacement better than themselves.
5. The fifth addition to this list is not an audiobook, but a course: the Landmark Forum.

In the book *Good to Great,* author Jim Collins introduced me to the Hedgehog Concept.[7]

3. Eliyahu Goldratt, *The Goal* (North River Press, 1984).

4. Stephen Covey, *The 7 Habits of Highly Effective People* (Free Press, 1989).

5. Brian Tracy, *The Psychology of Achievement* (Simon & Schuster, 1989).

6. Jim Collins, *Good to Great: Why Some Companies Make the Leap . . . and Others Don't* (Random House Business, 2001).

7. Ibid., 95.

Collins contends that the area where all three circles overlap is where a person or company is most powerful. The intersection is where founders and their companies are intertwined and the greater the overlap, the better the business. For my own life, and in considering my new venture, I drew the following:

Circle 1: What was I "passionate" about? Athletics.
Circle 2: What could I be the "best in the world" at? Black stretch pants.
Circle 3: What would be my "economic engine"? Vertical retail.

The idea of designing technical clothing to suit athletic activity drove me. My brain worked full-time on athletic solves. Design sketches littered my day timer. Throwing myself into solving the apparel issues of yoga was exciting, and I was ultra-passionate about maximizing the athletic experience that produced an endorphin rush.

As I further considered the way the Hedgehog Concept[8] applied to me, I realized the convergence of my three circles was not yoga apparel. It was people development. I knew people development was the key to my specific business philosophy.

Linguistic Abstraction

Culture is a way of operating such that people act consistently, inside and outside the company.

Consistency arises from a belief in the vision, values, and linguistic abstraction (a common set of terms and definitions that all employees understand) of the company. Lululemon's linguistic abstraction was composed of a series of twenty to thirty

8. Ibid., 95.

terms and definitions that arose from the previously listed books, audiobooks, and participation in the Landmark programs.

Our linguistic abstraction allowed the company to communicate with speed and efficiency across all departments and geographies. A person in Vancouver had to be able to communicate effectively with a supplier in Beijing. Just like the Gutenberg press or the fax machine or email, abstractions enabled exponential communication. A company of developed employees who understand the same business terms also grew exponentially.

A few examples of lululemon's linguistic abstractions are as follows:

- **Committed Listening**: Listening without obligation to act, paying attention to both verbal and non-verbal communication.
- **By-When Date**: The date on which a project or task is promised to be completed.
- **Condition of Satisfaction**: An action or criteria against which completion can be measured.
- **Looking Good**: a protective way of being that is inconsistent with how we declare ourselves to be.
- **Talking into the Listening**: Within a conversation, each person's position is based primarily on how they were raised and their life's experiences. For a conversation to be effective, the person speaking must consider the filter through which the listener hears.

The Fabric

From my first yoga class, I knew exactly the fabric I wanted to use to make my yoga apparel. I had used a version of my dream fabric as a first layer under snowboard clothing for the emerging fourteen- to eighteen-year-old female snowboard market. At the time, it was thick and shrunk too much, but the cottony feel of this particular synthetic fabric was amazing. It was unique because I could apply technical properties to a synthetic fabric to manage sweat and stink. As a bonus, it was matte-black. Globally, with Westbeach, I wholesaled fifty-seven pairs of those pants. All fifty-seven women who purchased them wrote to me pleading for more.

I realized that a lighter version would be ideal for yoga clothing. My key invention was to cut the pattern extra-wide—effectively using twice the fabric of existing dancewear pants—so when the fabric stretched, it would not be see-through or shine. I worked with a fabric mill to improve on the shrinkage, weight, and technical capabilities. The fabric still shrunk too much. It was good but not great.

The next thing to consider was the stitching and seaming of the apparel. From my time as an athlete designing triathlon clothing in 1979, I knew damp, snug clothing combined with repetitive movement always resulted in chafing.

I couldn't believe anyone at Nike had ever run ten kilometres in a pair of Nike shorts without developing a rash on their inner thigh. They left their inner leg seams wide open. The result was very painful for anyone with prominent muscles. I guessed Nike runners were too skinny or were paid too much in sponsorship money to complain.

The problem was athletic designers didn't exist in 1998. I was it. One-hundred percent of designers coming out of schools focused on runway fashion or wedding dresses. Designers were first and foremost aesthetically driven. Apparel function was way down on the list of priorities.

Over the previous year or two, I'd been reading about a new type of garment construction in which two pieces of material abutted one another in something called a *flat seam*. That meant there'd be no raised seam inside the garment and, therefore, less chafing with movement.

I immediately understood that flat seaming was vital to solving the number one athletic problem of rashing. But, the prohibitive cost of the sewing machines combined with the challenges of training inexperienced and unsophisticated retail staff to educate the customer on this hidden technology meant that the consumer would probably not understand the value.

Refining the fabric took over six months. During this time, I also made a major purchase—two Japanese flat-lock sewing machines for a total price of $80,000.

By the time I'd imported the machines and developed the fabric, I'd spent more than 10 percent of the money I'd made from the sale of Westbeach. It felt like a huge outlay of cash, especially given that I was still a long way from having a final product.

With the flat-lock machines, I could cut labour time down to about six minutes per pant. It was almost like using a robot. I had expensive fabric, expensive machines but low labour costs. With robot-type machines, I could match the price of Asian manufacturing in Canada.

Before flat seaming, all seams were ugly, so fashion designers hid them. With beautiful flat seam technology, I pulled the seams outside as a functional solution to prevent all rashing. This meant the seams were visible on the outside of the garment. By doing this, I inadvertently discovered that I could use these seam lines to accentuate the female body.

I believe this seam idea changed fashion design for the next twenty years.

A New Generation of Women

A few years earlier, I'd dated a top-level track athlete. She was incredibly fashionable, passionate about the environment, and had a great mind for business. She was younger than I was, and she gave me a new context for the next generation. Our relationship didn't work out, but she'd given me the experience of observing a new market of women that had never before existed.

As fashionable as she was, her athletic clothing never fit well, and it wasn't flattering. I'd long wondered why.

The answer lay with the mantras of Adidas and Nike. At that time, both companies were all about men, shoes, competition, and winning at all costs. Their idea of women's athletic clothing was to take men's apparel and "shrink it and pink it." It didn't perform well for women, but there were absolutely no alternatives.

Shrinkage

While vacationing in Mexico in the '70s, I remember seeing a homeless man wearing a twenty-year-old Aca Joe sweatshirt. It struck me, at the time, that despite its age, the sweatshirt still looked solid.

Aca Joe colour-dyed their fully sewn garments in a hot-dye process resulting in zero post-purchase shrinkage and a it had a velvety hand feel.

Considering that Aca Joe technique in the context of my new venture, I knew I wanted my company to be known for goods that would not shrink when a customer brought them home and laundered them. I wanted everything I sold to look, feel, and perform as well as it did when it was purchased five years earlier.

At that time, women often had only one set of athletic apparel and would reuse the same outfit day after day. A hot wash eliminated stink, but ensuring the garments wouldn't shrink was key. The only way to achieve this was to put every garment through a hot water wash and in a hot dryer before selling it to the customer.

Devising the Business Philosophy

From Westbeach, I'd gained a superior understanding of Canadian and Asian manufacturing. I'd also acquired the business skills to manage a small-to-midsized company. I had eighteen years of vertical retail experience, which was about eighteen years more than any other person on Earth.

I also loved to interact with people. I believe this made me unique because a person in the apparel business tended to be either a manufacturer who did not like people, or a retailer who loved people but had little understanding of manufacturing. I straddled the middle. I was not an expert in anything other than knowing how the vertical retail puzzle worked.

I had a healthy chunk of money for start-up costs. I was starting from scratch, but I already knew what I wanted the company to look like in five years. All I had to do was work back from that five-year vision to create a plan.

Choosing to be unconstrained by my past experiences, I knew I could create this new company any way I wanted. All the little things that hadn't worked for me at Westbeach could be easily solved in my new business philosophy. The model I was formulating was so counterintuitive to "normal" apparel methodologies that I wanted to think clean. Each piece of the puzzle had to work with the others. A change in accounting procedures could easily mess up speed in logistics. A change in the design of a garment could mess up the layout of a store.

I also knew I wanted to call my salespeople "Educators,"

and that much of our success would rest on our ability to educate customers on the technical solves that they could not see (like the flat seaming). With education, I was confident that the customer would understand why our product was three times the price of what they were accustomed to paying.

I knew this model would only work if the Educators were phenomenal. It occurred to me that I could potentially transform a defined group of post-university women into Educators, using a catalyzed self-development program. Again, people development was the convergence of my Hedgehog Concept, as developed by Jim Collins.

Finally, I wanted to maintain 100 percent control over my brand without any dilution from middlemen. This meant staying as far away from wholesale as I could, and totally embracing vertical retail.

To explain vertical retailing, I need first to describe the wholesale business model: manufacturers (known as wholesalers) make a product and sell it to a retail store, who then sells it to the customer. The wholesale model has a middleman.

With the wholesale model, great technology is impossible. When I made a stretch, black, first-layer snowboard pant for women at Westbeach in 1996, it cost $40 to make, and we sold it to snowboard shops for $80. The shops would sell it to the customers for $160. I knew if I changed to a vertical model, I could bring the cost of the pant to $30 and sell it inside my own retail stores for $90. At $90, I was sure I could sell thousands!

With wholesaling, I couldn't get the customer to pay for technology they couldn't see. Retail stores like Dick's didn't have trained salespeople who could enhance the value of the product by educating customers on what was hidden. Further, retailers rarely paid on schedule—or sometimes went bankrupt—which meant the manufacturer had difficulty planning their budget (as was the case for Nike, Under

Armour, and Adidas with the Sports Authority bankruptcy of 2017).

When a company's primary revenue comes from wholesale, the store buyers call the shots. Typically, buyers review data on what has sold in the last quarter and extrapolate data from that to decide what they will buy in the future. In effect, wholesale buyers just want more of the same as last year. Therefore, successful but outdated designs are rewarded. Buyers are given bonuses for achieving annual budget metrics and are disincentivized to risk.

I wanted to design apparel from "amnesia"—as if I'd just woken up in the hospital with no memory of my past or any apparel I'd ever known. I wanted lululemon to be design-driven, not buyer-driven, which would mean that all final decisions would be made by designers and not buyers.

Another danger of wholesaling is the loss of control over markdowns. Too many discounts on products can cheapen the value of full-priced items. Deep discounts can also damage the overall image of a brand.

One benefit of vertical retail is the complete ownership of branding and customer experience. I wanted complete control of the store display and staff hiring. Every single detail the customer saw in my ideal store would go through a specific creative experience.

Vertical retail comes with its own challenges, however. There are more moving parts in a vertical retail operation. Because people are involved, a great retail company must love people. Hiring, paying, and maintaining staff can be arduous. The overhead expense of operating retail stores must be added to the price of the goods sold. Paying rent, storing inventory, making tenant improvements, and store infrastructure all represent major capital expenditures—and unfortunately, so does theft.

My new business philosophy would skip the sporting goods

stores. I would own my own stores and take both the manufacturer and the retail store revenue. I would make enough money to be able to develop and pay highly educated people. I would make women's technical athletic apparel beautiful, and then sell it at a premium. I would do what had never been done before.

Yet again, the time had come for me to risk everything.

Defining the Target Market

My experience taught me that if I saw something three times within a short period of time, it would show up in the mainstream public five to seven years later. In 1998, I read an article about yoga, heard a random person mention yoga in conversation, and saw a poster on a telephone post promoting one of the very first yoga classes in Vancouver.

But those three things were not the only trigger points for me. That year, I also read a statistic that said 60 percent of the graduates from North American universities were women. I was stunned. When I'd attended university in the '70s, it seemed like female graduates numbered about 20 percent.

Before 1998, a common assumption was that most women in North America would get married, then get pregnant, and leave the job market before the age of twenty-four. That was the case with many of my friends. But, because I'd read articles about diminishing poverty in Africa through educating women to affect lower birth rates, I saw a different future. I believed that a new demographic of highly educated women would wait much longer to have children.

I believed this would be the new North American order; a specific market segment that had never before existed. This market segment was the twenty-four- to thirty-five-year-old woman who was single or engaged, had no children, was highly educated, media savvy, athletic, and professional. These women travelled, owned their own condos, earned $80,000 year, and were very stylish.

The more I considered them, the more of an identity, context, and social history unfolded in my mind. I believed this entire pool of women would be untapped by other businesses because the prevailing thought was still: "Why invest in a female employee if she will just leave our business at age twenty-four to start a family?" I knew I was on to something.

Power Women and Super Girls

I often develop a sort of "thesis" as a means of truly identifying and understanding various market segments. It's a branding exercise that provides a historical context for me and enables me to design into the future of that specific target market. I have also found that there is power in giving market segments a name as other social scientists have done (e.g. Generation X, millennials, and so forth).

As I considered this particular group of women, I looked first at their family history and who their parents might have been. It occurred to me that in the 1960s and early '70s, the birth control pill had come into widespread usage. The pill immediately transformed the sex lives of anyone under the age of forty, sparking what is commonly known as the Sexual Revolution.

Women suddenly had significant control over conception. If they did want children, they could decide when, and how many. There was a newfound sense of independence in this ability to delay childbirth. There was also the opportunity to pursue careers that had, to date, been dominated by men.

Meanwhile, men's lives did not change as much with the arrival of the pill, and they had no idea how to relate to this newly independent woman. Thus, came the era of divorce, with divorce rates peaking in the late '70s and early '80s (rates that have since undergone a steady decline).[9]

With all the publicity around divorce and equality, a new female market segment was created in the 1970s and 1980s. I came to think of this segment as *Power Women*. These women put in twelve-hour workdays, kept a clean and orderly home, and did their best to give their children all the love they'd had pre-divorce. What they gave up was their social life, exercise, balance, and sleep.

Unfortunately, I read that the hormone dosage in the original birth control pill was too high. That dosage, combined with the Power Women's lack of sleep, work-related stress, poor eating habits, and three-martini lunches worked together to cause the terrible upswing in breast cancer rates in the '90s.[10] Too many Power Women had looked to their fathers to define business success, emulating both their drive and their toxic lifestyles. Regretfully, for many Power Women, this would ultimately cost them their health and, in some cases, their lives.

With the rise of the Power Women came a societal shift. These women wanted to be invested in, to rise to the top, and to be treated the same as their male counterparts. The belief that all women would leave their careers at twenty-four to have children had become a thing of the past.

The 1980s also produced new fashion trends and Power Women were seen in the boardroom wearing power suits with big shoulder pads, a look that spoke to their confidence and their newfound place in the business world.

9. Claire Cain Miller, "The Divorce Surge Is Over, but the Myth Lives On," *New York Times*, December 2, 2014, www.nytimes.com/2014/12/02/upshot/the-divorce-surge-is-over-but-the-myth-lives-on.html.

10. Roni Caryn Rabin, "Birth Control Pills Still Linked to Breast Cancer, Study Finds," *New York Times*, December 6, 2017, accessed August 16, 2018, https://www.nytimes.com/2017/12/06/health/birth-control-breast-cancer-hormones.html.

The daughters raised by these Power Women subconsciously knew that education was essential because divorce seemed inevitable. They knew that education and a substantial income were critical to managing both a household and a career simultaneously.

Many of these daughters spent weekends with a newly divorced father who had no manual for how to be a single dad. These fathers did what they knew best: they got their daughters into sports and became their coaches and mentors.

As youngsters, I suspect these girls were influenced by Saturday morning cartoons, which traditionally featured men, wearing capes and stretch fabric outfits, running around and saving the world. By the '80s, most of these cartoons had incorporated a female superhero—also wearing tight, stylish, form-fitting suits and capes.

I felt these powerful cartoon women became iconic to these girls, who were doing what most adolescents and teenagers do: dress in a manner opposite to their mothers. They did not need to look like boys or men to compete with them; cartoon superheroes were depicted as equal to men. I coined this market segment the *Super Girls*.

In my mind, Super Girls didn't have any context for gender inequality. It just didn't exist for them in the way it did for their mothers. They knew they were just as well-educated as men and had been brought up in an era that, if anything, favoured girls in education. The Super Girls that I knew had no use for Women's Events or Women's Achievement Awards. They were playing in a bigger pool and were the "best of the best," not the "best of the women."

The thesis I created for these Super Girls worked for design and branding purposes, so brand and design had only one person on which they needed to focus. I defined a single Super Girl to be thirty-two years old and born on September 28. I called her *Ocean*. Each year, since 1998, Ocean never got a day older or a day younger. Every Ocean in the world would be our sponsored athlete, just like Nike choose a few specific men to sponsor. If Nike or lululemon couldn't make sponsored athletes excited about their product, then the rest of the market wouldn't be excited either.

For twenty-two-year-old university graduates, I speculated utopia was to be a fit thirty-two-year-old with an amazing career and spectacular health. She was travelling for business and pleasure, owned her own condo, and had a cat. She was fashionable and could afford quality. At thirty-two, she was positioned to get married and have children if she chose to, and to work full-time, part-time, or not at all. Anything was possible.

For forty-two-year-old women with two to three children, her former thirty-two-year-old self represented an era when time seemed so available—a time without the pressures of motherhood and when keeping fit was easy.

As my ideal customer and demographic, the thirty-two-year-old in 1998 did not yet exist. In 1998, she was twenty-four. Essentially, I imagined who she would be eight years before her thirty-two-year-old self existed. I then designed for who I knew she would become in eight years' time. Because Super Girls were iconic to women of all ages, I felt they would best represent the perfect way to dress for a busy life.

The Church of Athletics

The stage was set for yoga wear in 1998. The Super Girls had just graduated from university. They averaged twenty-four-years-old but would soon become the thirty-two-year-old urban professionals I'd envisioned. Super Girls were determined not to fall into the health trap of their mothers.

Yoga was a great way of maintaining balance, and because it was feminine, noncompetitive, time-saving (in comparison to surf and snowboarding), and mentally calming, it struck to the centre of what women wanted. I'd experienced the endorphin rush of yoga for myself—I knew it would be on par with other great endorphin producers of our age: sex, drugs, Starbucks, surf, skate, snowboarding . . . and the soon-to-be-developed "ding" of a smartphone.

Why Women Would Pay Three Times More

Even though my product would be three times the price of the most popular existing brand, I could deliver a quality product the customer would buy in volume by going with a vertical retail model. Starbucks was doing the same thing with coffee.

At first glance, no one could believe a person would pay three times the average price for better quality, but I knew the Super Girls would have the professional jobs that would pay them well. I knew they would *invest* in their wardrobe. I knew that after owning a lululemon piece for five years, women would know it was the best investment they ever made.

They would have money, devotion to health, organic food, and athletics. They were fit and were waiting four to eight years longer than previous generations of women to have babies. Therefore, they could invest in their wardrobes without any concern about how their bodies might change with pregnancy. There was a propensity for Super Girls to buy fewer, better-quality wardrobe staples that would stay in style longer. Quality material and fastidious construction would cost more.

The clothing was also designed so that it could be worn outside the gym. Workout clothes could now be worn to go for coffee. Before lululemon, people had never felt comfortable walking around all day in athletic clothing.

I had met my ideal customer, at least theoretically. To take this to the next level, we had to speak with the Super Girls themselves and ask them to help us create a new future for athletic apparel.

While I believed women would respond positively to the designs taking shape in my mind, my experience told me it was imperative to contact my target market and listen to what they had to say. My tried and tested way of connecting was to host design meetings and find out exactly what women wanted.

Initial Design and Formation of lululemon

Female athletic fashion seemed to die after the short run of Reebok's step classes and Jane Fonda workouts in the early '90s. Athletic companies were making most of their apparel money from T-shirts with big logos on the front. There was no such thing as an athletic, technical apparel designer. Finding a designer who was 99.99 percent focused on the technical was nearly impossible. Most designers went to design school so they could showcase their individual creativity and design flair on the runway. Design was all about *the look*. There was no glamour in technical function. If it was good, *technical function* was virtually invisible to the naked eye. Lastly, yoga was rare in big cities. I was entering unchartered territory.

Amanda Dunsmoor was a designer I had hired at West-beach to design outerwear jackets. She was athletic and had the perfect style of a fresh, healthy Vancouver athlete. From my kitchen table in a decrepit one-bedroom Kitsilano apartment, we developed samples in anticipation of conducting focus groups.

In Amanda's words: "There was Nike, there was Adidas, there was Reebok, but there was really nothing that catered to women who wanted workout clothes that actually fit and felt good. Chip was really keen on finding the perfect technical fabric."

I would sketch something on paper and give it to Amanda

to expand into a design. Even though my sketches were usually rough, I made sure I was very specific about certain aspects. I would tell Amanda: "I want reflective here; I think it's important that the seams are flat and away from underneath the arms and inner thighs so that there's no chafing; I think it's important the pants have a diamond crotch gusset to solve for camel-toe and make pants palatable for women to walk to the studio in public."

Even in the beginning, the most important item was the pants. Most of the pants in the marketplace at that time were high-waisted, non-gusseted, and shiny with open seams in the worst places. They were just dance tights women only wore when other women were around. Women did not yet wear running tights. I wanted something with a bit of a flare at the ankles so that it was more flattering to women with rounder hips.

I was adamant that the rise of the pants would mimic that of men's surf shorts. I knew athletes had a bigger butt and a higher thigh-to-waist ratio. That meant the back rise had to be significantly higher than the low-rise front. Then athletes could bend over or squat without exposing their butt cracks and without having to put up with the doubling up of fabric in the front. I wanted crop tops to vent body heat as yoga classes had moved to dedicated heated rooms. This was a radical departure from the high-rise front and back of the mid-'90s and of styles since 2014. Pants with high-rise fronts in 2018 are in response to women wanting their pant to shape them. In 1998, fit women did not want a high-rise front and wanted a low rise to expose more skin to the air to control sweat when doing hot yoga.

The first line was simple. We had two pants, a pair of shorts, and three tops. There were six designs and around four or five sizes of each style. As the fabric was so expensive and a dye-lot was about 2,000 metres, we could only buy one colour. That colour was black.

Even with those constraints, I developed an idea to make the pants with black thread or multiple coloured threads and then multiple colours of fabric trim taping around the neck and armholes of tops. From one black fabric, we created various colourways to give the customer options.

The more we reworked the styles for fit, the more confident I was we had a great product, but I still needed a name for my new company. The Westbeach name had been vital to the success of my surf, skate, and snowboard brand. I needed something for the new line that would have the same iconic and memorable feeling.

The Name

I came up with about twenty name and logo possibilities, including *Athletically Hip*. Another name, *lululemon*, has a history attached to it.

At Westbeach, we purchased a skateboard brand called *Homless Skateboards*. We produced Homless for two or three years, and it was becoming very popular in Japan, so I proceeded to trademark the name. But through the trademarking process, I found there were already countless variations on the name—mainly since *hom* (or homme) means man in French. Trademarking the name was not a viable option.

Skateboarding had crested, and snowboarding was blowing up, so I told all our distributors and salespeople that Homless Skateboards was done. It didn't make sense, I thought, to put any more resources into the brand or skateboarding.

To understand the Japanese psyche, when you deliver something they love for two years, and then you stop, it becomes doubly valuable, like rare art. That year—1990—as I brought Westbeach's new snowboard apparel to our Japanese buyers, they said, "Mr. Chip-san, where is Homless?"

"We're not doing Homless anymore," I told them.

The next year, even as snowboarding apparel exploded in popularity in Japan, the Japanese buyers asked me the same thing. "Mr. Chip-san, where is Homless?"

Again, I had to tell them we weren't doing it anymore. At that time, the Japanese yen was at its very pinnacle, and Japanese people were buying up hotels, property, and brands in North America. We got a call from my Japanese buyers.

This time, it was an offer to buy the Homless brand name. This surprised me, especially since I couldn't trademark "Homless" and Westbeach didn't own it. So, when I gave the Japanese a price I thought was ridiculous and they came back after mere seconds to say "okay," I was astounded. This felt like the easiest money I'd ever made.

After that, I often thought about why my Japanese buyers liked the name Homless so much. I could see how the big Japanese trading companies were coming up with North American/Western–sounding names because the Japanese consumer at the time wanted "authentic" Americanism.

On further consideration, it seemed the Japanese liked the name Homless because it had the letter L in it, and the Japanese language doesn't have that sound. Brand names with Ls in them sounded even more authentically North American/Western to Japanese consumers, especially the twenty-year-olds.

This felt like a neat idea, so over the next few years, I played with alliterative names with Ls in them, la la la, jotting down variations in my notebook. This continued until the time came to develop a brand name for my new yoga apparel concept, and during this creative experimentation, lululemon was one possibility I wrote down.

It came out of nothing. Absolutely nothing. And it was risky at the time because the word "lemon" was attached to poor-quality 1980s Detroit automobiles. However, the word lemon also represented freshness. Either way, I would have to see how the focus groups responded to it.

I wanted a lower-case L to start the word lululemon because I wanted a less in-your-face men's athletic name. Meanwhile, I sketched a bunch of logos for the focus groups to discuss, then worked with a graphic artist, Stephen Bennett, who put a circle around a stylized "A" that I had sketched. The "A" was made to match the name Athletically Hip.

The Focus Groups

As I only intended to be a vertical retail operation, I hired a woman named Amrita Sondhi to assist me in dealing with the hundreds of operational details involved in opening a retail store, including assembling focus groups.

As far as the focus groups went, we invited ten groups of ten women. Their ages ranged between twenty and forty. The focus groups took place over a couple of months at an apartment I'd recently moved into, about a block from Kitsilano Beach.

"The focus groups were fun," Amanda Dunsmoor would later recall. "We would just gather around Chip's kitchen table. Most of the people he knew from the community; some were yoga instructors. I remember there was an artist there, reworking a logo. The focus groups helped me understand what people were wanting in yoga wear, and that was essential for me because I had never done yoga. I would not have been able to do it if not for their feedback."

It didn't take long for us to create an effective way of running our focus groups, despite having no real training. Our questions included asking the participants what they thought of twenty possible names, twenty possible logos, and their favourite running shoe brand.

We also asked about vitamin usage, emerging trends in athletics, and whether our participants had ever visited a massage therapist, homeopath, or chiropractor. We even asked about their favourite music and what could be improved about women's changerooms and the entire shopping experience.

Most importantly, we asked each person in our focus groups to bring one piece of athletic clothing they loved or wanted improved.

One of our first designers, Summer Gray, says, "The focus groups were so important to the evolution of lulu's product design and became part of the design process for many years. We asked people to bring their favourite pieces of athletic clothing. We were able to learn from all types of athletes what they loved and what they felt was missing in the market. We were able to learn what companies were doing it better than us and how we could leapfrog what they were doing."

We started to see trends. We learned that asking open questions about a wide variety of topics encouraged the participants to engage in conversation with one another, rather than just replying to us. This, we found, was what got us the interesting and useful information we needed.

Usually, during each group, I would have three "aha" moments. But I also found this was the same for the participants. One woman would say something that would cause the rest of them to suddenly get animated and think of the topic or question in a whole new way. When this spontaneous conversation happened, we would sit back, listen carefully, and take notes.

Something I'd learned through personal development was that you can't create the future without first clearing up the past, so we made a point of having the participants talk about what *didn't* work for them in the athletic clothing or the retail experience that were currently available. Once this clearing was finished, and the participants got any background issues out of the way, we could move into questions to solve the unknown future.

We wanted to know what our participants thought of the future of athletics, and what athletic apparel needed to perform to provide for changes. For instance, snowboarding had gone from hard-boot, ski-racing clothing, to free-ride, to pipe-riding, to powder—each stage in this evolution requiring different apparel. Likewise, as it grew in popularity, yoga morphed from one version to the next: power, Bikram, flow, sports yoga, meditative yoga, etc.

The most satisfying part of the focus-group experience was watching people's reactions as they touched our fabric for the first time. No one had created a technical fabric that felt like cotton before. I already thought this material was special (although it had yet to be perfected), but the feeling of seeing someone's eyes open wide as they touched it demonstrated that we'd made something unlike anything that had come before it.

I believed in my gut this pant innovation would affect people's behaviour and the way they lived their lives. Once our focus group participants felt the fabric with their hands, they could hardly wait to put it on and feel it against their bodies.

The people in these focus groups could see the possibility of performing without all the hang-ups of transparency and fabric turning shiny when it stretched. But it went beyond that: what I really saw was the possibility of customers using our clothing not just for yoga but to the studio, or gym, and back. Solving the camel-toe problem was probably the key invention. Without that solve, the pants couldn't be worn on the street. I knew Super Girls valued time above all else. If they could go to a yoga class and then to coffee and onto shopping without needing to change between activities, I could save them forty-five minutes a day.

Westbeach succeeded in surf, skate, and snowboarding because the athletic look of those sports transferred out onto the street. I failed at street clothing for triathlon, beach volleyball, and mountain biking because they did not make that transition. I knew the real success of lululemon would be in the ability of the apparel to perform twenty-four hours a day, in several settings, if needed.

Voting

At the end of every focus group, I came away with three or four improvements I'd never even considered. The groups talked about the length of pants and the psychology of sizing. Because of taking the time and effort to run these groups, I not only came away with what has since become an iconic name and logo, I also avoided countless mistakes that would have proven costly, or even disastrous.

I took twenty names—including Athletically Hip and lululemon—to the focus groups. I was almost certain the participants would go for Athletically Hip, but to my surprise the overwhelming favourite was lululemon.

Also, to my surprise, the participants selected the subtle, stylized letter A intended for Athletically Hip.

To this day, I answer the, "Where did the name come from?" question daily.

Long Pants

In 1996, I was selling snowboard boots at Westbeach, and in the first week, all the size thirteen to fifteen boots sold out. Further back, in 1973, when I was a six-foot three teenager, I was five inches taller than almost everyone I knew. By 1997, my height felt normal. The population was getting taller.

I'd never been able to find pants of a decent length for me, especially with shrinkage after a wash. So here was another issue I could solve. As I had spent considerable time in Japan, I noticed most stores had sewing machines for on-site tailoring. The Japanese body is generally long in the torso but short in the arms and legs. For Japanese retail stores to sell American goods, every pant needed to be hemmed on the spot.

I loved this idea and wanted to incorporate it into the very early stages of lululemon. As I saw it, with our own stores, we could build the cost of hemming into the product and provide a pre-shrunk pant that was the perfect length for tall women. I decided I was committed to making perfect pants for tall girls.

Styling and Design

On my trips to Europe in the '70s, something that stood out to me was how people dressed—specifically, how *well* they dressed. The design lines in their clothing created an illusion that their bodies were more fit than they were. I could see how much thought Europeans put into styling. It differed greatly from what I'd seen in New York fashion magazines or nonexistent fashion on the West Coast. There was nothing functional about European fashion—it just looked really good.

I would think about how to bring these two dichotomies (European style and West Coast function) together into something that had never existed before. That was the birth of the idea that eventually became athleisurewear, and its inception can be largely credited to my seeing the world at a young age.

Until lululemon, fashion dictated that either the top or the bottom was tight, but not both. Incorporating stretch yarns made fabrics more form-fitting, and for the first time in history, women wore a tight top and a tight, low-rise bottom. Because of hot yoga rooms, a crop top was a functional necessity and the combination of all three created a look no one in fashion would have ever thought possible.

My success at Westbeach and then at lululemon was due to honing a perfect combination of Euro-style and West Coast function, but function always came first.

Accentuating what made people feel confident—wider shoulders, smaller waists, slimmer hips—meant Guests would feel good and look good in our clothing. I realized that the shape of our logo provided a perfect contour to enhance the natural shape of a woman's body. I designed the lululemon logo right into tops and hoodies. This was a critical shift in brand design for us because we could subtly show our logo without it reading as such.

I wanted the same for pants. There was a huge debate about where to set the seam lines on pants. Women told me they preferred side seams because when they looked in the mirror, side seams slimmed their hips. I wanted to move the side seams to the back to frame the bum and make the bum appear smaller.

I persisted because I believed that eventually, men would tell women the pants looked great without really understanding why. It was like what I'd observed in the '90s surf industry; girls wanted their boyfriends to wear the Australian-inspired surf shorts without realizing it was the cut that made them so flattering on their boyfriends' athletic bodies. The same occurs when men wear tighter jeans.

I wanted beauty to be where the visible meets the invisible. More than anything, I wanted lululemon to stand for great quality, and I wanted our Guests to be proud to wear it. That's how lululemon athletica came to be.

CHAPTER 12:
LULULEMON TAKES SHAPE

Great ice creams start with the best ingredients, but what elevates them beyond the competition is putting two disparate ingredients together like salt and caramel or chocolate chunks and cherries.

An Elevated Location

It was exhilarating to create something from nothing, to put into place the early blocks of the business, to put together that totally original puzzle. Although I listened to the input of others, I knew what I heard was just more of the same. Lululemon athletica was not born to play by the normal rules of retail, because we didn't know the rules in the first place. The time had come to put a lifetime of failures and experiences together. To do that, I'd need a concept store.

There was nowhere I wanted to be other than West 4th Avenue in Kitsilano, just up from the beach, not far from where Westbeach's Vancouver store had been located. I wanted the newly-named lululemon to be associated with Kitsilano and the people who lived there. It seemed inhabiting a location on West 4th would be important, perhaps vital, to our success.

Lululemon was inspired largely by university graduates drawn to this unique, athletic, semi-hippie-like part of the city.

I didn't have enough money or product to rent a regular store location, so I found a space behind an inconspicuous door and up a drab-looking flight of stairs, instead of an inviting street-level storefront.

I decided there had to be a way to use this central yet cloistered location to my advantage. This required maximizing large floor space and strategically displaying products, so people would enjoy the experience and stay as long, or as little, as they wanted.

The store, I thought, could be made into a sort of interactive design laboratory. We built a sewing lab right there. I felt the process of designs being conceived on the spot would be part of the brand and would create word-of-mouth excitement about what we were doing.

As Amanda recalls: "We had our office area in one corner and racks of clothing set up on the other side. It created a fantastic design environment because I could interact with customers and find out directly from them what worked and what didn't. I would take their feedback, and I would incorporate it into the next cut or the next design. Even though many people doubted our upstairs location, I loved the vibe we had in that store. It was so barebones that it had this very cool boutique feeling."

As the store got going, we dedicated a third of the space to design, and a third to stocking inventory. The remaining third was the clothing display area. It was clear I couldn't fill our display area with lululemon's six to eight styles, so I brought in other brands to plump up the inventory, ensure our customers had a reason to come up the stairs and to research competitors' pricing. I brought in Champion, Adidas, Fila, Gaia, Calvin Klein underwear, Cannondale cycling gear, and even some of the existing dancewear apparel that I'd set out to improve upon. I bought T-shirts from American Apparel and changed the neck labels to say "lululemon" and printed reflective graphics on the front.

Summer Gray was responsible for ordering and meeting with the sales reps from these other brands. From observing the items to which customers were attracted, she was able to determine if the top-selling products were about fit, function, fabric, or price. She used this background information to assist in designing new lululemon styles.

I knew building word-of-mouth about lululemon quality would take time. Meanwhile, I wanted our space to be as efficient as possible. We painted the space white and put down the cheapest carpeting I could find because the linoleum floor was ugly. Even though it wasn't a storefront at street-level, it was still very memorable. The front windows had an amazing view of the mountains, and the whole space had innately good energy.

One day, my yellow Lab, Bagels, tripped and spilled essential oils over a part of the rug. This turned out to be a stroke of good fortune: the amazing smell lasted for eighteen months, and customers loved the aroma.

Good energy, the tunes of Al Green, and a view of the mountains meant I didn't have to sink money into too many adornments. Instead of buying racks, I put screws in the ceiling beams from which I hung wood doweling with rope. These were used to display our clothes. Little tricks like this helped me to outfit the first ever lululemon store for less than $4,000.

A Functional Design

During our focus groups, women expressed that the cost of their time was critical. I thought this through and calculated how long it took a customer to find a garment in a store. I then compared that to what that customer would have earned at work had they not gone shopping. This information drove the store to be set up for function rather than by colourways or outfits (as is typically done in fashion stores). Our pant wall allowed our busy Guest to visually and expeditiously locate the perfect garment for her athletic function, in her size, and in her desired colour.

The thought of maximizing the working woman's time ultimately drove the functional store design. I was fanatical about creating the right combination of store size, store location, number of Educators on the floor, number of change rooms, number of cash desks, and the price/quality of the clothing.

It was a worthwhile exercise. Over time, lululemon stores would yield the third highest sales-per-square-foot in the world . . . behind only Apple and Tiffany.

Logoing

When I was young, I wanted T-shirts with big logos. I wanted other people to understand who I was, and because I was inarticulate and insecure, the logos spoke for me. When I wanted to meet a girl, I hoped the logo on my shirt would tell the girl I was cool. With surf-skate-and-snowboard, the target market was fourteen- to eighteen-year-old boys, so the logos were large, necessary, and driven by sponsorship. A company would pay an athlete to wear their branded apparel, which would inspire young boys to buy that apparel.

As I grew older, became confident, and stopped growing, I could afford better quality clothing that lasted longer, so I no longer needed the big logo. I didn't want disposable T-shirts, and I didn't want my apparel to be dominated by a logo. I wanted my clothing brand to match the quality of person I aspired to be.

I always believed a well-educated, marketing-savvy consumer could easily see through the purchased loyalty of sponsorship. A more sophisticated consumer was looking for a product that had better quality and a smaller logo. The size of the lululemon logo was one inch in the first year. We shrunk it to half-an-inch the second year and placed in on the backs of garments. We made the logo reflective, so it would be functional.

Educators

Back when Westbeach had become popular, competitors had set up around us, making Kitsilano one of the most concentrated areas for sports apparel retail in the world. I knew I did not want customers to enter lululemon and expect to get the same treatment that they would get elsewhere, where a salesperson approaches them, suggests such-and-such would look good on them, that this item is discounted, or that clearance apparel is in the back.

One of lululemon's very earliest Operating Principles was never to tell a customer something looked good on them. We assumed our intelligent customer did not need to be talked down to. Talking fashion used up our customers' time; it was fake and added nothing to the experience.

My next step was developing a staff training system for how best to deliver a technical product. I wanted to rename every component within our unique business philosophy. I didn't want to call staff "salespeople" because I hated the connotation of one person attempting to fool another.

While making snowboard jackets, I had wanted to insert technology not visible to the customer. Salespeople and hangtags at a wholesale sports store frustrated me because neither could explain the superior hidden value of technology-enhanced apparel. On the other hand, in my Westbeach retail stores, I could describe hidden technology to customers, which, in turn, meant there was no problem getting top price. I had to have my own stores and educate the customer.

Considering how little my father earned as a university-educated teacher, I wanted to create a retail business that could pay Educators top dollar. I believed using my vertical retail model to remove the middleman would allow me to pay my staff—my Educators—30 percent more than they were earning elsewhere. For a manager, I could pay double the salary of a public-school teacher.

The First Store

Lululemon athletica opened in March of 1999. You had to be in the know because the second-floor location was so obscure—but that made the store even more special. The people who came were the invitees to our design meetings, their friends, and the small number of people who were in the yoga scene at the time.

The first store functioned a bit like a showroom. If we were going to expand to other cities, the idea was to set up in an inexpensive location in a Kitsilano-type neighbourhood. From there, we would softly educate while creating community via design meetings and developing relationships with forward-thinking athletes we would call *ambassadors*.

Each piece of lululemon clothing had its own name, its own identity. I believed by naming a garment, the customer would better understand the spirit and technology, which was a part of the educating puzzle. Our first pant, for example, was a black Lycra flare-fit pant that reminded me of the '70s. We named it the Boogie Pant (in 2017, the MoMA in New York presented the Boogie Pant as a catalyst for social change in a show called "Is Fashion Modern?").

That particular pant evolved to be the Groove Pant with a built-in band as a design feature, inspired by the look of a low-slung hippie-style belt on a woman's hips. As a woman's hips moved, so did the built-in panel. The original did not sell well until it was redesigned to slim out the leg to the knee and bring the flare out wider (the designer of this innovation was Summer Gray, whom I would marry a few years later).

Despite the fresh paint, the good energy, and the view of the mountains, our second-floor location on West 4th proved to be as difficult as I'd worried it might be. Being so tucked away from foot traffic was a real problem. The staff did what they could to get potential customers up the stairs, including setting out a rolling rack of our samples at the bottom of the stairs and talking to passersby about our products. It was heartening to see how much our small staff believed in what we were doing.

From the outset, profit was never the goal. I was driven by providing athletic and health information to our customers, and if they wanted to buy something, then that was a bonus. The way to make this model work was to ensure everyone I worked with was wonderful. My personal desire was to ride my beach cruiser to work every morning and never get on a plane again.

In fact, lululemon's original vision was to provide people with the components to live a longer, healthier, and more fun life. In my mind, it was as simple as that.

I was also confident that once a woman tried on our clothing, learned its functionality, and felt the fabric on her skin, she would become a loyal customer. Generally, we only needed between three and five people coming in per day to break even, but my big problem was selling enough units quickly enough. I had too much money wrapped up in inventory, as I had to make between 500 and 2,000 units to achieve economy-of-scale. I couldn't build more styles until I had more sales. That was the big problem with starting a vertical retail company. Success would take capital and time. I began to understand why few people would even contemplate trying to make this business model work.

I needed to push things along while we waited for word-of-mouth about lululemon to spread.

In-Store Yoga

Fiona Stang was still teaching yoga at Ron Zalko's gym, which wasn't ideal because you couldn't heat the space enough to teach a proper power yoga class. I, however, happened to have just the place for such a thing. We had our clothing on rolling racks, and in the morning and at night, we would move them to the side, so Fiona could teach. The smell of spilled essential oils and sweat became synonymous with the lululemon brand.

Lucky for us, Fiona taught the only yoga class in town. People who showed an interest in yoga found out about us while they attended a class. They realized the yoga class also sold clothing and brought their friends back to peruse the merchandise.

I knew once women were exposed to our location and our pants, it would create authentic word-of-mouth. Word-of-mouth was the only way I wanted to expand lululemon. This was going to be a long, arduous branding journey but I knew the effects were exponential and demand would correlate with my ability to expand production.

"Chip had figured out a really organic way to get all these people—more importantly, the right people—into the store," Fiona recalls. "It was a brilliant idea."

Advertising

Yoga Journal magazine was a mediocre publication wallowing in the depths of the granola world. I don't even know how they made money. But I knew the future of yoga was akin to the surf, skate, and snow business, so I thought, if I could be the top advertiser and control the first few pages—much like Burton Snowboards did in the snowboarding business— then I could set lululemon up to be the international leader in yoga.

My approach to marketing with lululemon was just as unconventional as it had been with Westbeach. I didn't want to advertise what the brand was—I wanted to advertise what the brand was not. We wanted to be clear about who our nemesis was, who we were fighting. Lululemon was against big pharma pushing unneeded drugs, unhealthy food companies, and anything that would shorten a person's life. We were against false advertising that provided short-term gain and long-term pain.

In the '90s, with the high buying power of the yen, Japanese people were coming to Vancouver and spending their money.

Also, at that time, Roots Athletics was marketing their apparel as being athletic. That was maybe true for canoeing on a lake in Canada, but Roots apparel had no use in athletics as I understood it.

Drawing on Roots and Japanese tourists alike, we created our first of three ads—a girl wearing big glasses with the words *"Trendy Clothing for Rich Japanese Tourists"* with a girl wearing a Roots sweat top.

First, I wanted nothing to do with the word "trend," despite what the New York fashion and business media said about athletic fashion. Second, I wanted to make fun of tourists that buy inauthentic tourist clothing. Third, I wanted to take a fun stab at Roots for calling themselves athletic.

I knew our targeted Super Girl would look at the ad and understand the nuances and subconsciously want to be part of the lululemon "tribe," a phenomenon described in Malcolm Gladwell's book *The Tipping Point.*[11]

Our second ad revolved around Vancouver's number one gym—Ron Zalko's—where I had attended my first yoga class. Ron had marketed his business around sex. He did an ad in the *Georgia Straight* in Vancouver showing a girl, her arms draped over his shoulder, saying "It's bigger than I thought." This apparently referred to the size of his workout facility. I found this ad pretty gutsy. Many Super Girls I knew who had seen the ad found it outright creepy.

Creepy, gutsy, or otherwise, the ad was so well known, I decided to mimic it. I had Amanda wrap her arms around me, and we used the same, "It's bigger than I thought" slogan. Any Super Girl in Vancouver knew exactly how tongue-in-cheek that was. The ad showed us being egoless, irreverent, and risk-taking. Most importantly, it brought our market together.

A third ad, a few years later, was in response to someone who knew nothing about Asian production accusing Nike of child labour. I felt bad for Nike because producing a quality product is impossible without having great conditions for factory workers.

In North America, I noticed some kids who weren't made for school, who dropped out with nowhere to go. In Asia, if a kid was not "school material," he or she learned a trade and contributed to their family. It was work or starve. I liked the working alternative.

11. Malcolm Gladwell, *The Tipping Point* (Little, Brown and Company, 2000).

The accusation of Nike was the first time I saw untrue social media "journalism" come to the forefront. I learned of the damage one uninformed person can do when they publicly accuse an innocent party. Once in digital, always in digital. Everyone wants fifteen minutes of fame.

I decided to get in front of some wildcard individual who could falsely accuse lululemon. We shot an ad for *Yoga Journal* magazine with three or four of our employees, including me, dressed in diapers and baby outfits at sewing machines in one of our factories. The caption below said, "We believe in child labour." If we were ever accused of child labour, I would just agree.

(As a side note, my own children have worked in the business from the age of five with no pay; working young is excellent training for life.)

CHAPTER 13:
A RETAIL OPERATION

Failure is simply an opportunity to try again, but this time, more intelligently. —Henry Ford

Mounting Expenses

While I was waiting for lululemon athletica to reach true profitability, the costs associated with running a retail operation were mounting uncomfortably.

The ratio of buying customers to expenses wasn't yet in our favour. I had to weigh out what I could afford. Something that fell by the wayside was theft insurance. Area break-ins were common—especially on weekends—but surveillance cameras were not, so I took a cost-effective approach. Saturday nights became camp-out nights on the second floor with my boys.

"Brett and I did security for my dad when we were ten and twelve years old," says JJ. "Of course, Dad made sure it didn't feel that way. We were just having fun and spending quality time together. Other little kids camped in their backyards. We did it amongst Boogie Pants and Y Bras in the store. What we'd have done if someone had broken in, I'm not sure. The sight of my dad barreling out of a tent would probably have made them take off in a hurry."

We'd move the clothing aside, set up a tent, and sleep at the store before going for breakfast the following morning. This wasn't strange for JJ and Brett because they'd been raised in the retail business and had spent considerable time at Westbeach.

I had no choice but to bring them with me on Saturdays and Sundays, but they didn't seem to mind. They'd hang off me as I interacted with customers or make forts out of boxes while I worked in the warehouse. The operations of the business became ingrained in them—from logistics to sales to branding. They took it all in from an early age, and at last, I found myself spending quality time with them.

A Pivotal Moment

Then, by the summer of 1999, I noticed something on the streets of Kitsilano. Women were wearing lululemon as they did their shopping, walked their dogs, or sat in cafes with their friends. Lululemon wasn't just in yoga studios. It was on the street.

Somehow, we'd made clothing that women wanted to wear for yoga—and wear *after* yoga. Any reservations I'd had about making clothes for a new, niche sport suddenly evaporated. Yoga was not only gaining in popularity, but lululemon had also made the leap into streetwear.

Enough signs pointed in the right direction to make me feel I had to hold on and grow organically without the drug of conventional advertising. The question I asked myself, as my cash dwindled, was: How?

Ambassadors & Product Testers

I had developed a strong relationship with my first instructor, Fiona Stang, and, as lululemon became a hub of yoga culture in Vancouver, a handful of other yoga instructors in the city joined us. This included people like Eoin Finn, a Vancouver-based philosopher who'd been a leading figure in the yoga movement since the late 1980s. I kept coming back to the invaluable information and ideas these instructors offered, always asking questions and getting their input on our designs.

It quickly became a synergistic relationship. We supported one another and believed in what we were creating. We not only believed, but our livelihoods also depended on yoga picking up momentum. These yoga instructors had started to act as spokespeople for lululemon. I decided at this point lululemon would never set up its own yoga studios as it was not our job to compete with our best partners and brand builders.

As Fiona recalls: "People ask me what it was like to be one of the first lululemon testers. I don't really remember it being that official. It was like, my friend Chip is starting a yoga clothing company, and he's asking me to test designs and tell him what I think. I loved the clothing and was happy to share my thoughts about it, but mainly it just seemed very natural and fun."

I decided I would formalize the relationship by asking these leaders to become brand testers, providing them with new designs in return for their invaluable feedback in regularly scheduled design meetings.

As time passed, the testers became known as *ambassadors*. They realized how serious I was about perfecting the products. They recognized that I was listening to what they said, and they saw the results of their feedback in the designs themselves.

The ambassador program was also a unique marketing opportunity. We would photograph our ambassadors and put the pictures in the local newspaper with the name of the ambassador's yoga studio . . . and then we'd put a small lululemon logo at the edge of the picture. The first goal was to make the ambassadors' businesses work. The second goal was to provide just enough financial love to the media publications to allow them to justify an occasional editorial piece on lululemon.

Old-school marketers would not have understood our desire to build an authentic tribe with community-based yoga, but within a short period of time, people wanted to be part of the ambassador team. This all contributed to maven yogis pulling for the lululemon brand and creating an underground surge on our way to the tipping point. Slowly we were getting more people up the stairs and into our world.

Hemming

I thought about the inconvenience of purchasing pants, washing them, shrinking them, and taking them to a tailor. I wanted to eliminate that need entirely. I surmised that Super Girls did not have time to go to another business, try on the pants again and get their pants hemmed. Of course, women are particular about the exact length of pant and need the pant to be 100 percent functional for a yoga class. I wanted someone to buy a lululemon product and wear it beautifully the first time.

If Japan had seamstresses in each store, I wanted hemmers in ours. I took that one level higher and hired not just hemmers, but design graduates fresh out of school. Not only could they sew and hem, but they could also create. Starting with Amanda Dunsmoor, I'd set up a studio where the designers could work but also talk to customers.

If the store got too busy, the designers came into the sales area to help. They'd interact with customers and then create, create, create. This approach replaced traditional buyer statistics. It laid the foundation for lululemon to listen to its Guests and ambassadors and create amazing new products that directly addressed their feedback. Statistical sales print-outs don't tell the buyers what shade of purple a customer would have preferred or what size they would have bought if we had it in stock.

Over the years, these early insights became cultural practices that included company-wide design calls, product testing in local communities, and design meetings based on climate, lifestyle, and the popular athletics of that region.

I refused to allow algorithms or metrics to run lululemon.

Design Meetings

Through our early days, focus groups and design meetings remained a critical part of our growing success. With the second-floor location, these meetings were another way of bringing people in to see where our store was. We'd have sushi, I'd give the participants a $100 gift card, and we would ask a series of questions that prompted an open dialogue.

This customer perspective—whether I agreed with it or not—helped to move lululemon ahead of its competitors, because the information for which I was listening was the future. I designed meetings with Guests and then a separate meeting with our ambassadors.

I welcomed negative feedback and made sure we invited people who had made store complaints. Design meetings gave us a face-to-face platform to disseminate information to Guests and ambassadors who spread it to their clients. I also held meetings with the store Educators, which gave me a third and equally important viewpoint with which to work.

Focus groups and design meetings were some of the very best branding exercises for lululemon because during these interactions I would be asked very pointed questions about the business. Sometimes I'd have a good explanation for why something was the way it was. Other times the question would flag a need for follow-up or change.

Despite these rapid innovations, business was growing too slowly. I had a lot riding on whether lululemon could hang on through those first few months. The wholesale prospect crossed my mind more frequently as lululemon struggled to remain profitable.

A New Approach to Wholesale

I was always thinking about how to get the product on more people more quickly. I knew anyone who wore our product would be an instant convert and would tell six other people within a week. I visited the venerable Glencoe Club in oil-rich Calgary with a new branding idea.

I proposed they sell eight of our main pieces in their shop. It was a wholesale agreement in which I would make no profit. I would move through styles at break-even and build up my base to get to economy-of-scale. This was part of my developing break-even marketing mantra.

I suggested I control all buying and fulfill inventory as quickly as they could sell it. I knew how in-demand our clothing would be at a place like the Glencoe, and how profitable it would be for the club. Lululemon would get in front of the perfect high-end customer, and the Glencoe could make millions of dollars.

Unfortunately, this meant butting heads with the merchant system the Glencoe (and all other retail stores) already had in place. The buyers whose job it was to curate clothing (and other wholesale items) wanted the product, but they weren't willing to give up the ego of their job or look at a new model. They didn't understand lululemon was a design-led company because they had never dealt with one before.

Once a brand matures, the Midwestern North American consumer buys in heavy and deep. This natural evolution warps sale metrics, so buyers in a merchant-led company direct the designers to make more of what is selling. While overbuying for these Midwestern North American consumers, companies lose their focus to deliver market-leading styles for the trend-setters of the next year.

(As a modern example, lululemon men's line creates too many nine-inch inseam shorts that work for golfers and Mid-west Americans. If you look at the world's trendiest beaches—Tulum, Jose Ignazio, Kits Beach, St. Tropez, Ibiza—you'd see that no one has been wearing nine-inch inseams for the past three years. Five- to seven-inch inseams are the standard on these beaches).

To us, design would always trump every other system—even old-school merchants and buyers.

Selling a Stake to Employees

Another attempt to enhance cash flow was to get employees to work the same hours, or produce the same services, for less money upfront. In exchange, I'd offer them a small piece of equity in the company. I viewed a 1 percent stake in lululemon as a way to motivate my staff by giving them a sense of ownership while reducing my wage expenses.

I made this offer to five people. Of the five, only one employee, Anthony Redpath, took my offer. Anthony was a friend and a photographer who had been shooting a lot of promotional material for us.

"There was a point when Chip was starting to have cash flow concerns," says Anthony. "He was on his own, and he was stretching himself to make it work. His idea was to offer 1 percent of the company if I agreed to work for cost. He thought he would keep the company for ten years and eventually sell it for $10 million. It was only me who bought in. Nobody ever dreamed lululemon would actually get to where it is now."

Every little bit helped, but deferring Anthony's payment would not make a precarious situation better. I needed to think of other ways to avoid a financial meltdown, but I felt like I was running low on options.

While disheartened that I was running up against the same old issues that had exhausted me with Westbeach, I had enough reasons to be optimistic about lululemon to make me feel that I needed to find a solution. If I could just make it through the next few months, I was sure we would reach critical mass.

Running Out of Money

I don't think I've ever been driven by money or profit. I've been driven by the beauty of a process, and that's what I was perfecting with lululemon. My worst fear, at the time, was seeing the little money I had left disintegrate while waiting for lululemon to turn cash positive. I had taken another loan and maximized the equity of my house with nowhere else to go.

One option I considered was taking on a partner. I was happy to have the autonomy of going it alone with lululemon after some of the partnership issues I'd had with Westbeach. I liked the clarity that a single vision, core values, and quality control provided my new brand.

On the other hand, having a partner onboard had huge advantages, including shared risk, an infusion of capital, and expertise in other areas of business.

My friend Dave Halliwell had been helping me off and on in an advisory position. I approached Dave with a partnership proposal. Dave believed in lululemon, he told me, but needed to think about it before giving me an answer.

I had reservations about this. Not reservations about Dave—a great guy who would be a strong addition to the company—but about taking on a partner altogether. I didn't know if I was offering a partnership opportunity because it would take off some pressure, or if I was choosing an easy way out by reverting to a familiar formula. Was I losing confidence in what I'd learned, or was I doing what I had to do to give the company the time it needed to grow?

Dave's expertise was wholesale. I was unsure about how to evaluate the importance of a financial infusion from Dave, knowing that with him as a partner we'd likely go back into a wholesale model. I loathed wholesaling, but time was running short.

Then, in the fall of 1999, six months after lululemon had opened its doors, an unexpected lifeline presented itself. Morrow, the company that had purchased Westbeach from us two years earlier, was forced to sell the company at a loss to Wyndcrest Partners. Wyndcrest were based out of West Palm Beach, Florida, but they brought Westbeach back to Vancouver. They also contacted me to ask if I was interested in taking the CEO position.

I had stumbled on the perfect solution to my issues. The company I had founded, grown, learned from, sold, worked for, and then left, wanted to hire me back to run it. I could then funnel the salary they offered back into lululemon—the company that Westbeach had moulded me to create—and keep it going while being patient and letting word-of-mouth about our quality reach a critical mass. It kind of blew my mind to think about it all.

A New Option

While returning to Westbeach felt like a step backward, there was no question in my mind that it was a means to an important end. I took the job. Working at the company I'd started at an outdoor mall in Calgary two decades prior meant extra money to pour into my new venture, but it would also take me away from day-to-day operations at lululemon. I would have to separate myself from lululemon to be fair to my new employer.

If I left to run Westbeach, I would need people at lululemon I could rely on to execute the vision I had laid out. I wanted people with the same energy, enthusiasm, and belief I had in what we were doing.

I only had a few part-time people and Amanda Dunsmoor as our designer. As I departed lululemon, our little company would live or die by the hands of the few people running the business in my absence.

Amanda was doing great work in her design role, but I asked her to come to Westbeach with me. Part of me knew I'd be walking into a company that needed to recreate itself, and I would benefit from having a talented, dependable ally. Snowboarding and snowboard apparel were Amanda's passions. I felt sure that bringing Amanda back to Westbeach with me was the right decision for Westbeach, even though it meant creating a void at the very heart of lululemon.

I also wanted to exit Amanda from lululemon because she didn't enjoy working the retail part of the store. Loving being an Educator and working on the floor is a big part of what would make lululemon great. Otherwise, I felt, another mediocre American business would be created. That was not for me.

Summer and Jackie

Fortunately, I'd recently interviewed a young woman named Summer Gray. Summer had a fine arts degree, an education degree, an apparel design degree, and two small entrepreneurial ventures of her own. I'd received hundreds of design portfolios, but Summer's was the first I had ever seen that included work with stretch fabrics. She'd been making stage clothing for bodybuilders, male and female.

Here I was, a forty-one-year-old divorced male with two children who had worked with fourteen-to-eighteen-year-old boys for twenty years—and in walks Summer. The perfect Super Girl. She was twenty-four, highly educated, a top athlete, and passionate about goals, athletics, and apparel design. Frankly, I was taken aback. I thought to myself, "she is going to make some man a very lucky husband someday, too bad it won't be me."

The designs in her portfolio were great. She had been a competitive swimmer and later competed on the Canadian water polo team, so she understood everything I was thinking about rashing and how stretch fibres functioned and moved from an athlete's viewpoint.

She told me she'd initially gone to get a degree in science. That's what her parents wanted, but she more or less snuck out and got a Fine Arts degree on her own. From there she went into teaching, hated it, and went back to school for her design degree. What I liked about her was how she knew what she wanted to do, she knew her calling. I wasn't dealing with someone who was just figuring out what they wanted to do.

Summer was the first person I called when the opportunity to go back to Westbeach presented itself. I contacted her about a week before I left for Westbeach and told her I needed her to start immediately. She could still only commit a limited number of hours, but her strong design eye and unique energy were exactly what we needed. To my relief, Summer accepted the offer.

Around that same time, I also hired a woman named Jackie Slater, first as a designer, then to lead our production. In turn, Jackie and Summer took on some people to help them with weekend shifts. Amanda and I gave them an intensive crash course in what lululemon was all about.

As Summer says: "Jackie Slater had just been hired when I got an emergency call from Chip on a Sunday night. He met us at the store with the keys and showed us the layout and merchandising and talked us through the sales. There wasn't even a cash register. We just added stuff up on a calculator and wrote out the receipts. It was like starting over, just Jackie and me. We were both brand new when Chip left. I was still substitute teaching high school in Surrey.

"There was so little money," Summer adds, "that anyone working had to be motivated by pure love and passion, or pure desperation. Most of us in those early days were united in this intense belief in lululemon. Jackie and I did almost everything. She was mostly concerned with production, and I was working on design. I remember doing anything I could, from making patterns on my kitchen table during the night to working the floor selling all day." With Summer and Jackie at the helm, I felt that lululemon was in good hands.

It was tough for me to step away at such a critical time, but I wanted authentic word-of-mouth growth, and it would take time.

Back to Westbeach

Returning to my first company was not without its challenges. The new owners recognized that I had a significant history with the company and a lot to offer, but the people working there had their own inertia and were not interested in change. Westbeach needed change, as it had still failed to be profitable. Many employees were new people who had no idea who I was. The experience felt very different than it had when I was an owner.

The snowboarding business was in crisis and needed command-and-control leadership to right a sinking ship. There was no time to enroll employees in a shared vision, but I needed them to align with me if we were going to move forward together powerfully. The company was between a rock and a hard place, and in hindsight, a "bottom-up" leader like myself may not have been what this "top-down" company needed at the time.

Despite these hardships at Westbeach, I had faith in the way I'd left things at lululemon. Summer's and Jackie's jobs were to fulfill the vision and maintain quality. I believed if I gave them the tools and space to feel creative, motivated, and empowered, good things would happen.

"Chip was out of the picture, and it was really our business to run and make a go of," says Summer. "We had a lot of power to make decisions and steer the product line. We chose fabrics and decided how many pieces to make. Chip gave us an incredible amount of freedom. We were so excited that when we hired people, they quickly picked up on our enthusiasm. People saw a future in the company, so it was a great fit for those with an entrepreneurial and business drive. Lululemon was wide open, especially for women with an education who wanted to see where the company could go."

This is an important point about the founding of lululemon. Except for my own part in it, the company in its earliest days was run *by* smart, independent Super Girls, *for* smart, independent Super Girls. We seemed to be the only people that believed in the possibility and greatness of Super Girls.

I stepped back and tried to look at things more critically,

to ask questions that needed asking. Was the yoga market strong? It was. I felt the yoga movement was still gaining momentum. We were in the right place, at the right time.

Was our product great? Yes. There was no question in my mind that we were the best in the world. Anyone who put on the clothes confirmed that. Jackie and Summer had built on the foundational concepts and refined the designs beautifully.

We had to get people in the door to make purchases, and it was becoming increasingly apparent to us all that the upstairs location on West 4th was making this a serious challenge. The traffic up the stairs to the store was low, and consequently, so was our sales volume.

I made tough long-term decisions that were affecting our short-term survival. Not going for the easy money of whole-sale, not looking for comfort in a partnership, and not running any conventional advertising campaigns. I could certainly see the downside of my choices. Without wholesale, the exposure of the products was minimal. If a customer didn't find our store, they would not find the clothes anywhere else.

Before I allowed myself to consider wholesale—to prosti-tute myself and go against all I knew to be wrong—I made a commitment to think laterally and exhaust all other possible options.

But the more I dwelled on it, the more it seemed there were none.

The Superstar Sports Experiment, Part 1

It seemed I had too much money wrapped up in perfect, unsold inventory, but not enough cash to continually deliver new designs to ensure the customers I already had would return. The bottom line was that there was more cash going out of our bank account than coming into it.

If we explored wholesale, our product would reach more

people. The revenue from wholesaling would create money to outfit a new location and help with the higher rent costs. From Dave Halliwell's viewpoint, one hand would wash the other.

It didn't take long to put together a sizeable wholesale deal with a company called Superstar Sports and with many other cross-Canada yoga studios. This helped seed the market so when we did grow, we had brand awareness. Superstar had thirty stores and stocked a wide variety of sporting goods, but mostly Nike.

Superstar looked good—and that had to count for something. We increased production and stretched our resources to the limit. Everyone put in extra time to fill our first wholesale order. Wholesale was not the option I'd wanted to go with, but we were desperate. With the Superstar deal, it seemed we had a lifeline . . . if only for the time being.

CHAPTER 14:
MOVING ON

Life is full of setbacks. Success is determined by how you handle setbacks.

The Superstar Sports Experiment, Part 2

We got word from Superstar that our product was selling well, and we just had to wait for our payments to come in.

Over breakfast, shortly after getting this good news, I read a newspaper article describing bankruptcy proceedings that had started against Superstar Group. The same Superstar Group in possession of lululemon product worth $30,000. There's no way to describe how this felt—especially finding out in this way.

Lululemon's small staff, run by Summer, had bent over backward to make the production schedule work. We had been far from cash flow positive before wholesaling. Losing the receivables from Superstar was a devastating blow.

Hoping to salvage something, anything, for lululemon, I attended Superstar Group's bankruptcy meeting. The room was packed with representatives from companies that, like mine, stood to lose money. Everyone there wanted to secure a piece of the bankruptcy pie for themselves. Initially, I held hope that we might be paid out in the proceedings, but it didn't turn out that way. We never saw a single cent from Superstar. For a young start-up like lululemon, it was a huge hit.

A year and a half later, the same owner of Superstar, who'd essentially walked away with everyone's money, formed the corporation that opened Nike BC retail franchises. I must say it hurt having someone use my money to compete against me.

I was frustrated that I hadn't listened to my gut instinct. I had ignored the learning I'd gained from Westbeach, and the results were disastrous. I promised myself this was one mistake I would never make again. If I could somehow pull lululemon out of this mess, I would stick to my guns.

Now that the Superstar money had vaporized, it looked like we would have to defer the cost of moving to a new location until our financial outlook improved. I realized it would be impossible to keep going until the unknown point when we had more cash. Now, more than ever, we needed a new space to generate sales volume that would dig us out of the hole in which we'd landed, but the cost of moving felt prohibitive.

Still, it was move or die. At least housing prices in Vancouver were skyrocketing. This meant I could take out another equity loan on my house—it was the only way we could afford to move the store.

2103 West 4th Avenue

I had been keeping an eye out for any good space on West 4th Avenue. Ultimately, we didn't have to look far. In November 2000, an excellent location opened right across the street. We could see into its front windows from our own.

The new spot was formerly an electronics store. It was

rundown and in bad shape. Wires were hanging everywhere, and the walls were covered in ugly pegboard. $20,000 was all the money available, and we would need to spend every last cent moving in and getting the new store into a somewhat workable condition. We wanted to set up before Christmas, and it was already November.

"Ugly," says Summer. "The new space was just really ugly. Since we were operating on such a tight budget, we couldn't do that much to fix it up. The plan was, paint it white, put in new carpet. We didn't have enough money to pay professionals to do the work, so we did it ourselves. We closed the store for four days which, for a small, start-up business, was a long time to have our doors closed. We pulled all-nighters trying to get it finished. One day, an Australian guy who was backpacking across Canada poked his head in to see if all these people frantically working needed some help. We pulled him inside and gave him a paintbrush."

My day job as the CEO of Westbeach had taken me away from the original lululemon store for the better part of a year. Now, the four-day period we needed to move our little company across the street and renovate our new store coincided with a European business trip. Summer, Jackie, Dave, and some people they'd hired took on the bulk of the move. I wished I could've been there with them, pitching in on the work.

"We rented a five-ton cube van with a driver and a motorized tailgate," Dave recalls. "There was a big posse of us—store employees and friends. We moved everything over in three trips. Fixtures, rolls of fabric, sewing machines, the entire stock of inventory, cash desk, etc. The truck and driver cost us $200, and I remember I tipped him $40."

When the crew finally moved the inventory over, it was immediately clear the space was too big. We had an empty second floor. I'd chosen to stop selling other brands at our new locale, choosing instead to focus solely on lululemon. I knew it was the right choice, but once we had our products in the new store, it looked distressingly sparse.

After devoting so much to wholesale production, we had little inventory. At a push, we could only fill half of the main floor store. I knew I wanted the store to feel like a busy "kitchen party," so I built a huge moving wall on wheels that expanded the store on weekends and shortened the store during the week. We had moveable change rooms so we could add or subtract those for traffic, too.

The familiar elements of today's lululemon stores didn't exist in that first street-level location, but it did solidify a deep faith in being able to create something from nothing. It was teamwork for a higher purpose. We brought over our community boards from the old store and made do with bits and pieces of furniture that I'd found at distress sales. By the time we were ready to open the doors, we'd completed a marathon, bare-bones renovation.

It felt surreal to return from my European business trip and find that the store into which we had poured all our faith, experience, and belief had changed completely. I didn't even have to be anywhere near the store to see that.

My one indulgence was commissioning a massive mural for the outside wall of the store's building. It depicted a silhouette of Fiona Stang, my first yoga teacher, in Warrior Two pose. I could see it from blocks away as I approached. Lululemon was now a visible player in Kitsilano. This was a new beginning.

Then, right before Christmas, Westbeach fired me.

The Firing

It had been hard coming back to Westbeach. Much harder than I'd thought it would be. I was just starting to understand what it was to be a manager. I was just learning how to align others with a vision effectively.

As CEO of Westbeach, I had only a few options. I could license the Westbeach brand to a company in Europe or move it into direct vertical retail and get out of wholesale altogether. A vertical retail shift of a wholesaler like Westbeach would have meant two tough, unprofitable years shutting down wholesale and opening stores.

I would have lost my economy-of-scale production with the loss of wholesale, without enough sales coming from the retail stores. Opening our own stores would cost money we didn't have. Westbeach needed an entirely different structure—almost a complete reinvention of the company.

Then there was a move at the ownership level. Westbeach merged with Sims Skateboards. Although Sims was a major force in its own scene, skateboarding was also in a period of decline. If it would survive, Sims, like Westbeach, had to consider mergers and acquisitions. The merger was with Westbeach. The two brands now eliminated a lot of redundant warehousing and administrative processes.

They also eliminated one of two $100,000 CEO positions. That was me. Merry Christmas.

It was a weird position in which to find myself. The Superstar Sports fiasco had set lululemon back tens of thousands of dollars in product. Our move to the new store cost another $20,000. Westbeach had just let me go. I had borrowed $200,000 against my house to start lululemon, and I'd borrowed the final $200,000 to keep it afloat. It suddenly seemed like everything was on the verge of falling apart . . . but it turned out to be the best possible scenario.

First, Westbeach let me go with a healthy severance package—half of my annual salary. That quick infusion of cash couldn't have come at a better time.

Second, I wasn't the right CEO for Westbeach. Lululemon represented exactly the work environment I wanted, but Westbeach had no money to change, and it was the antithesis of the future I had envisioned.

Third—and most important—I could now give lululemon my full attention. The $20,000 store move had paid off immediately, and business was growing by the day, particularly as Christmas drew nearer. I could now turn my focus to marketing and possibly, expansion.

Now that I'd returned, Summer, who had been the de facto CEO in my absence, was concerned that her days of creative freedom in steering lululemon were over. "I'd been having such a great time," she says, "enjoying an incredible amount of autonomy . . . but now the boss was coming back."

In my absence, Summer had done a phenomenal job of maintaining powerful forward momentum in design. The vibe she and Jackie had created and promoted in the store was exactly what I wanted. Plus, I knew it was important for our success that they felt personally invested in the company. Summer and I made extra money on the side by designing outerwear jackets for another Vancouver company called Aritzia and setting them up with Asian manufacturing.

I could understand how they felt about my return, so I stressed to Summer and Jackie that they were still in control of day-to-day operations. I wanted to focus my energies on marketing and growth, not looking over their shoulders in the store, micromanaging everything. I was choosing a leadership style of mentoring and training. My job was to develop people in the culture and get out of their way. I adhered to the principles of Michael E. Gerber's book *The E-Myth: Why Most Businesses Don't Work and What to Do About It.* I developed Operating Principles and processes that would allow the company to operate without me so I could focus on the future. Because our training and development program was implemented at the beginning, we could grow exponentially faster than other companies. The employees didn't need adult supervision; they needed empowerment and the opportunity to be great.

Farewell to Dave

Now that I had the time to flesh out my ideas, I knew one thing I wanted to prove was our business philosophy. I didn't want to take shortcuts, but it was all a big risk.

After our busy Christmas period ended, I wanted to have a serious talk with Dave Halliwell about the partnership issue. Even though he had done a massive amount for the company in my absence, he had never committed to an official partnership. He'd been "thinking about it" for months.

For both our sakes, I told Dave he had to make his choice by January.

Luon

With Christmas right around the corner, lululemon was appearing in several articles about hot gift-giving options. One article mentioned a polar fleece bra Summer had designed. The bra hit it big that Christmas.

The bra was a peripheral item in our inventory as our focus was on our Lycra clothing. But the interest the bra generated was a perfect marketing vehicle for introducing our clothes to new customers. The people who came in the door looking for the fleecy bra inevitably left with one of our signature garments.

Meanwhile, I felt we'd finally perfected our fabric and

trademarked it as something called *Luon*—a proprietary blend of nylon and Lycra. We trademarked the name for reasons similar to ones held by those who trademarked Gore-Tex and Velcro. Many competitors may use a similar product or invention, but if you're the first to define a category and trademark it, then it builds a moat around the brand, and the name becomes synonymous with the entire industry.

I sensed lululemon was very, very different in the apparel world and I continually considered how to build a wider and deeper moat that would make future competition difficult.

In January, as promised, Dave Halliwell and I sat down for a meeting about his future with lululemon. I could tell right away it was a "no." The decision wasn't easy on Dave. He told me that although he believed deeply in what we were doing and was more optimistic than ever about the direction the company was going, he was saying no to our partnership.

I didn't have to, but I wanted to remunerate Dave for his passion and commitment to our success. In 2001, I paid Dave $60,000, or $5,000 per month over a year. This amount was a fortune for lululemon at the time, but Dave's work had been a vital part of our success.

We parted ways on good terms.

CHAPTER 15:
GOALS, CULTURE, AND PEOPLE DEVELOPMENT

People don't want a pat on the back. They want to contribute and be effective. My superpower in life is I give people the opportunity.

Goal Setting

Many people might now be bored by the concept of goal-setting, but in 1998, it was almost nonexistent. There are always those who won't try goal-setting because they fear the feeling of failure if a goal is not attained. In my view, learning to fail might be the most crucial learning of all. Most people don't like goal-setting because it makes them responsible for their lives and what they get out of them. Often, people want to dream about their ideal life, and then vote for people they think will give it to them without their actually having to work for it.

SMART

As lululemon's early culture developed, we used the SMART template set out by Brian Tracy in his monumentally great work *The Psychology of Achievement*.[12] SMART stands for Specific, Measurable, Attainable, Relevant, and Timely goal-setting.

Our brains are like computers. Garbage in, garbage out. A goal that is measurable, with a by-when date, is something with which our brains can work. It has the right information for our subconscious computer to work on 24/7, even when we're asleep or doing something else.

One fundamental idea is that a goal must be so specific there can be no grey area as to if the goal was met.

Unfortunately, most goals I see look something like this: *I will make my family happier.* While a noble idea, as a goal, this cannot be measured and has no date for completion, therefore, it does not adhere to the SMART template.

Conversely, a workable, SMART-oriented goal looks like this: *I will take my family to Europe for ten days by December 31, 2025.*

At lululemon, we developed a template for staff to set out a ten-year vision for their lives, their three top personal values, and eighteen goals. The goal template was split between family, career, and health goals. The goal-setter established two goals each for family, career, and health, to be attained within three different periods of time: ten years, five years, and one year.

The goals fed into and were aligned with their vision. In this way, lululemon became a leadership development company disguised as an apparel brand.

Where I differed from Brian Tracy was in my belief that a

12. Brian Tracy, *The Psychology of Achievement* (1984).

person should fail at great goals 50 percent of the time. Failing is a part of life. It is merely a setback and an opportunity to reset the goal with new conditions of satisfaction, and new by-when dates.

I also believed that the teachings of Landmark combined with vision and goal-setting produced an even more powerful synergy.

I wanted a way to keep the transformational concepts of Landmark alive well after people had taken the course. By combining vision and goal-setting with insights around integrity, choice, and possibility, it created something very tangible and real that people could action in their own lives.

As I said in my purple shirt story, my past constrained my future. Prior to investing in transformational development, I would set a goal like this: *I will be 220 pounds by December 31, 2013.* The problem with that goal was 220 pounds was based on the weight of 240 pounds around which I had fluctuated for at least five years. I was setting my goal from what I knew, not from what I didn't know. If I didn't know my weight and I researched the optimum weight for my age and height, I would find my goal would be 208 pounds. Setting goals from a vision-based future, unconstrained by my past made my goals audacious.

Setting goals from my vision-based future also enabled me to create a plan. I first set my ten-year goals based on my vision for my future. Then I asked myself, to be there in ten years, where do I need to be in five years? And if I am there in five years, where would I need to be in one year? This way of goal setting freed me up from the pitfalls of mediocrity; it had me create goals from a desired future as opposed to a future that was going to happen anyway.

lululemon's Culture and Training

In early 2001, I decided we would take advantage of a relative lull in the higher pace of business to codify lululemon's core culture and training, which took its inspiration from *The Psychology of Achievement*.[13] I only wanted to go to work with people I loved to work with. That was the basis for lululemon's culture.

I had listened to *The Psychology of Achievement* on audio cassette. As soon as I was done listening to each cassette, I passed them along to Summer and Jackie. They responded positively to Tracy's teachings. I told them I wanted anyone they hired to hear the same lessons, so Summer and Jackie gave the cassettes to new hires to take home and digest. That was the very beginning of the lululemon training program.

I assumed each new lululemon person was already great and all we had to do was catalyze their lives. I believed it was important to train people for their own benefit, not because I was expecting some sort of return. I wanted to develop employees to their full potential and then set them free. They could then choose to work at lululemon or to fulfill other goals. With choice, the ones who stayed were outstanding employees and the ones who left, left happy and always spoke well of their time at lululemon.

It was critical for everyone to attend the Landmark Forum. I had experienced such a positive, transformative impact on my own life that I wanted anyone working with me to have the same access to understanding what a great life looked like. I wanted people around me who were excited to live a long, fun, and fulfilled life.

Dave Halliwell had been involved with Landmark for a long time. "I was an introduction leader for the Forum," he says. "Landmark is an intense transformational experience

13. Brian Tracy, *The Psychology of Achievement* (1984).

that allows people to embrace breakthroughs in their lives. It's clear that the relationship between lululemon and Landmark has been fundamental to the company's success. Like anything so dramatically effective, there are people who love it and people who fear it, but to my mind, there's no question about its power."

I knew if the people who worked at lululemon could communicate using a common language, and if they had the same context for what greatness was, we would build an amazing launchpad for success. I knew if we could build a solid educational platform that could be absorbed in two weeks, our people could grow faster than the company.

Even with a handful of people, a unique culture was already taking shape. Part of it was the series of audiobooks we shared. These books set the foundation and the context of who we could be. As I look back on everything now, I want to thank the authors of *Why We Buy*,[14] *Tipping Point*,[15] *Pour Your Heart Into It*,[16] *Jack: Straight from the Gut*,[17] and *Built to Last*,[18] among others, for offering the wisdom and insights that helped make lululemon what it was.

More than that, our development training showed Jackie, Summer, and the women they'd hired that we were *investing* in them.

In a sense, I was exceedingly selfish about people development at lululemon. I wanted to go to work with people I loved, so I was willing to invest in their greatness. I believe

14. Paco Underhill, *Why We Buy: The Science of Shopping* (Simon & Schuster, 2009).

15. Malcolm Gladwell, *The Tipping Point*, (2000).

16. Howard Schultz & Dori Jones Yang, *Pour Your Heart Into It* (Hyperion Books, 1997).

17. Jack Welch, *Jack: Straight from the Gut* (Grand Central Publishing, (2003).

18. Jim Collins and Jerry I. Porras, *Built to Last: Successful Habits of Visionary Companies* (HarperCollins, 1994).

when a person is transformed, they become leaders to themselves, then to their family, and then to their community.

A transformed person loves themselves and has the mental focus to generate a wonderful life. A fulfilled person has so much evidence of success, they automatically want the people around them to be trained in the same way. The leadership of one person automatically begets the leadership of those around them.

With the development culture, I wanted to be able to send a twenty-three-year-old to another city to run a $10 million store with twenty employees, knowing that twenty-three-year-old would act with integrity, be responsible, be creative, and because of this, be well-paid. They would reach their goals, then the company's goals, and be rewarded for being a leader first to themselves and then to others.

As Foundational lululemon Trainer Jenna Hills puts it, "Something that gets hidden about lululemon is that the company wants its people to have goals way outside of it. Goals that may take them somewhere other than working at lululemon. The way it succeeded was by having people understand they could develop the skills and leadership at lululemon to attain their personal goals outside of the company. Conversely, if this was forgotten, people were consumed by the company and no longer did their best work. Leading by this principle requires strong leadership that is 'all about people'—leaders who love to get out of bed to watch their teams grow and flourish in their work and are not focused on company profit."

Educators and Super Girls

Lululemon had become something truly unique. This started with the Educators working the floor of the store. They were excited because they were part of the future of how businesses could run. The Educators we hired were living, breathing models of the Kitsilano life. Each morning, our Educators chose to bring happiness into their lives, which, in turn, brought happiness to the lives of those around them.

I was fascinated by the convergence of the employees' self-interest and our company vision. As much as I believed our employees were interested in the betterment of the world, I knew that they each had their own personal motivators as well. I wanted to create an incentive-based model that prioritized the employee's personal life over the company as a new way of driving a profitable business.

I had engaged a group of dynamic and enthusiastic university-educated women who were contemporaries of the highly educated customers I knew would pay for technology.

I wanted Super Girl employees to interact with Super Girl customers. No company had ever put this puzzle together because wholesale apparel was focused on the lowest common denominator. The lowest common denominator was cheap labour with high turnover.

Everyone in the company created their own vision and goals. Our Educators were so excited about their own lives that they began to spread that sense of living fully in the now to everyone that entered the store. This Super Girl Educator created a sense of belonging; she listened to the commitments of our Guests and partnered with them on the big things they were up to. The relationship between the Educator and the Guests was based on finding the perfect item for the Guests' specific goal or need.

I also trained our Educators to point the customer to Nike or Adidas if their product provided a better solution for the Guests. I felt that everyone should win; even the competition. Lululemon was to be agnostic and egoless.

Our training worked. I overheard real conversations shared between friends over coffee about the authenticity of our brand. It was exactly the experience we wanted for our customers.

Super Girls were defining lululemon, and I was learning from them.

The 6/13 Rule

Part of our formula also depended on our customer experience—how we educated our Guests once they were in the store. Using our Kitsilano store as a sort of laboratory, I studied how people interacted with our products and thought about the optimum way for us to engage them. We assumed the number one thing the Super Girl wanted us to solve was her compressed time. She was busy and needed a new way to shop.

We had the best quality, so she would rarely have to return a garment. We supplied free hemming, so she didn't have to go to another location to get the right length of pant. Our store was set up on function, not colours or outfits, so she could quickly find what she needed. We were fanatical about having the perfect combination of Educators, change rooms, and cash desks to make the shopping experience friction-free.

I came up with several new procedures. One was something I called the "6/13 rule"—if a Guest was looking at a product for six seconds, an Educator had a thirteen-second window to educate them about the item. Barring any follow-up questions, the Educator would then leave them alone until they looked at another item for around six seconds.

There wasn't anything scientific about it. I'd come up with those numbers by looking at people and observing their body language to see what they were comfortable with. I wanted our Educators to impress customers with their sheer knowledge of and enthusiasm for the item.

Our Educators were on the front lines and knew more

about the customer and the product than most people at the Store Support Centre (the SSC was lululemon's answer to the "head offices" of other companies). When we made big decisions, we made sure the decision was heavily weighted toward the person who works in the store.

Nothing on Hold

Our success also came from breaking retail rules at the store level. For starters, we put nothing on hold. Some people couldn't believe we wouldn't put products on hold, but we were selling our clothing quickly, and I always felt it was our responsibility to prioritize the Guest who was actually in the store.

If something was on hold behind the shelf and someone who wanted to buy that same garment was out on the floor, it didn't make sense to hold it for the person who wasn't physically present.

This rule wasn't accidental—I'd noticed that a large percentage of people who'd asked for something to be put on hold never returned. The product would sit there in the back of the cash desk for several hours. A store Educator might remember to put it back out at the end of the day or the next morning.

So, I decided I would never put our products on hold. Sometimes people got mad because we were the only retailer to do this, but, in 95 percent of the cases, customers would immediately buy the product.

We broke another retail rule by rarely answering the phones in our store. We would answer the phone if there were no customers on the floor, but our priority was always the Guest who had dedicated their time to come into the store, and who was maybe already at the cash desk. I wanted us to be really, really good at being present with in-person customers.

The New Year

The move to the new store had been expensive, but the location was already bringing excellent returns. Local media had started to take an interest in the company since lululemon was in a unique position at the forefront of the yoga movement. The press was approaching us and not the other way around.

Pre-e-commerce, every retailer knew the holiday season represented 30 percent of a year's revenue in forty days. Most retailers go on discount and suffer massively during January and February.

I was feeling great about our sales through December 2000, and January 2001. Lululemon had surged because of New Year's resolutions to get back to the gym or get into yoga.

The biggest sales day we'd ever recorded in the old store was $2,000. Our slowest day in the new store was multiples of that figure. It was thrilling, but I knew to prepare for the sales dip sure to come in February and March. I scaled back production to ensure we didn't get in over our heads with inventory.

But then, the end of January 2001 came, and our sales volume still showed no signs of slowing. Every day I looked at our sales figures for the telltale dip in volume. And every day, I saw our volume increasing instead.

I knew what was happening was abnormal. Experience told me I was observing concrete evidence that lululemon was over the awkward stage of retail infancy. Our patience was paying off. The spring of 2001 arrived, and sales still had not slowed down.

It was incredible to watch this happen, but it also meant our little company had to change to keep pace with our new-found popularity.

The Power of Attraction

The recent change in lululemon's revenues also coincided with the growth of our small staff.

As we hired more Educators, I noticed a higher number of them were older Super Girls (generally aged twenty-eight to thirty-four), with stories similar to Fiona's. They had been working fourteen-hour days in finance, were not dating, and could see no prospects for marriage or children. They dropped out, looking for a better balance in life. Lululemon and yoga represented their myopic ideal of achieving that balance. We hired them as Educators, but their Type A Wall Street personalities swung the pendulum in the opposite direction.

Utopia for these women was to be Zenned out, but this was not lululemon. Lululemon was not in the wellness business—we were in the good to great business. We soon had to rid ourselves of these *Balance Girls*.

Balance for lululemon was maximizing every moment in life. It was knowing when the bank line-ups were short and jumping on that opportunity so as not to waste a second more than was necessary. We had great things to do and waiting in line at the bank was not one of them!

Around that time, I got talking to a woman who lived across the back alley from me. Deanne Schweitzer had been on a swimming scholarship when she became pregnant in her final year. Now a mother of two with no steady job, she was highly stylish and the overall perfect candidate to become an Educator.

"I remember thinking Chip may be a little bit crazy," Deanne laughs. "One day, I was running in the rain, and this car pulls up alongside me. The windows are all steamed up. The window opens, and it's Chip, naked, except for these tiny little shorts. He says: 'Hi Deanne, wanna lift?' I was like, 'No thanks!' Later he'd told me he'd just come from hot yoga—

which I'd never heard of at the time—which explained why he was driving around with little shorts and steamed windows. Sort of."

I'd initially asked Deanne to work for me in 1999. I'd wanted her to promote lululemon at the high-end athletic clubs, same as I'd tried to do at the Glencoe. However, Deanne wanted to focus on an accounting course and taking care of her children, so she said no.

Then, when our sales picked up around Christmas of 2000, I approached Deanne again. This time, she said yes. Deanne first came to work as an Educator, helping with the unprecedented sales volume we were experiencing. Within four weeks, she became our first store manager. Bright and quick, with an ability to hire the right people, Deanne would eventually go on to become lululemon's head of product.

Deanne's sister Delaney, who was managing a bar in downtown Vancouver, joined the team in 2001. Delaney was also a single mother and not living a healthy lifestyle. "I loved what the company stood for and the people it attracted," Delaney says.

Like her sister, Delaney started as an Educator, but she soon moved into a managerial role. I loved being in Delaney's presence because she so easily absorbed everything I knew about retail, and in the years to come, Delaney would move on to run all store operations and e-commerce (in fact, Delaney would someday become my pick for CEO). Both Schweitzer sisters were superstars; they were cornerstones to the growth and culture of lululemon.

Eric Petersen, like Deanne, was a neighbour of mine. When I got to know him, he was director of marketing for EA Sports.

As Eric recalls, "Chip drove by my house one day—with no shirt on, of course—and he reached out the window and said, 'Hey Eric. Come over here. I want you to listen to these tapes.' He hands me some of these cassette tapes by this guy named Brian Tracy. I think he handed me tapes one, two, five, six, nine, and eleven. He said, 'I want you to listen to these; give them back to me when you're done.' I thought 'Well great, my weird neighbour has handed me a series of cassette tapes with several missing—he's going to think I pinched them.'"

After I had invited Eric to a Brian Tracy event, he said: "I had no idea what type of business Chip ran up there," Eric adds. "I knew it was some sort of apparel company, but I was blown away by the energy in the room, these young women who felt that they could change the world. I went home that night and told my wife that in thirty years of team sports I'd never seen a group of people who were so passionate about achieving something."

Eric would join us as Director of Marketing and would play a pivotal role in our disruptive plan for the 2010 Olympic Games in Vancouver.

One of the next people to join us was Darrell Kopke. Darrell was another person I'd known through Westbeach—he'd been doing sales for a zipper manufacturer, with which Westbeach (and then lululemon, in its first stages) did business. Having just finished his MBA at the University of British Columbia, I hired Darrell as general manager in November 2001.

"Chip told me he didn't want to get on another airplane," says Darrell. "He knew what he was good at, but he wanted me to grow the business. We were an unusual group of people that had no business being successful. We didn't come from pedigree. We didn't listen to what anyone else was saying. It was fun. It was exciting. It was us against the industry."

Darrell was the perfect person at the perfect time to grow lululemon. Like Delaney, Deanne, Summer, and Eric, Darrell became another lululemon philosophical icon, because he understood why our specific development model connected to the value of the brand.

To have core Kitsilano people understand my vision and trust that the company would become something great was all I ever wanted. There was no traditional recruiting. In my mind, lululemon was built organically through the Power of Attraction. By sharing my love of athletics, fun, and greatness, I attracted people who were all about the same things. I am completely blunt and transparent, and everyone knew where they stood. We had zero internal politics, and immediate direct feedback was the norm.

As lululemon grew, our teams were often assembled using the same technique. We went out into the community and practiced yoga, we joined local run clubs, and we attended athletic events. We did the things that we loved doing, and in doing so, we met great people that we wanted to spend time with. Relying on the power of attraction instead of recruitment analytics or traditional channels allowed us to quickly attract people that were interested in what we were up to.

Most of the people I hired from within the community were athletic, educated, and had a healthy West Coast approach to living. They withstood the growing pains as we morphed from entrepreneurial to professional—growing and shining. It was a synergy thing—one plus one equals three. Lululemon would never have achieved what it did without these core players.

CHAPTER 16:
TORONTO

I will never stop working because all I see is possibility.

Syd

In the spring of 2001, I was approached with an offer from Syd Beder, a Canadian apparel veteran based in Toronto.

Syd had at least twenty-five years' experience in the industry. His business partner, Alexandra Bennett Morgan, had happened upon lululemon in Vancouver and liked what she saw. Syd knew the ins and outs of production, so he immediately recognized the quality of construction and materials we used. The two of them believed in yoga and its growth in popularity.

Syd wanted to open a lululemon franchise in Toronto.

The offer was a dilemma for me. A big part of me just wanted to keep my little shop in Kitsilano and preserve lululemon as it was, simple and local. However, sales had taken off so much I was having a hard time thinking small. Back when Westbeach had become successful with snowboard apparel, there was just never enough money to facilitate the growth we'd needed to take us to the next level. I didn't intend to repeat that with lululemon.

I wanted us to reach a larger audience—I just didn't want to start our expansion in Toronto. Saying no would have consequences, however. Syd was experienced, and I got the feeling if I didn't jump at the franchise offer, he would give the concept a try and create a lululemon knock-off of his own. If he copied us, he had enough background to do it well and corner the whole Eastern Canada sales market before I even got there.

It seemed I could ink a contract with Syd and make an ally, or I could say no and create an instant competitor. So, I signed the agreement . . . but did so without legal advice. In those days, even though we were becoming successful, every penny still meant something.

Once the agreement was signed, Syd Beder paid $25,000 for the right to sell lululemon clothing in Canada's most populous city.

A Declaration

My first business goal was to have a single store and ride my beach cruiser to work every day. I had achieved that goal. My second business goal was to have five stores, enabling us to increase in quantity, and drive down production costs. My third was to compete against Nike.

As Syd and Alexandra got to work on opening in Toronto, I thought a little more about my own expansion plans. I knew that making an amazing product at a reasonable price would get a lot easier once we got to five stores and could take advantage of economy-of-scale production. Eventually, I knew, making several times more of something and having enough space in which to sell it would work better for us—especially since I'd committed to never doing wholesale again.

I could see long-term success. I knew if we didn't grow, Nike would figure out what we were doing, set up across the street, and put us out of business.

But the real reason to grow was our people. They were just ageing into the stage where they were thinking of marriage. They wanted a bigger possibility in their career and to take on more significant challenges. We all knew if the company grew, we could afford children and mortgages and schools. I felt I had an obligation to give them every opportunity to fulfill their lives.

One day in mid-2001, I gathered our staff together and told them, "Nike is our competitor." Considering we had only $4 million in yearly sales, it was a crazy thing to say. My handful of staff didn't know whether to laugh or run for the door.

As Delaney Schweitzer recalls, "There were fifteen of us in a room—the whole company—and Chip declared we would open three hundred stores, that we'd be across North America, and that soon we'd be mentioned in every board meeting at Nike. As crazy as that sounded, every one of us was like: 'I'm in.'

"A few years later, we hired a production person from Nike," Delaney continues. "He told us that the second he gave his notice and said that he was going to lululemon, they immediately had him escorted out of the building. At that point, Nike had created a small team to dig into the lululemon story and understand our stores. They couldn't figure out the connection we were making with people. When he said, 'You're on the agenda at Nike, they're talking about you, they're trying to figure you out,' it was proof positive that Chip's declaration had come true."

Small as we were, we were united in the opinion we had a better product and business model than Nike. We were reaching the female market in a way for which Nike didn't have the culture. We were doing so well that I could envision if we didn't expand, Nike could replicate our business. This was closely related to what I'd considered when taking Syd Beder's offer. It was sobering to consider the demise of our company while the brand was still in its infancy.

I knew our staff were more than up to the challenge of growing lululemon. By that point, I'd paid for our core people to attend the Landmark Forum, and I'd seen them come back empowered and communicating in a way they'd never known before. They'd become people who were no longer willing to settle for mediocrity in their lives—or in the company to which they'd devoted themselves.

In fact, instead of targeting Nike as competition, it even occurred to me to model lululemon after McDonald's and become a real estate company. Our stores were profitable enough to pay for their own real estate.

The possibilities were endless.

Showrooms Defined in Toronto

Meanwhile, Syd's plans to open in Toronto were progressing. I liked the way he was building enthusiasm by word-of-mouth. In June of 2001, he invited people to his own loft apartment where he'd set up a few racks of lululemon clothing. Since it was invite-only, Syd's loft had an exclusive, underground feel to it, much like the feel of our original second-floor store. People had to know someone to get in, so it generated a lot of curiosity. It was *pull* instead of *push* marketing.

Syd partnered his exclusive "loft store" concept with a focused campaign targeting Toronto's yoga studios. He took rolling racks of clothes to the studios for people to try on their way in and out of classes. It was precisely the grassroots marketing that had worked for us in Vancouver.

Eight months later, in February 2002, Syd opened the lululemon store on Queen Street West. By then, the customer base was already established, and right away the store started putting up fantastic numbers. It felt like a well-executed success.

More than that, the Toronto opening reassured me that if a similar plan was followed—opening inexpensive show-rooms, educating the public, networking with yoga studios, and inspiring grassroots word-of-mouth conversations—the lululemon concept could work just as well almost anywhere. We had a successful formula for growth and expansion. We just needed to stick to it.

Our First Quality-Control Problem

We had fundamental confidence in our products. We didn't even do sales or discounts. Then, in 2002, we experienced a quality control problem and had to recall approximately 2,000 pairs of pants due to the pilling of the fabric.

I knew that authorizing the recall would nearly kill the company but was prepared to take that risk to maintain prod-uct integrity. I fully acknowledged the flaw in that batch of fabric.

With technical knits, a thousand things can go wrong. Most bolts of fabric have one flaw, and that's okay. Some have two, and it might be a problem, but three is a big issue. The problem comes when no one can predict what combination of three things out of a thousand creates a massive error.

From this moment on, I became the "King of Luon." I checked everything we made, and when I couldn't check it, I made sure there was a designated king or queen to check it on my behalf. Our livelihoods were based on the quality of our proprietary Luon.

After we pulled all the affected pants off the shelves, we had our Educators speak to every Guest that walked into our stores. We posted a notice above the cash register. We told our

Guests we were responsible, and we knew it was a problem. We wanted them to return the subpar pants they may have already purchased. We would replace them with another pair from a different batch.

Though we did a good job of taking care of our Guests and maintaining our integrity, I was now sitting on thousands of pairs of defective pants. I looked at them and realized that despite not living up to our high standards, they were still really good pants. The question was, what to do with them.

We held a design meeting. At the meeting, it came to my attention that many customers had complained about how they would love to take their dogs walking wearing our Luon pants, but they couldn't because the dogs' hair would stick to the Luon.

Here, I thought, was a unique solution.

We took the pilling pants and built another pair of loose, woven, slick nylon pants over top of them. Dog hair wouldn't stick to the woven nylon. What started off as a pragmatic way to put superficially defective pants to good use became lululemon's "dog walking pants"—one of our bestselling items of all time.

Around that same time, a woman entered the West 4th store determined to be refunded for a pair of pants that was pilling. This style pair of pants was not from the previously mentioned run. An object—I suspected a metal buckle on her hip purse—had repeatedly been slicing into her lululemon pants, as the flaw was specific to one location on the pant. She berated me in the middle of the store, in front of other Guests and Educators, demanding that I reimburse her for a faulty product.

My dedication to selling quality clothing—and honest admittance of past flawed production—gave me the confidence to refuse this woman a refund.

CHAPTER 17:
OTHER EXPANSIONS

Do it now, do it right fucking now.

The Trip with Summer

In August 2001, I planned to attend the Outdoor Retailer Show in Salt Lake City for our third time. The OR Show specialized in technical fabrics and outerwear and was a great source of inspiration for the company. I asked Summer Gray, now lululemon's head designer, to come along for the trip.

By this point, Summer and I had been working together for almost two years. During the first year, we didn't see one another day-to-day, but during the second year, I got to know Summer a little better. I had huge respect for her work ethic. As a designer, she was phenomenal.

My own sense of design was far more obtuse than hers. I would experiment more and often go too far. Some of the products I came up with were home runs, others were disasters. But Summer had an ability to look at something and fit it, colour it, or make it look a certain way so that people would buy it in volume. This made us the perfect combination because I would have the far-out and technical ideas, which she would then hone to sell in volume.

Thank God I let Summer drive the product because I soon realized she was the best in the world at stretch-fabric fit. Lululemon would have been a shell of itself without Summer's expertise.

Although I knew her well in a work capacity, Summer and I had not spent time getting to know each other personally. We boarded the plane to Salt Lake City and chatted, not as boss and employee, but just as two people. Ten minutes into our conversation, I was struck by what an incredible woman she was.

Away from work, I realized I was seeing her in a whole different way.

We arrived in Salt Lake in the afternoon, but the trade show didn't start until the next day. We were travelling on a shoestring budget, so as was standard for the usual three to four people we took to the shows, I'd only booked one room with multiple beds. We saw it as camping.

After checking in, we dropped our things off, headed out for a city art walk, and then caught a free outdoor concert before dinner. We talked and laughed and then went for a swim.

After a nice evening, we went back up to the room and stretched out on our separate beds. I turned on the TV.

I was older than she was, I had no way of knowing if I was her type, and I was her boss. Summer was the most valuable employee I had, in responsibility, integrity, and trust. I would never risk ruining our professional relationship and having her leave the company because I knew how hard it would be to get anyone else at her level of capability. She was far too important for me to risk making a romantic move.

We each lay on our own beds while I flicked through the television channels. Then, Summer got up. I assumed she was heading to the washroom. Instead, she came over to my bed and asked me to move over. After some time, Summer put her head on my chest and closed her eyes, and we both fell asleep like that.

In the morning, we woke up to a new reality. We hadn't even kissed the night before, but everything had changed.

As Summer says: "Chip interviewed me for a job at lululemon in October of 1999. He was late for our meeting. I saw him peel into the parking lot, no shirt, no shoes. I then watched him rummage around in his car for something clean to put on. That was my introduction to Chip, him frantically picking up shirts, sniffing this one, sniffing that one, trying to find a matching pair of shoes . . . When my mom asked me how the interview had gone, I told her I wasn't sure I'd get the job, but I did think I would marry him."

I couldn't believe I had been working side by side with this incredible woman and did not understand how she felt. At that moment, in a hotel room in Salt Lake City, everything changed.

Many years before, as a little kid, I'd thought my grandparents had the best possible kind of partnership. They not only loved each other, but they also *worked* together in almost perfect synchronicity. My whole life since I'd been searching for something comparable and had so far never found it.

Even in those first few moments with Summer, I felt like I'd found what I was looking for. As crazy as it may sound, that morning in Salt Lake City, I asked her if she wanted to marry me and she said yes. Then we kissed. It wasn't a great kiss (we both agreed). We were both unprepared. Still, our chemistry was powerful.

Summer told her parents right away. They were surprised, but okay with it. My own mom, dad, sister, and brother were all a little more apprehensive about the whole thing because they didn't know Summer. There seemed to be a sentiment of not being sure it would stick, or if it was just a brief, happy delusion.

My sons, JJ and Brett, were the two people whose feelings about this new development in my life were most important. In the past, the two had been a challenge for the handful of women I'd brought home to meet them, understandably out of allegiance to their mother.

But since I'd started lululemon, the boys were always in and out of the store, so they'd met and spoken with Summer many times prior to me explaining what was happening between us. In many ways, she'd already won them over. JJ's own growing interest in design meant that he and Summer had a lot in common from the get-go. He was only thirteen, but his vote of confidence helped to smooth things over with their mother, who'd been worried my new relationship might be disruptive for our sons.

Workplace romances can be tricky, and it was reasonable for people to be concerned there might be favouritism, or that the work environment would change. But ultimately, the people we worked with knew how important integrity was to Summer and me both, and how we would not let our relationship hinder lululemon's success.

We immediately fell into a routine. We worked twelve-hour days, went home together, worked out, ate dinner, went to bed, and woke up to do it all again. There was nothing to explain or apologize for since Summer knew what the business was going through all the time. I could talk to her about issues and count on her to understand. I loved her and the life we were already building together.

I also made good on that promise to put a real ring on Summer's finger just a short time later. We were in Paris at a fabric show. The ring I brought—which wasn't extravagant by any stretch of the imagination—meant a lot. I was nervous to leave it in the safe in the hotel room, so I carried it with me everywhere, waiting for the perfect moment to ask Summer to marry me.

This trip was a week after 9/11, and security everywhere was heightened. I was worried that the ring would set off an alarm and I'd be forced to get down on one knee beside an x-ray machine. Luckily, that didn't happen, and I finally popped the question at a nice little Parisian café. It was perfect.

Initially, we figured we'd get married as quickly as we could. "We'll just go to the justice of the peace, or we'll just get the boys and pop off somewhere," says Summer. But then a good friend of hers insisted on putting something together for us. "She knew how busy we were with lululemon, working flat-out, seven days a week. She started planning a little backyard affair for the following spring, allowing Chip and me to grow the business we were both so passionate about."

April 20, 2002, was a Saturday and our wedding day. I went into our West 4th Avenue store to work as I usually did. The number of Guests in our store had been steadily growing for a long time, but on that Saturday afternoon, I was taken aback by how many people were coming through the doors.

The change rooms and cash desk had huge line-ups. The Educators were lit up with enthusiasm, and there was energy in the air. I immediately jumped in to help and worked at the front of the store, directing traffic.

As the day went on, the store became even busier. I didn't feel I could leave. I kept an eye on the clock. I was cutting it close, but I wanted to stick around to find out how our sales had gone. Plus, we needed every extra pair of hands we could get. It felt like we'd reached a critical mass.

A seemingly random day in the calendar was doubling the best day of sales in the history of the company—$30,000.

At the last possible moment, I rushed out of the store, ecstatic with the revenue and the experience of everything coming together. I had a dozen things to do, and I was running late, but the first thing I did was call Summer. I couldn't get over the fact there was no logic behind that day being so extraordinary. It wasn't a holiday of any kind—it was just a weekend in the middle of spring.

For the first time in a long time, I felt like a whole new future was ahead of me. I believed I could pay for a mortgage and raise a family without working myself to death. I felt like we would be fine. I rushed home, threw on my tuxedo, and with JJ and Brett as my best men, I married Summer Gray in our backyard, surrounded by our friends and family.

Summer and I had turned a significant corner in our personal lives that April, and it felt like lululemon had too. Our store was doing huge amounts of business week after week. A few years earlier, I'd noticed women wearing our clothing here and there on West 4th.

Now it seemed I was noticing the same thing all over Vancouver.

The Manifesto

At a certain point, I became aware it wasn't just our designs that were becoming ubiquitous—it was what we were putting them in.

The shopping bags we gave our Guests were suddenly everywhere I looked. Women, men, and even children were carrying them, using them as grocery bags, lunch bags, gym bags, shoe carriers, and just about everything in between. People had come into the store just to ask for bags and not even purchase anything. Our culture was being broadcast far and wide.

In 1998, I spent thirty minutes compiling a list of sayings I called *the manifesto*. It was just a list of random statements about how I lived my life with authenticity and integrity. *Friends are more important than money*, was one. *Do one thing a day that scares you*, was another. *Children are the orgasm of life*, another yet. Most of these thoughts had come from my life experiences, my parents, my commitment to transformational development disciplines, and our lululemon library.

I thought these observations were interesting enough to post beside the cash register so people in line could read something thoughtful while waiting. I quickly found other people liked these observations and aphorisms and were asking for their own copies.

I asked some surf and snowboard graphic friends of mine (Cowie and Fox) to make the manifesto look like artwork. Then I photocopied a bunch to leave at the cash register. Most customers who came in the store wanted to take a copy, so we automatically started putting them into every bag.

Soon afterward, I thought of creating a bag with the manifesto *on* it, instead of *in* it. I reasoned that the biggest waste in the world was pretty, useless packaging that came from the luxury fashion world. I wondered if I could develop a reusable bag that with the manifesto, which would add to people's lives instead of being another piece of garbage. I didn't want people to walk around the street with a bag with a logo on it or lame words that showed to others that the person with the bag was wealthy enough to buy luxury. I was all about function, with fashion being a distant second.

I wanted customers to be sitting in their car or on the subway or at home and pick up the manifesto and read it. I noticed the transformational effect the manifesto had on people. It validated the way I wanted to live my life, and I saw this occur for others too. The manifesto was not inspirational, but aspirational.

I researched a few different options and came up with a 100 percent polypropylene reusable shopping bag that was durable, waterproof, and recyclable. We created them for Christmas gift-giving, so that the present was "wrapped" in our manifesto. As far as I know, we were the first company to make these expensive, recyclable shopping bags.

As Darrell Kopke, our first general manager, recalls: "The fact that the word 'orgasm' was on the bags caused a bit of a stir. I got a call from an outraged customer not long after the bags came out. She was particularly upset, she said, because as a result of bringing the bag home, she had to explain the meaning of the word orgasm to her twelve-year-old daughter. I listened to her patiently and when she was finished, I said, 'You're welcome!' That was the end of the conversation."

As I reflect on the lululemon shopping bag, I realize just how great our branding was. The popularity of the bags was spectacular. Not only did they create conversation, but they were recognizable around the world! It was proof that our Guests aligned with our psychology of health, athletics, and a West Coast way of living.

the original lululemon manifesto 2003

(these were the quotes on the side of the lululemon shopping bags)

- Coke, Pepsi and other pops will be known as the cigarettes of the future. Colas are NOT a substitute for water. Colas are just another cheap drug made to look great by advertising.

- Drink fresh water and as much water as you can. Water flushes unwanted toxins and keeps your brain sharp.

- Love.

- Do yoga. It lets you live in the moment and stretching releases toxins from your muscles.

- Your outlook on life is a direct reflection of how much you like yourself.

- Do one thing a day that scares you.

- Sunshine absorbed into the skin might be worse than no sunshine. Get the right amount of sunshine.

- Listen, listen, listen and then ask strategic questions.

- Life is full of setbacks. Success is determined by how you handle setbacks.

- Compliments from the heart elevate another person's spirit and will often result in an encouraging word for someone else—a domino effect.

- Write down your short and long-term GOALS four times a year. A class study at Harvard found only 3% of the students had written goals. 20 years later, the same 3% were wealthier than the other 97% combined.

- A daily hit of athletic-induced endorphins will give you the power to make better decisions and help you be at peace with yourself.

- Let SWEAT FLOW from your pores once a day to regenerate your skin.

- Jealousy works the opposite way you want it to.

- One hour of aerobic exercise will release endorphins to regenerate cells and offset stress.

- Wake up and realize you are surrounded by amazing friends.

- Communication is COMPLICATED. Remember that each person is raised in a different family with a slightly different definition of every word. An agreement is an agreement only if each party knows the conditions for satisfaction and a time is set for satisfaction to occur.

- Friends are more important than money.

- Live near the ocean and inhale the pure salt air that flows over the water. Vancouver will do nicely.

- Do not use cleaning chemicals on your kitchen counters. Try vinegar and lemon. Someone will inevitably make a sandwich on your counter.

- Stress is related to 99% of all illnesses.

- Don't trust that an old-age pension will be sufficient.

- Do yoga so you can remain active in physical sports as you age.

- Observe a plant before and after watering and notice the benefits water can have on your body and your brain.

- You ALWAYS have a choice and the conscious brain can only hold one thought at a time. Utilize your freedom to choose.

- Just like you did not know what an orgasm was before you had one, nature does not let you know how great children are until you have them. Children are the orgasm of life.

- Lululemon athletica was formed to provide people with components to live a longer, healthier and more fun life. If we can produce products to keep people active and stress free, we believe the world will be a better place.

- DO IT NOW. The world is changing AT SUCH A RAPID rate that waiting to implement changes will result in you being two steps behind.

- Will you choose a life of a glass-half-empty or a glass-half-full?

- Take various vitamins. You never know what small mineral can eliminate the bottleneck to everlasting health.

- Nature leads us to mediocrity for safety and reproduction. Average is as close to the bottom as it is to the top.

- Dance, sing, floss, and travel.

- Visualize your eventual demise. It has an amazing effect on how you live for the moment.

Calgary

In late 2002, my cousin Russ Parker came from Calgary to see the lululemon store in Kitsilano. After showing him around, Russ told me he wanted a franchise.

"Although I had been considering a couple of business opportunities," says Russ, "I knew within a day of seeing lululemon in operation that it was something I wanted to be involved in. The electricity was palpable, and I loved the vibe in the store. People were communicating with each other in the office in an open, honest way you rarely observe in an office environment. I wanted in."

This time, I also brought on a lawyer to help me make my franchise agreements just right—including an easy buyout. The buyout clause stated I could buy back the franchise for four times the profit and pay for all depreciated leaseholds and inventory at cost. This meant no negotiations in a buyout; it also meant that I could buy the sales of the franchises for four times profit and the public market would give me ten times the profit if we ever went public.

It was a great deal for me, and it was a great deal for Russ—he would stand to make about $10 million over the next five years.

So far, the desire I had to get to five stores quickly to get my production costs down was becoming a reality. Syd Beder was running a very busy store in Toronto, my cousin Russ did extremely well as soon as his Calgary franchise opened, and Summer's sister and brother-in-law had started a successful franchise in Victoria. This, I believed, put us in a strong position to open our second Vancouver store.

Naked on Robson Street

Every city has its own premier shopping district. While lululemon's origins were tied to Kitsilano, Vancouver's shopping mecca was Robson Street. Even though the focus on Robson was high fashion and not athletic apparel, it was almost impossible to run a store in Vancouver and not think about the possibilities Robson offered.

At that time, Robson was one of the most expensive retail areas in the world, primarily due to the value of the Japanese yen and the influx of well-heeled Japanese tourists. We wanted to set up next to the Robson luxury stores with a product that was completely different. A luxury brand is usually defined as a company with impeccable quality, sold at a price available to only a few. At lululemon, we believed we had impeccable quality that could be sold at a price accessible to anyone who appreciated technology and fit.

Luxury customers, meanwhile, could buy "time" in their lives and were consequently often in great shape and very healthy. These wealthy women were unconscious trendsetters who helped to propel the lululemon brand.

On the other end of the spectrum, we already had the hard-core yogis and athletes in community street stores and supplied them with the best-functioning athletic garment in the world. I knew that once people used the best of something, it would be almost impossible for them to use anything else.

We signed a lease on Robson and designed our first professionally-built store. Then I took out an ad in our local weekly newspaper offering a free lululemon outfit to shoppers if they came naked on the store's opening day. The response was unbelievable. It was so strong that I became concerned there would be a naked riot, and we would be forced to hand out our entire inventory free-of-charge.

I went back to the paper and placed a second ad. This time

I clarified that only the first thirty naked Guests would score free clothes. I had forgotten about Vancouver culture, and that given a chance, the whole city would show up naked.

On the day of the opening, at around 4 a.m., people started lining up outside. It was a drizzly, cool October morning in Vancouver, but groups of people were showing up wearing raincoats and nothing else. It was still dark outside, but I could see the numbers were growing. The inside of the store was still swarming with our efforts to get it ready.

Not long after the line formed, the media showed up with trucks and vans. As dawn broke, a large crowd of spectators had assembled. Milestone's—the restaurant across the street—had a balcony packed with people craning over their breakfasts to get a look at those lining up. Even lululemon's meek, mild accountant who couldn't have looked more out of place had shown up not willing to miss the spectacle.

As we got ready to unlock the front doors, I was very excited . . . until I got a good look at the group of people clustered by the front door. The first two customers lined up were young girls who couldn't have been older than fourteen.

I turned from the door and went to find Darrell Kopke in the back. I was verging on panic, thinking about the media and the video cameras filming, the crowd of spectators, and these kids about to strip down. What was supposed to be a funfest was suddenly verging on becoming a PR catastrophe.

After a couple of minutes to assess the situation, I asked Summer to help greet the naked Guests. We went to the door, opened it up, and stepped out to the crowd. I shouted, "You guys are fantastic—thanks for coming!" The tension broke that instant and there were cheers and clapping. Then we counted off the first thirty naked people over the threshold.

As it turned out, those girls at the front of the line weren't alone. They were sisters—and they came with their equally naked mother and grandmother.

Dozens of Guests continued to show up naked to the store all day, just because they could do it. Three naked men came in the morning and just didn't want to leave. It was a little creepy, but we went with it. We had no issues with the police, and this reminded me why I love Vancouver so much. There are plenty of cities in North America where this kind of event in 2002 wouldn't have gone over nearly as smoothly. By closing time, it was clear the day had gone phenomenally well. The publicity was worth millions, and so much more fun than a standard press release.

Our store on Robson enjoyed a strong start and did not let up from that first day. The volume of foot traffic on Robson Street brought in tons of new customers and introduced many people to our world. We made use of our prominent store windows and used them to reach our community authentically. We treated every lululemon store window as a living, breathing expression of the empowered team of Educators in that store. It was theirs to create as often as they wanted. Unlike other retailers that had pre-set merchandising and window dressing, we encouraged our stores to be locally relevant and entrepreneurial with the "advertising" that the window represented for people walking past and into our stores.

The challenge I'd anticipated before opening on Robson was maintaining our ability to do retail our way in a high-fashion environment. People may have come to Robson expecting the usual luxury fashion commission sales pitch, and they would have been surprised when they didn't get it.

Jenna Hills, one of the first Educators hired at the Robson Street store, says: "Chip would visit a few times a week. He always selected a few Educators to do a walkthrough. Nothing got by him. He was fastidious about approaching every single person in the store with a sense of urgency. Time was a huge value. He gave feedback with clarity and was generous with his love.

One story I remember was at the end of a monthly staff meeting. Everyone from Vancouver would gather at the West 4th store in the evening after closing. I was sitting on the floor, like we did, when Chip said we couldn't grow this company without those of us in the room stepping up. He said any one of us could be making $100,000 per year in five years' time. It was up to us, and the company needed us. I knew it was the truth. It struck me like lightning. Five years later I broke six figures for the first time in my life. At that staff meeting, I was making ten bucks an hour. But I'll say it anyway—it wasn't about the money. It was about creating possibility.

CHAPTER 18:
THE BUSINESS OF FAMILY

This is not our practice life.

Big News

In early 2003, Summer and I found out we were going to have a baby of our own. As the news settled in, I felt a tremendous amount of satisfaction with my life. With Summer as my partner, we had grown a business from nothing. Now, that business was set to provide for the family we were creating.

Summer was lululemon's phenomenal designer. In fact, a few months earlier, the owners of Roots had come into our store, asking who our designer was. "My wife," I told them, and that was the end of that.

Summer also provided design continuity for the brand, her work representing our original intent. Having a child might lessen Summer's involvement in our operations and successful formula, but by then we'd hired and trained great people underneath her (Andrea Murray, Cassandra Tse), and had tried to mitigate against her inevitable absences.

Things at lululemon were going exceptionally well. As an

entrepreneur, it's sometimes hard to believe you'll ever have a company that's bringing in enough money to create a rainy-day fund, but lululemon was now in a place where it would do just that. I paid off the debt I had taken on our house. That meant Summer and I could start our family without financial worry and stress.

Partnering with the Hons

Meanwhile, the lululemon concept was translating smoothly across our locations. The success of the five Canadian stores confirmed we could thrive while doing business our way.

We'd put into place an exclusive manufacturing deal with my friends Frankie and Elky Hon. Their Vancouver factory was working at 80 percent capacity, and they were always scrambling for business. I made them an offer. I said I would guarantee 100 percent production with one fabric for 50 percent of their business.

My 50 percent of the manufacturer's profit meant I had eliminated yet another middleman. When great factory people like Frankie and Elky do not have to look for business and can focus on efficiency, amazing work can occur. We ended up making $2 million a year profit on the factory, and I continued to build a deeper and wider moat to protect against future competition.

As Frankie says: "We started with very small orders, a hundred pieces at a time. Then Chip's business bloomed crazily, and Chip suggested an exclusive partnership with us." Much like my relationship with Josephine Terratiano, my relationship with the Hons grew organically, and, to this day, they're like family. Eliminating two middlemen by owning our manufacturing and our own stores was a key reason for lululemon's rise to greatness.

Around the time of this partnership, a man named George

Tsogas came in as a consultant to look at our inventory, distribution, and overall logistics. "When I first walked into the office," says George, "all I remember is this big West Coast dude sitting on a yoga ball, shirtless, in board shorts and flip-flops. His first words were, 'You're way too serious—do not wear a suit again to this office.' That was my first taste of Chip's unique culture."

At the time, George was a recent graduate of a Vancouver technology school. He was a young, natural leader who quickly modernized the processes in our warehouses and distribution centres. Not only that, George introduced the people working in the warehouses to our culture—he brought in fitness equipment, personal trainers, and development coaches.

Where there'd previously been high staff turnover in our warehouse, people now stayed for the long-haul. This concept was almost unthinkable for part-time seasonal workers. Over the coming years, George would prove to be a major asset to the company, eventually rising to the position of VP of Global Logistics and Distribution. He was one more addition to our core team.

Toronto: Growing Concerns

There was one exception to the excitement—I was developing serious concerns about our Toronto franchise. While Syd Beder understood how to sell, he wasn't embracing our business philosophy. Contrary to our training, he told the customers how pretty they looked and was attached to the old-school fashion model. He was going about things in his own way. He wasn't investing in his Educators, and without our training, they were unable to connect with our Guests authentically.

What Syd failed to recognize was that the success of our brand was driven by our people development. No matter what the company's goals were, the most important objective for lululemon was to remain true to our culture. That culture—and how it related to both our staff and customers—underpinned everything we did. Keeping to our core philosophy was what would give us long-term success.

To me, the culture of the company was so critical that it needed a valuable person to lead it—a person who had a major commitment to training. "A huge focus of this was training people to live great lives," Delaney remembers. Because she was a poster child for personal success, I asked Delaney Schweitzer to be our first training manager.

The Buyout

The Toronto franchise was doing the same sales as Vancouver stores, or about $1,500 to $2,000 per square foot. This was double or triple what most retail stores did, and we were just in our infancy. This provided a hint on the sales multiples we could do if we implemented our business philosophy in Toronto.

Jill Chatwood was one of the first Educators at the Toronto store. As she recollects, "There was always a waiting list for products. At one point, we had a binder with lists of people waiting for certain items to arrive. We would call them and make no promises, simply letting them know we had received new stock. Changing room line-ups were regularly waitlisted for longer than forty-five minutes. We had people on the floor whose jobs were simply to bring up more stock by the armload and hang it up as fast as they could. Every day was like Boxing Day (or American Black Friday)."

I was happy with this. So was Syd. He wanted to sell lululemon clothes, but he didn't want to run a lululemon store the way I'd intended. Every management issue led to a disagreement. Our communication was broken. Our differences were fundamental.

Part of this was Syd's refusal to attend the Landmark Forum. Already in his sixties, perhaps Syd felt he'd already learned everything he needed to be successful. His business partner, Alex Morgan, was also disinterested in the course. If the two of them weren't willing to conduct committed, guided self-improvement, their employees wouldn't get the opportunity to experience our culture. I experienced a divide between a West Coast athletic concept and an East Coast fashion context. To me, the fashion model was old and dead.

I needed to get the store back to ensure the cultural integrity of our brand. In my mind, without integrity, lululemon was nothing. What had to be done was clear: I needed to buy Syd out of the deal.

I went back to our franchise agreement to acquaint myself with the details of our buyout clause, only to discover there wasn't one. The lack of a buyout clause in my Toronto franchise agreement wasn't the first time I was responsible for a bad contract.

Syd was a shrewd person, and it would not be easy to come to terms with him. He also knew I could set up five stores around him and put him out of business, but I had better and bigger things to do.

The dollar figure we settled on was $2.5 million. I had sold the franchise to Syd for $25,000 just two years earlier. Even though the number we agreed to was enormous, it was clear the Toronto store, along with other stores I could quickly build, would be enough business to justify the price. I had little alternative but to find the money.

Over the years, I'd learned hard lessons about borrowing money and the downward spiral that can result when financial liabilities overwhelm a company. My days at Westbeach had left me with a strong aversion to debt. But while learning fiscal responsibility had been an essential, valuable lesson for me, I also learned it's just as important to know when *not* to be so dogmatic and when to adapt to a new situation. The situation with Syd Beder was shaping up to be one of those times.

I had nothing close to the money I needed to buy back the franchise. I went to my former private equity (PE) partner from Westbeach, Don Steele, whose children were both working at lululemon. I asked Don to buy 30 percent of lululemon for $2.5 million, but he declined as he had too much on his plate. He said with my cash flow I should be able to borrow the $2.5 million from the bank. It was such an unbelievable number I couldn't believe a bank would lend it to a four-year-old business. It turned out the cash flow from the one Toronto store could cover the loan.

I had paid off the mortgage on my house, but the only way to secure a new loan was putting up the house as collateral. "Geez," I thought. "Here we go again!" This hit even harder, as the house was now where I lived with my pregnant wife.

I told myself that as daunting as it was to borrow such a huge amount of cash—and to put up my house as collateral—this was nothing like the old days when we borrowed money to keep the wolves from the door. This was a calculated risk with a huge potential benefit.

The biggest difference between the stress of borrowing money during my Westbeach days and this situation with lululemon was cash flow. The lululemon stores were all cash cows.

I had two factors in my favour: I knew what I could expect for income from the Toronto store, and I knew I could set up more Toronto stores to help pay back the loan in one year. I also knew that if I was going to buy back the store, sooner was better than later. It would only get more expensive, with more tense negotiation and more complicated terms.

Within a few months of realizing what had to be done, the negotiations were settled, Syd Beder was bought out, and the Toronto store was ours.

Briar Hill

The Briar Hill area of North Toronto was the residential centre of our customer base. I was 100 percent certain if we opened a new store in Briar Hill, it would be an instant success. We put our plan to open in Briar Hill into action, choosing a location that would be our flagship store. We wanted it to be iconic in the same way the first store in Kitsilano was.

I didn't even want to put the store name outside, just a discreet logo and nothing more. I started to understand that just a logo was much more powerful a branding statement than a name alone. I became averse to using the lululemon name on stores going forward. It seemed like push marketing. I knew Super Girls loved the confidence we showed with just our logo.

This was radical thinking at the time, as no one in run-of-the-mill, old-school marketing would believe it was a good move to just go with a logo. I knew old-school marketers did not understand the subconscious thinking of our customer and her need to discover and not be pushed.

There was enough potential in the existing staff to make it worth investing in retraining them in the true lululemon way. Syd had hired a woman named Karen Wyder from Vancouver as his conduit to the head office. Karen was also the perfect Super Girl and took on the culture naturally. With Karen's help, we rounded up the most amazing group of Torontonians who moved to Vancouver over the next few years and were powerhouses for the company (hats off to Erin Westelman, Jill Chatwood, Julie Ball, and Carla Anderson).

Bree Stanlake

Around that time, I was working as an educator in the West 4th store. One day, I started talking to a Guest who told me she had just graduated from the MBA program at UBC in Vancouver, just like Darrell Kopke had.

"Great," I said. "Want a job?"

This Super Girl—whose name was Bree Stanlake—said yes. The next day she was up and running. Lululemon was, by then, attracting a lot of lawyers and MBA-level women, but I could tell Bree was special. She had the West Coast fresh, athletic look and feel about her, and was obviously intelligent. She was also looking for a great future. As the lululemon model was producing amazing cash, I knew we were entering an era where our executives could make a better salary than they could doing normal corporate work.

Bree would go on to become lululemon's General Manager for Canada until 2012. As she says, "I started as an Educator in Vancouver, and worked in the Vancouver stores for about four months. Then one day Chip said, 'Emergency meeting at the 4th Avenue store tomorrow at 9:00 a.m.' I showed up. He said, 'Okay, it's game time, you're off to Toronto.' I went over for the franchisee trip with Chip and Summer and a couple others, and just got kind of thrown into the fire from there.

"At that point, there was only one store in Toronto," Bree continues. "Then we opened all the other stores out there. I went from Educator to the regional manager."

One part of the training consisted of reintroducing people to the company's ethos. Taking the focus away from sales and fashion, I educated the Toronto employees on the philosophy of the company. I enrolled everyone who hadn't taken the Landmark Forum or written their vision and goals and ensured they had everything they needed to be successful. Within a month, everyone was reenergized and excited to be a part of lululemon—the way it was meant to be. They were fired up about moving forward, using a common language to communicate, and thinking big. Many people who stayed through the transition of the Toronto store would remain with lululemon for years to come.

In retrospect, there were a lot of unknowns in the Toronto buyout. A lot could have gone wrong. But in the end, it was an example of the importance of our culture and the areas in which we could not compromise.

"This was a major success in the history of the Canadian apparel business," says Darrell Kopke. "There was a tribe, and that was a core element of it. There was a cultural distinction that this was not a product company. The tribe had an entrenched social infrastructure, and that created a virality. We deliberately created an industry through a long and painful process."

We set up the store business model to take advantage of the highly educated, well-developed employees we were attracting. Each store manager was an entrepreneur, and we paid them accordingly. We sent our managers (all women) full company financials until 2006. We helped them to be financially literate so they could make their own decisions as we were totally decentralized. Our managers had complete control of their windows, hiring and training, etc. We knew if we didn't give them almost total control, we wouldn't be able to keep their intelligent minds active and they would get bored and quit. Our best branding came from stores that created tongue-in-cheek windows with a controversial political or social point of view. Customers talked and debated, and our managers' intelligence shined because they questioned the status quo. This made our work fun and edgy.

This model proved so profitable that we could pay a manager two to three times what other retailers could. We completely upset the low-cost wholesale-retail model. The part of the business model was critical because we had to educate customers on what they could not see visually. We needed extraordinary Educators to deliver our message and to connect on the same educational level as our Guests.

Duke

Summer was admitted to hospital on the morning of October 15, 2003. I remember it raining as hard as I've ever seen it rain in Vancouver. Things happened quickly once we were there. We didn't know whether we'd be having a boy or a girl until the moment our son, Duke, took his first breath. As soon as I could, I picked up JJ and Brett from school and brought them to the hospital, where they each held their little brother. At that moment, life couldn't get much better.

Summer was eager to strike a balance between being a new mother and remaining a creative force at lululemon. She'd worked right until Duke's arrival, and made her return to the office when our baby boy was around ten days old, bringing him in with her every day. But, after three weeks of doing that, as much as she loved being back in the office and working, she felt she needed to spend more time at home with Duke.

"Designing for lululemon was my absolute dream job," says Summer. "It just fit me perfectly. Though it was uncomfortable to let it go, there was a bigger goal that needed attention. I'm fortunate that Chip has been so inclusive with me about the business. There's never been a line between what's his job and my job. He's always open, always sharing. We got to have those conversations before the actual changes happened."

I fully supported her decision to step back for the time being.

Besides adding Duke to our family, 2003 was a watershed year for lululemon. I felt as if we'd reached a tipping point in

Canada. We had systems in place for each new store opening that laid the essential groundwork for entering a new market.

The essential building block to our growth other than our people development program was what I'd learned from the book *The E-Myth*.[19] The myth holds that entrepreneurs have control of their lives, when, in fact, they don't—entrepreneurship is a 24/7 operation with no downtime. The solution is to set up the business from day one with processes in place like it will be franchisable, so that the operation can work without the founder.

I was meticulous in setting up our quality-control, brand, design development, people development, and store operations. Because the first store operated so well on its own, I was able to operate according to my expertise, that is, five years in the future.

Yoga and athletics were becoming ever more popular among our target market of educated women in their early thirties. I also believed the prudish way Americans dressed for athletics was ready for a change. I envisioned a future when West Coast functional clothing combined with flattering European design lines would change the way the world dressed.

We knew how to generate interest by working with yoga studios and the community. Plus, as more people in Canada grew to recognize the lululemon brand, it would be even easier to break into new retail environments.

In the life of any company, there are cycles of growth that force those driving the bus to figure out the direction they need to steer. This was the point we'd reached. Business was taking off, and I had to choose where we were going next.

Addressing this plan meant asking critical questions. Who were we? What did I want lululemon to be? Were we a local

19. Michael E. Gerber, *The E-Myth: Why Most Businesses Don't Work and What to Do About It* (HarperCollins, 2009).

company that thrived on being quirky and small? Or were we on the cusp of becoming a major international brand?

As I faced the questions of where we were going next, I also kept investing in our culture and people. Bree Stanlake recalls, "It was just unbelievable. It was a group of people who just truly believed in what we were up to. It was grounded in our belief in the product, and everybody's almost maniacal, fanatical adherence to product quality, innovation, and walking the walk.

"We all wore it all the time, and exercised in it, and did yoga in it, and really just believed in what we were doing, which was elevating the world from mediocrity to greatness."

Honing the Culture

A key component of the lululemon culture was family values. As part of our hiring practice, we screened for people who wanted families. We wanted our people to meet the perfect mate, we wanted people to have children, and we wanted the family nucleus to be an energy generator. I believed if our employees' families worked, then our company worked.

Delaney Schweitzer's team put together a training checklist that included chapters on Culture, Product Knowledge, Store Operations, Community, Inventory, Guest Conversations, and Guest Experience. Everything was covered. One of their first assignments was to create a curriculum called Foundation, which would serve as lululemon's onboarding program.

Jenna Hills, one of our Robson Street Educators, became part of Delaney's team. "We were accountable to ensure that every single employee got invited to attend the Landmark Forum," Jenna recalls. "Landmark Education was our other foundational training program. It gave us a common language and allowed us to be real with one another. By living the principles of personal responsibility and integrity, we became unstoppable.

"We believed if we did a great job of providing people with the tools to be 100 percent accountable for everything in their lives, not much else was needed," says Jenna.

We made a big cultural shift by changing our vision. I decided that our existing vision of "making components for people to live a longer, healthier, and more fun life" wasn't big enough. Our vision became our mission, and our new vision became "elevating the world from a place of mediocrity to greatness."

This vision aligned better with our mantra of "giving before expectation of return."

Before we had an HR department, a brand team, or any of that, we had Training and Culture. Training and Culture was our brand department and HR, all in one.

New York Fashion Media

Even as we grew as a company and changed the way women dressed and lived, New York fashion magazines overlooked us. To this day, I think the media turned a blind eye to lululemon because we did not fit into their co-dependant business model of paid advertising in exchange for editorial coverage.

The fashion media model of that time relied on getting wholesale clothing samples months before publishing a magazine. Wholesale companies made samples to show store buyers on an eighteen-month production cycle from design inception to in-store sales. The samples that wholesalers used to sell their product to retailers were made available to the fashion media for magazine photo shoots.

Because we were accountable only to ourselves, lululemon had a nine-month production cycle. We didn't prioritize samples for photoshoots. There was no reason to as we only sold in our own stores. The value of lululemon products was in the feel and function of the garments, which could never be effectively relayed to the customer through glossy photographs.

Our nine-month production calendar also kept us ahead of the fashion houses in regard to the demand for this new athletic apparel with all-day performance. We had created the future of apparel, and our business model made it too easy for New York fashion media to ignore.

Looking back, I wish I had documented more of the lululemon story in a diary or taken more photographs to capture the context of our early years. We didn't make samples, and we didn't believe in New York media advertising, so we never did photo shoots. My personal culture (and therefore lululemon's) was never one of self-promotion or "look at me." This came back to bite me in the future as social media evolved. Because there was no documented history of lululemon, the media took control of the story.

There is a brilliant book out now called *The 4 Billion Dollar Tweet,*[20] by Ryan Holmes of Hootsuite. This book describes how social media is here to stay. Companies, politicians, and individuals need to use it to speak directly to the customer or voter.

As lululemon was successfully eliminating the wholesaler and going direct to the customer, proper use of social media would have allowed us to eliminate the media middleman and communicate directly with the consumer. I would then have had a voice to offset the skewed filter of old-school media and noncustomer social media comments. Unfortunately, I didn't change with the times—but that's a story for later in this book.

---

20. Ryan Holmes, *The 4 Billion Dollar Tweet* (Hootsuite, 2017).

Throwing Logs on the Fire

The opportunity to grow, to expand lululemon sustainably, was an opportunity to share what made us unique. The more we grew, and the more new markets we encountered, the more opportunity we had to elevate the world from mediocrity to greatness—one Educator and one Guest at a time.

I was really clear that we were not in the wellness business. We were not interested in making sick people well. We wanted to give normal people the opportunity to be their best. By being their best, they would elevate those around them. It seemed to be an idea everyone was excited to get behind. People were calling us a cult, and employees were in on the first wave of lululemon tattoos.

"Lululemon could have died in November 2003," says Darrell Kopke:

> The problem was cash flow, like it is for every other apparel business. We went from two to eleven stores and invested all our money in inventory. Our warehouse was piled to the roof with clothing, and we had no readily available money to pay the factories. We bet the farm that we would sell everything that Christmas.
> "By the second week of December, we knew that lululemon was going to be unstoppable. Our sales were through the roof. We sold through tons of inventory, and we had our first million-dollar month in one of our stores. We would open a store, and within three months it had paid itself off. We were just throwing logs on the fire.
>
> We made a ton of mistakes but we were able to make them because we were allowed and encouraged to, and we had the kind of revenue growth that enabled us to make mistakes and still live through it.

Darrell is right. We were really good at celebrating mistakes and learning from them. A big part of our growth was driven by empowering people and creating an environment that would foster creativity and new ideas. This was especially relevant as it related to our Guests and our community. For example, we originally did yoga in the first store to increase foot traffic coming up the stairs. When we moved to the street-level store, we had as much foot traffic as we could handle, so we stopped offering in-store yoga.

A while later, our community people came up with the idea to reinstitute in-store yoga at every location. I'll admit I was not aligned with the idea at the time, but the employees wanted to do it, and it ended up having fantastic results. It proved that allowing our people to take ownership was a vital part of our company's successful formula.

At Westbeach, I'd often led by command and control. At lululemon, after I set the culture and documented the operating principles, I chose to be a leader by developing and mentoring others. I was fanatical about developing people because the future was so huge that I had to get out in front of it. I made it my job to do nothing. Inside of nothing was the ability to be the future before it occurred. For the first time, it was the right moment for me to think about how to establish lululemon outside of Canada.

CHAPTER 19:
LOOKING SOUTH

Jealousy works the opposite way you want it to.

Victoria's Secret

Toward the end of 2004, I received a letter from Victoria's Secret expressing their interest in lululemon. I sat back and savoured the moment. If Victoria's Secret was interested, it meant we'd succeeded in bringing something special to the world.

I discussed the letter with several people at lululemon. We were flattered, but it didn't take us long to agree that this wasn't a direction in which we wanted to go. The letter confirmed what we already knew: we had a successful formula of our own.

It occurred to me that Victoria's Secret might use our concepts to develop their own line. Although our focus was athletic pants, I decided I wanted to look at athletic bras as well. I knew we couldn't be a complete women's athletic company without being best in the world at athletic bras by 2013, still ten years away.

I considered our position. A lot had changed in our first five years as a business. I was very happy with our jump on the market and the moat we'd built around it. We had an industrial trademark on all innovations and had trademarked the lululemon name and logo worldwide. Our profit margin was twice that of most other apparel retailers.

With interest coming in from US companies, it was time to increase our growth and get a solid foothold south of the border.

One Step Closer to Global

In my view, there are two classic reasons that Canadian companies meet their end at American hands. They either stay in Canada too long and get run over by an American competitor with economy-of-scale, or they expand into the US with a product only viable in Canada.

I knew lululemon had the potential to be a global company because health and the desire for longevity crossed all cultures. I also knew our philosophy of transformational people development was a revolutionary international brand driver. Our success in America would depend on knowing when conditions were just right and then making a calculated move.

The conditions were right. The steady stream of US interest in our company was showing no signs of letting up. Americans were buying a lot of our product when they ventured north, and we'd proven ourselves successful right across Canada. Our Canadian stores were generating enough revenue to justify the risk of an international expansion, and more importantly, we could afford to make a mistake.

I felt my personal ties to the US would be advantageous in introducing lululemon to the American market. Although my younger brother Brett was born in Calgary, my mom and stepfather had taken him and my sister to pursue the oil business in Denver when he was ten. Despite the time we'd spent apart, Brett and I had a history of influencing one another's plans at pivotal moments.

Brett and Susanne

After selling Wave Rave to Ride Snowboards in the late '90s, Brett and his wife Susanne began developing a social tech company called Two Jet in 2000, but they got caught in the 2001 tech bubble burst and lost almost everything.

After Brett and Susanne closed Two Jet's doors, I immediately spoke with him about opening the first lululemon store in the US. He said yes right away.

I trusted Brett, and not just as my brother. I also knew he had the entrepreneurial gene and had already run retail stores. Having someone with Brett's experience setting up our first US store meant I wouldn't have to divert the attention of our Vancouver people who were busy growing the business in Canada. This wasn't a franchise. The first stores in the US would be owned by the company, with Brett taking responsibility for the leasing, build-outs, hiring, and opening.

As the plan of opening a store in the US took form, the first question that came up was one of precise location. I wrongly chose to do a hybrid model of a showroom and a flagship store. I believed the core yoga culture wouldn't want us to set up on Santa Monica's busy Third Avenue Promenade and look like a big-shot retailer. I wanted to do it softly. I picked a location a block away.

When Santa Monica opened, things were much slower, even slower than we'd anticipated. In retrospect, we had a product the world wanted, wanted now, and wanted a lot of. There was nothing the world over comparable to what lululemon was doing. All I had to do was put lululemon on a busy street and let the maximum number of people discover it.

Brett recalls, "As the brand was taking off in Vancouver and Toronto, we opened in Santa Monica where nobody but travelling Canadians knew anything about the brand. Just getting a foothold in the US took work."

"The first time I had concerns about our company's future was when we didn't have instant success in Santa Monica," says Deanne Schweitzer. "When we opened up the Santa Monica store it was probably the wrong location and wrong size of store. The build-out didn't really feel like us, and we were really struggling to get Educators that were excited about the brand and what we were creating."

"There was a very naïve understanding of what it would actually take to begin the community-based branding process," says Brett's wife, Susanne, "but it needed to happen in the same way it had in Vancouver. Slowly, organically, and through word-of-mouth."

Fortunately, Brett stuck to the formula: he went straight to the yoga community and began a grassroots campaign. Slowly but surely, that strategy paid off.

Still, one store alone would not be enough. We knew we needed to get a few stores to accelerate the brand conversation in the US. Over the next year, following the Santa Monica store, Brett opened additional locations in Newport Beach, and then Cow Hollow in San Francisco. Cow Hollow was really a pivotal store opening because it was a launch beyond Southern California.

It wasn't easy to break lululemon into the United States, and I was constantly mindful of how hard it was for Canadian companies to take off in the US. But as we moved through 2004, it felt more and more like we were onto something unique and unstoppable.

The Tipping Point

I was starting to believe we'd reached our tipping point—that crucial moment where we moved from being an underground brand to becoming something everyone in mainstream society wanted.

When the tipping point occurs, the last thing posers want is for the company to advertise or make products for them. They want only to buy what the target market wants because non-target customers want to look authentic.

The underlying principle of surf, skate, and snowboard branding was to push the non-strategic customer away and play hard to get. The branding was clear about who the customer was not. It was also a strategy we employed again successfully at lululemon. I found this concept very difficult to explain to people and enroll them in if they did not understand the West Coast athletic subculture.

Lululemon's tipping point came when two things occurred. First, we noticed customers coming in with friends and educating their friends about our products, just as a paid lululemon Educator would.

Second, the stores got to be so busy that we could no longer fulfill on providing health and fitness advice to our Guests—there was simply not enough space. I shifted our focus from the Guest to our Educators, their families, and their communities.

I believed if we made our Educators icons of their communities, their presence would be of inspiration to our Guests. This was better for business, but more importantly, it was a better way of elevating the world from mediocrity to greatness.

Category Killer

Part of lululemon's success—even in our slow, early expansion into the US—was that we were a category killer.

A category killer refers to having so much of a desired product that a business becomes the only place customers will go for it. It effectively 'kills' the competition in that category. For instance, many years earlier, I knew of a ski shop in Whistler that was rather mediocre, selling every product everybody else sold. But one day I walked into that mediocre ski shop and saw they had devoted their entire store to selling only ski or snowboard gloves. Before long, if you had to get a pair of gloves, you knew there was only one place to go . . . that formerly mediocre ski shop.

I wanted to do what no one else had done before. I dreamed of a large athletic store whose stock was 80 percent women's clothing. What I believed missing in the market was the ability to buy a hundred styles of technical clothing in one store that all worked well together. The store would match luxury store standards but be set up in a functional way.

Instead of buying in outfits, a woman would go to sections for pants, shorts, bras, etc. The change rooms would have five hooks and a bar, so a woman could hang her purse, jacket, and street clothing, and still have five garments she could try on in the change room.

The lighting would be perfect, and each room had to have a three-way mirror so a woman could be self-critical of her backside and choose freely whether to buy or not. I didn't want to force a woman outside the change room to get beauty validation from a commission-oriented salesperson.

To expand on this concept a little more, you might be best in the world at making something, the way lululemon was the best in the world at making black Lycra pants. But to become a category killer, pricing also had to be considered. One option is three-tiered pricing: a low, medium, and high pricing model that all depends on levels of quality.

I preferred not to use that model because lululemon couldn't make a low-price garment in the first place. I wasn't reaching for a discount product or demographic (I recently saw a documentary about Steve Jobs, where he said something along the lines of: "Make them pay full price, make the best in the world, and the best will come." I was aiming for the athlete who wanted something that worked. I couldn't think of producing a profitable medium-tier garment that didn't work for the athlete.

As the three-tiered pricing model was not an option, another option was to make sixteen pairs of pants all look different. These included high-rise, low-rise, crop, long, and even loose-fitting. We did just that.

In this way, we appealed to the woman who appreciated quality and would spend $90 to $100 on a pair of pants. She would recognize that she was buying the best black Lycra pants in the world and would likely want to buy ten of the variations we were offering, rather than one of this and that from ten different companies.

This truly set lululemon apart as a category killer.

Dumpster Diving and Headbands

Once we'd started making decent profits as a category killer, I thought of different ways to own the yoga market. Yoga mats, straps, and blocks were the only things we bought from other suppliers to round out the store's offering. Because of yoga clothing, we were a natural stop for mats.

The product was difficult to differentiate, but yoga mats were really a commodity. It wasn't rocket science, so to speak. But I realized if I could sell yoga mats at cost, it would bring more people through the door, which would sell more clothes.

I could envision hundreds of lululemon stores selling millions of yoga mats. I also wanted to encourage people and provide them with a low-priced gateway to experiencing yoga. In the era before great search engines, I had no idea how to find a manufacturer. So, I got scrappy.

I decided I had to find the source of production. I waited until after dark and then went dumpster diving in the alley of a mat supplier. I figured all I had to do was find a cardboard box with the return address of their Asian supplier.

I was successful.

I sold yoga mats at cost. Store sales jumped and so did profit even though we made zero margin on yoga accessories. Once I controlled the market, I raised the price on the mats to a point where I could make a small profit but kept it low enough so that it wasn't economical for anyone else to enter the market. This was part of my ongoing build-a-moat-around-our-success-and-don't-let-the-competition-in model.

Another cool idea came from seeing scrap fabric. When I was abroad, I remember watching fabric fall to the floor of a sewing factory and thinking, "God, that's a lot of waste, what can I do with those scraps?"

As Summer recalls, "The lululemon headband was born out of the hemming process. One of the seamstresses used to take the ends of the pants she cut off and wear it as a headband because her hair got in her eyes while sewing. We thought, 'What a great idea! Let's take these pant ends and sell them.'"

Thinking back to my mother's talent as a quilter—we cut scraps from the pants into small triangles and squares and made caps and headbands. It seemed like a natural next step.

Every headband looked different, which was always a bonus of quilting. I extrapolated this idea of variability to the drop-down waistband on the groove pant. Women would sift through twenty pants looking for the colour combination that would best suit them. I had figured out how to do mass production and still make each garment different. Guests loved this.

Headbands were especially popular with younger girls who used them to differentiate themselves amidst a sea of school uniforms. They would become one of lululemon's best-selling items.

Contemplating the Future

The year 2005 had arrived, and I still couldn't see any competitors on the horizon. No one wanted to spend the kind of money necessary to build the retail stores they'd need to compete with our vertical retailing model. No one could match our successful formula, unique designs, high-quality Luon, free hemming, flat seams, or anything else that made lululemon so unique.

Nevertheless, I'd recently begun to wonder if the time was coming—sooner rather than later—when the growth of the brand would outpace my ability to keep up with its demands. So many people started to tell me that I didn't have the expertise to run a billion-dollar brand. My stated vision and goals were focused on family goals. This meant choosing to prioritize family while doing the best for both lululemon and its employees. JJ and Brett were young teens, and I only had a limited amount of time to be the best dad I could be to them. I had three other boys under the age of two—I wanted to go to every school concert and every bike ride to Kits Beach with them.

With that in mind, what were my next steps? Would I partner with a larger retailer? Did lululemon need a more experienced CEO? How could I ensure my family was taken care of for life?

I had turned down the offer from Victoria's Secret, but I

still had a stack of letters of interest from big public companies and private equity firms. Everyone, it seemed, wanted to participate in lululemon's phenomenal story.

I knew the business of my business, but I was frightfully naïve about businesses that invested in businesses and the motivations of the people who run them. Who would I get to advise me, I wondered? I knew no one inside my small circle of friends who qualified. I had been working hard, and the speed of growth of the brand was phenomenal. Every step was exhilarating. But I had not taken the time to develop the relationships I would need in the future. I thought I could get the advice I needed with private equity (PE).

CHAPTER 20:
THE VALUATION

The conscious mind can only hold one thought at a time. Choose a powerful thought.

Selling Part of the Company

If we were going to get involved with a big company or private equity, the first step was understanding the value of lululemon. Naively, I had a ballpark figure in my head of about $25 million—a number which seemed intangible, surreal, and very weird to me. But my CEO, Darrell, and CFO, Brian, had determined that the company was worth about $225 million, more than ten times the number I'd come up with.

From my end, I knew we had a great brand. All our profits were being reinvested in the company because the return on each dollar doubled each year. Summer and I were not drawing salaries, and we were only pulling enough out of the business to cover living expenses. In retrospect, I could have borrowed $40 million unencumbered from the bank to give my family a lifetime of security. I had told the top-tier of our senior employees that I would give them 10 percent of the company if we ever went public. This incentive probably drove the wrong actions, but I didn't understand that at the time.

I had three boys under the age of two, and my priority was to be present as a father. I knew lululemon's future meant a lot of travel around the world to find perfect store locations, and to Asia, specifically, to maintain my partner relationships with mills and factories. I was not astute enough to talk to advisors. This may seem counterintuitive, but in retrospect, I needed to talk to people who had been through the experience of PE before. I limited my options to either continuing as CEO and prioritizing the business, or to selling part of lululemon. Selling would allow me to bring in advice, partners, and financial oversight, and give me an opportunity to prioritize my family. I chose family, and I will never regret this choice.

"We had the best of both worlds," says Darrell Kopke, our GM. "Highly profitable growth in the front end, and timely, accurate, and useful information in the back end. We implemented software and payroll systems and then had to replace some of them as we grew. This paid off when we looked for the outside investors." The reality was that we had such a great foundation of Operating Principles, a world-class people development platform, and a strong employee pipeline (based on ideas from the book *The E-Myth*) that the company was relatively easy to run. The hard work had been done, and we simply needed to replicate what we had built. The company's profitability and cash flow were best-in-class.

I felt out of my depth, and I wasn't confident that I could broker the deal I believed we deserved. Corporate finance and tax were a weak point for me, and I'd never been a natural negotiator. I was the best in the world at making a product and asking a fair price for it (my theory always has been that customers could take it or leave it). I didn't know what I didn't know, and I wasn't even sure where to look for help.

I needed help with negotiations and valuation.

The Beauty Contest

I decided to work with a local Vancouver business broker who had come highly recommended. It took a month to create a package to send out to the private equity companies and retail operations that had asked about lululemon. The package profiled the brand, explained our history, and showcased our culture. We wanted to give them all the tools they needed to evaluate our company and understand who we were.

This was a process called a *beauty contest*—introducing a client to people who could provide financial solutions or make potential investments in their company.

One of the first retail operations we met with was Liz Claiborne. Executives from the longstanding women's apparel company were in Vancouver conducting due-diligence on another deal when they came across lululemon. The Liz Claiborne people offered $500 million at $100 million per year to be paid out over five years. They also asked that lululemon perform within their overall corporate structure, meaning we would have to conform to their system for finances, shipping and receiving, and technical infrastructure.

After some deliberation, I turned down the Liz Claiborne offer. I felt the $100 million for five years was too thin a spread, but more importantly, that their culture was not the right match for us. I was worried our people would have a tough time working under that much structure. All things considered, Liz Claiborne was a little bit too corporate, too big. I thought the culture clash would be too big an obstacle to overcome.

Another retail giant on our radar was the Gap, but it seemed nearly impossible to get a real read on what they wanted. As a public company, the Gap had to be very cautious about with whom they met and what they reported. The whole thing was secretive to the point of being unproductive.

They couldn't discuss concrete terms or put a single word on paper.

When the Gap finally made an offer, it was inadequate. $200 million for a full buyout, which was much less than valuations we were getting from private equity.

I was frustrated because I felt it was a bad move by the Gap. The Gap was sucking on all cylinders. It was a commodity product, and the stores were underperforming. I thought they were too big. Their stores looked like bowling alleys. I thought if the Gap would replace half of all their oversized five thousand square foot retail stores, which had the best retail locations, and insert, in their place, three thousand square foot lululemons, the Gap would be victorious. The Gap would be stronger because they could better focus on their "best-in-class" product, and lululemon would be able to grow exponentially in one year.

I was bursting to tell Gap what I thought they should be considering. I wanted them to buy lululemon for $500 million. A rapid rollout of lululemon would be a home run for them. I believed that lululemon would have brought a lot to their organization, beyond what I felt I could personally contribute.

Over the years, the Gap suffered because they became driven by numbers and metrics instead of staying in touch with their core customers. I surmised the "new" digital e-commerce people were telling Gap's leadership to make more of the same thing because, at the time, commodity products were e-commerce's bestsellers.

I wanted the Gap to drop half of their merchandise and focus on innovation and selling only their best products. To me, innovation is delivering to the customer that which the customer does not yet know he or she needs. I felt if the Gap brought in lululemon's product development and buying principles, and shared store space, the Gap would quickly be worth $20 billion more by 2012. The Gap didn't know how to morph. It was resting on its laurels.

Interestingly, just after this, the Gap brought on a Canadian—Glenn Murphy—who had run Shoppers Drug Mart in Canada. A nice Murphy decision at the Gap was buying the e-commerce and catalogue-based company Athleta to propel the Gap into the future. I always wondered if the commodity thinking of Gap management would trickle its way down to Athleta. Because merchants, not designers, ran the Gap, past sales metrics told them that they should target a frumpier, cost-conscious older market that didn't sweat.

In any case, as of 2018, Glenn Murphy is now co-chairman of lululemon. More on this down the road.

Vetting Private Equity

There was a lot more appeal in a deal that got us less money but found us the right partner. That way, I could maintain a strong position in lululemon and find the right private equity people who could provide me with foundational guidance to build a billion-dollar company.

The things I wanted from a PE agreement were fivefold:

1. Expertise in US real estate locations
2. Help in hiring world-class upper management
3. To maintain a 70 percent interest in the company
4. Advice on future needs and processes so lululemon could skip usual growth roadblocks
5. To have $40 million to fulfill the goals my wife and I had set in 2002

By the summer of 2005, I was determined to find the right personality fit in a potential private equity partner.

Generally, interested private equity parties made a trip to Vancouver to have a look at our operations and meet our team. When they arrived, if things were going well, I'd take them up the Grouse Grind. Grouse is a local Vancouver ski mountain with a very popular, rugged hiking trail—the Grind—running up its side. If you're in reasonable shape, it's about an hour climb, straight up.

The Grouse Grind was a great way to measure culture fit. People were showing up at our office in suits, ties, and dress shoes. For someone not from the West Coast, or someone who doesn't understand the Silicon Valley surf, skate, and snowboard culture, a suit and tie is mandatory. On the West Coast, the suit and tie uniform subconsciously says you are not in control of your own life. As an aside, recently, I wondered with great fascination whether Mark Zuckerberg would show up to his congressional hearing in Washington, DC, wearing a suit or not. I am sure his PR people were adamant Mark toe the line so the political powers would appreciate his respect for their customs.

When I suggested a hike, some of these visitors acted as if it was a root canal. Not a great sign. But there were others who jumped at the opportunity to do the Grouse Grind. Doing a strenuous hike with someone was the first part of seeing if they might be the kind of person with whom I wanted to work. We had to be authentic. It was my way of meeting people in lieu of a round of golf.

"At one of our first meetings with private equity," Sean Morrison, my broker, says, "Chip was wearing flip-flops and shorts. If it was anyone else, I might have said 'How about throwing on a jacket and pants,' but that's totally not who Chip is. Lululemon was and is a lifestyle brand, and lifestyle brands were a mega-trend at that time. I didn't want to package it in anything fake. So, we ran a process, and we had a couple of really good partners to choose from."

We ended up with offers from all eight groups of investors who came to Vancouver. Their proposals ranged between $225 and $270 million, but in the end, it came down to personality match.

Tom Stemberg

Midway through the beauty contest, I got a call from a man named Tom Stemberg. Tom was the founder of Staples. He'd served as CEO of the company for sixteen years and as chairman of the board for another, taking Staples from a start-up operation to a leader in the office superstore market. Tom was also a partner at an equity firm called Highland Capital.

Tom first heard of us when both Staples and lululemon were up for a retail award. When we won, he decided to go and see one of our stores for himself. Tom's wife was from Toronto, so he visited the Briar Hill location. He walked into the store and was shocked by the crowds inside. He noticed the enthusiasm of our customers and the quality of the products. His wife, who'd purchased several items, loved our designs and technical features.

"People were practically fighting over garments in the store," Tom said. "I went outside and saw that there wasn't even a name on the front, just the logo. I went to another store, and it was the same thing. I had to know what was going on."

Tom and I met face-to-face in Vancouver. At the end of our conversation, he told me he wanted to invest if we ever took lululemon public. He would offer $20 million in return for a board seat. His investment meant lululemon would get the benefit of everything he knew about real estate locations in the US.

Tom also said we would need a board of directors to conduct lululemon's governance. My only experience with a board was the advisors at Westbeach. The Westbeach advisors had been very helpful, so I was enamoured by the board concept. It seemed I had an ally in Tom.

Advent

Advent International out of Boston had moved to the top of our list. Advent was founded in 1984, and since then, had specialized in the growth and restructuring of companies around the world, representing tens of billions of dollars in capital.

Advent valued lululemon at USD $225 million. It wasn't the biggest offer we'd received, but I still didn't feel I needed the cash nearly as much as I needed the right partners. I had a good feeling that Advent would fit the bill. We must have been incredibly appealing to a PE firm. We had trademarked our name and logo worldwide, we were set up to be global, and we had the best apparel metrics in the world. We were a cash cow with a product the world wanted, and we were the only company that knew how to manage a highly volatile technical knit fabric.

David Mussafer, the managing partner of Advent, seemed to take a long-term view of what lululemon could achieve. Besides that, David and some of the other Advent people had a super hike on the Grouse Grind, which spoke well about their fit with our culture.

David and his partner, Steve Collins, completed our full development program and set out their goals. I was impressed with their due diligence and their desire to understand lululemon. They seemed like they would be perfect for us.

While we were in Boston meeting with Advent, we also saw Tom Stemberg again. Tom was still very interested in getting involved with lululemon—so interested, in fact, that he told me Highland Capital would come in for 25 percent of the portion I would sell.

Advent had reservations about Tom Stemberg, but it

would take me a long time to learn their reasons. In any case, everyone agreed to the arrangement. All that was left was the due diligence that both Highland and Advent had to do on lululemon, plus the final negotiations. I had been clear with Sean (my broker) that negotiations were not my area of expertise. I trusted him to be great.

Months went by with everyone doing due diligence. It was a lot more time than I wanted. By late September 2005, we were closing in on a final deal. Summer was pregnant again and this deal coincided with the arrival of our twins. In retrospect, this put undue subconscious pressure on me to complete the deal.

I think Advent and Highland dragged on due diligence on purpose. They had their price set, and they realized we had a very junior negotiator. Each month the demand for our product increased in double-digit numbers, and the value of the company increased correspondingly. Advent and Highland were happy to let the deal drag on to confirm that our sales and profitability numbers would continue without their having to increase the price they would pay.

Summer went into the hospital on September 30. Our sons, Tor and Tag Wilson, were born minutes apart just before midnight. There wasn't much time for me to celebrate or relax. Advent and Highland had called for a meeting in early October.

I went into that meeting assuming an agreement had been made. I was confident that the due diligence had gone well and that the meeting was mostly a formality to sort out the details.

I was wrong.

Steve Collins went through a list of dimensions they'd used to evaluate lululemon. He said they were concerned that lululemon's current sales compared to last year's showed that sales were falling. Right away, he tried to bring the price down from USD $225 million to USD $200 million. I was stunned. I later found out we were just oversold and waiting for inventory.

Lululemon had been exceeding all its sales expectations, performing even better than was indicated in the previous year's numbers we'd shared with Advent in the summer. I didn't understand how we could over-perform and see our value take a hit. Another new development from Advent was that they wanted to take 50 to 51 percent of the company.

Looking back on it, I realize it was all negotiation and posturing. We didn't need to negotiate at all.

When I replay the scenario in my head, I wish I had stood up, told them that the price had just gone up to $350 million, and walked out of the meeting. The power was all lululemon's—I was in over my head.

In retrospect, the incentive for a business broker was no different than that of a real estate broker. Their number one goal is to do the deal. It is very risky for a broker to drive for the best price for their client and lose a deal. When the deal is lost, a broker gets zero. In final negotiations, the broker stops working in the best interest of the client and instead works to get the deal done. In retrospect, I paid for a negotiator, but I didn't get what I expected.

We agreed to USD $200 million. The next issue was the 51 percent ownership. Steve Collins argued that with Highland and Tom Stemberg in on the deal, they needed 51 percent of lululemon to share between them. I said no, but once again, I was just trying to hold my ground. Instead of the 30 percent I had originally proposed, I told them I would sell 48 percent so I would still have a majority interest. Advent agreed to this, and the deal was finalized. It was all a great learning experience for me.

When we were at $110 million in sales, even more people told me I would not be able to run a company from $200 million to $1 billion, and that I should get help. Of course, I'd also been told I didn't know how to run a company from $15 million to $100 million, despite how perfectly everything had gone. I think I had reinvented retail and people development models, and in retrospect, these new models would have gotten me a lot further than bringing in outside expertise with conflicting priorities.

Still, I was satisfied with the outcome. The people from Advent and Highland had proven themselves to be savvy businesspeople and skilled negotiators. It seemed that having Tom Stemberg, David Mussafer, and Steve Collins on my side in future negotiations would only benefit me and lululemon. Since I had not operated a company of $110 million in sales, I trusted this group to provide the guidance I asked for and hold my hand into the future.

I have made many life decisions that were strictly survival-driven, but never wealth-driven. In selling to private equity, I was motivated by a desire to develop an idea, a concept, a philosophy that was solid in its foundation into a global phenomenon to elevate the world.

To go from essentially owning nothing to having $100 million in my pocket gave me one thing above all else: an easier night's sleep. I could breathe easy knowing my kids would be taken care of. But after years of basic poverty, Summer and I still had a 1930s Great Depression mentality. We thought that at any moment it could all be taken away, or that it was all a dream, so we did our best to make sure our lifestyle didn't change.

CHAPTER 21:
CHANGE MANAGEMENT

Being in business is like playing poker. To keep the business growing it takes 100 percent of a person's time and money. The bigger and faster a company grows, the more it requires the profit to be ploughed back into the company. The entrepreneur can only get at his or her money by stopping growth. All living things die when they stop growing. At least in business, I can stack the poker odds for success in my favor.

Learnings

I want to preface this by saying this section may only be of interest to people who are taking on private equity (PE) to go public. Going into negotiations, I don't think my local Vancouver lawyers even knew I didn't *need* outside money to grow. Their experience was in big mining deals where substantial outside capital was required.

I am not sure we even told our lawyers how amazing our cash flow was. They'd probably never been in a situation where the seller wanted advice as the goal, so they didn't ask, and we didn't tell. I think my lawyers assumed that the PE people were in the driver's seat and the deal was done accordingly.

Hopefully, my learnings will help any entrepreneurs who are thinking of taking on investment from PE and going public! My learnings are as follows:

1. A broker works in his own best interest to close the deal. A broker shies away from hard negotiations for fear of losing the deal and the commission.
2. Select three experienced advisors with no vested interest in the deal other than your own. Lawyers, brokers, and company executives were not enough to provide the high-level, independent advice I needed.
3. Set aside time to talk daily to your advisors. The business will need you, but good advice will last a lifetime.
4. Keep two PE companies at the negotiating table until the final decision is made. Play the PE people off each other to get the best deal with the single PE firm you know you want.
5. If PE says they will be with you for a period of four to seven years and that they'll probably take you public in the first four, be cautious, as they must work in their own best interest.
6. Set a due diligence completion date and increase the price if the company's profit increases during the due diligence time.
7. PE will only be with you a short time. From their viewpoint, the shorter, the better. You must understand the different scenarios of governance and control that will be in place after PE leaves.
8. PE provides a stamp of approval to the entrepreneur and his or her idea. However, the entrepreneur should not let that feeling of approval affect financial negotiations.
9. My 51 percent control of the company after selling to PE meant nothing as I didn't control the voting at the

board level. I needed legal confirmation I would control the most board seats after the PE sale *and* after going public. (When I consider what happened—the way we went public, and what came to pass in the following years—I think of Phil Knight from Nike and Kevin Plank from Under Armour. Both have dual-class shares, which gave them control of their boards. When you control the board, you control the company's culture and vision. Nike never lost its vision, and that's what made it the company it is today. This is where I feel I missed the mark—not knowing how to keep board control.)

10. Create a special director onboarding program. Have them read three to four books critical to the company's culture and business model. Then, have them work in the store for a day—and, in a case like lululemon's, have the director go through the same development program as the employees. Have them verbally discuss ten points that would indicate their understanding of why the business model works, as well as their grasp of the company's linguistic abstractions, values, and vision statements. Ask them if they fully understand the hidden, subconscious reasons the business makes money.

Lululemon was a cash cow that provided me with all the negotiating power in the world. I held all the cards but played none.

The Governance Model

With the long-term possibility of going public, we needed a board of directors. They were to elect a CEO, set and oversee a compensation plan for upper management that would reward long-term value, define management succession plans, set our strategic plan, and ensure legal compliance.

I was getting to know our directors well. I treated them as my absolute equals and partners, a dynamic I felt was reciprocated. I had built an amazing company, and the directors had the experience to help me continue to put the building blocks in place.

The only thing that was weird to lululemon people was that the directors were a group of older men with button-down shirts, pleated khakis, and Blackberries slung on their belts like six-shooters. It was the opposite of lululemon apparel.

For any organization to succeed, a combination of different mindsets is critical. Organizational theory would tell you a successful team needs the right balance of conceptual, analytical, structural, and social people. An imbalance heightens risk and mediocrity.

My own abilities were (and are) creative and analytical. I wanted the directors to keep their eyes on the hiring of management and create structural processes into which we could grow.

The Advent people took on our employee development and slipped smoothly into our culture. I loved that they wanted to figure out why we were successful so they could transfer new knowledge to their other investments.

Tom Stemberg, I found, was very keen to offer his advice on how to set up a board. However, Tom did not want to do Landmark, perhaps because he already felt successful in his life. His wife was also against the ideas of transformational development, and I believe this contributed to the roadblock Tom hit with our culture. I wasn't worried. I thought he would come around once he saw how successful we were *because* of our development program.

But now that Tom was inside lululemon, he seemed sure our future value depended on "professionalizing" our company.

Culture took a back seat, since, in Tom's view, professionalization had little to do with culture.

Bob Meers

As the board took shape, Advent had a recommendation for an operating partner. An operating partner is someone a private equity firm puts inside the company, who is paid for by the company but works to the benefit of the private equity firm and acts as their eyes and ears.

Advent put forward former Reebok executive, Bob Meers. Bob had been with Reebok when it was the number one athletic company in the world, easily dominating the top position of the women's fitness market with step classes.

Where Reebok had failed, I thought, was in their decision to shift away from women's fitness, a business they knew well and at which they were the best in the world. They'd chosen to refocus on men's fitness and big sponsorship marketing and were rapidly swallowed up by their massive competitors in the men's market—primarily by companies like Adidas and Nike.

What I liked about Bob were the lessons he'd learned. He'd seen the mistakes and had gained experience through them. He also understood women's fitness, which was valuable to lululemon. Finally, he knew retail stores and real estate and came highly recommended by Advent. Most importantly, Reebok had been built on the foundation of Landmark, and Bob told me he had been through most of the courses.

After meeting Bob, I realized he might be a good fit as CEO as well as a member of the board. I was a father to toddlers, and I was tired of travelling. Where else could I find a Landmark-trained athlete who understood the future of the women's market? How else was I going to be the father I wanted to be?

On our way to dinner in Boston, I asked Bob if he was interested in the position of CEO. He immediately lit up. With the CEO offer on the table, Bob proved himself very smart in negotiating his compensation.

We announced both the private equity deal and Bob Meers's appointment to the CEO position in a press release on December 8, 2005. In January 2006, Bob arrived in Vancouver to begin work at lululemon. Bob and I shared an office for six months. Having a new CEO onboard didn't alter the number of hours I spent at work, but it relieved me of almost all business travel. I could come home at night and spend time being a husband and father.

Bob's arrival brought a mix of excitement and wariness. He was a new, older, experienced, East Coast executive coming in to run an unorthodox, highly personal, female-dominated, West Coast company that operated like a family. This time, I'd expected the wariness, and I knew it would take a while to foster trust in the people working for me. This was why Bob and I worked in the same office for six months—I wanted to ensure he understood who we were at every level.

Foreign Markets

Before Bob joined us, I'd looked at some expansion plans beyond North America. I was reluctant to open stores in Europe because human-resources complications were akin to those in California. I felt that their rules around hiring, firing, lunch breaks, vacation, cost of benefits, and the threat of legal ramifications created mediocrity at the retail level in Europe. In my opinion, that's why few great retail managers come from Europe or California. It's all due to the overregulation in those markets.

Fortunately, there were other locations in which to look.

Back when I was with Westbeach, a man named Kano Yamanaka was my Japanese distributor. In the years since, we'd maintained contact and become friends. As lululemon was picking up momentum, Kano and I decided that he would open a lululemon franchise in Japan with a view to opening a series of stores. Westbeach had enjoyed a lot of success in Japan, and I wanted to build on that with lululemon.

Kano's first store had opened a year earlier. Since then, it had performed moderately well even though it wasn't in a prime location, it wasn't big enough, it was spread over two stories, and so on.

Playing it safe was not what we needed, as we already had a proven concept. I needed a prime location to ensure that if lululemon wasn't great in Japan, it wouldn't be because of the same challenges we'd experienced in Santa Monica. Like a science experiment, I had to remove all external variables to validate our business philosophy.

It became apparent that Kano's financial resources were not as deep as they once were at the apex of the snowboarding business. Perhaps he had stayed in the market too long. While Kano was doing his best with what he had, I wanted someone committed to prime locations, who could afford to build out the brand.

We got an offer from Descente, a large Japanese company with a very modern CEO who wanted to westernize his staff and teach them what North American retailing was all about. He even wanted them to speak English. Lululemon bought Kano out of his franchise and made an agreement with Descente, who, under Bob's approval, opened three more lululemon stores in Japan.

If I had not stopped travelling, I would have seen that our new top executives were reluctant to work in our stores. Consequently, the top of the organization started to lose an understanding as to why our stores performed so well.

From the employees' perspective, we didn't necessarily want Bob's new hires working in the stores because they were not athletic and not the brand. We didn't have an executive onboarding program (that was my fault), and we eventually came to see new executives as inauthentic salesmen instead of authentic Educators.

We were beginning to understand the difference between "experienced" new management and lululemon's "self-developed" people. I had turned to experts to expand our business but discovered there were no experts for our new technical retail model. The self-developed people of lululemon lived to support others in being great and were "leaders creating leaders." This was part of the reason lululemon could grow so fast without ever losing control.

Australia

Lululemon's first Australian store was a brand-starter on Melbourne's Chapel Street. I was expecting a three-to-four-year brand build. There were many reasons I thought lululemon would be a natural fit in Australia. A love of the outdoors and a healthy, active lifestyle are a deeply ingrained part of Australian culture, just as it is on the Pacific Coast of North America. It's casual and laid back—a place where women would find functional athletic clothing a natural extension of themselves.

But I'd also looked at Australia to solve a problem. A big issue with North American apparel is that excess inventory is sold at a discount at the end of a season. I realized that if I could get stores open in Australia, I could move the end-of-season winter goods to Australia at the beginning of their fall season and vice versa. This would eliminate discounting in North America. It was a brilliant idea in my mind.

By moving inventory back and forth with Australia, I

could give each hemisphere something brand new, in the right season, at full price. Even if the product we transferred only "broke even" after the transfer, it was better than discounting.

A central part of our retail store rollout consisted of opening an out of the way, inexpensive showroom with open doors only a few days a week. We would educate, hold design meetings, and network with a local community before opening a store. We had the cash flow to play the word-of-mouth strategy in Australia and wait for the tipping point. We also had to learn about their labour laws, and customs and duties before going all-in.

US Rollout

An April 2006 analysis on Canadianbusiness.com described Bob's plans in the following way: "Meers . . . seems determined to relive Reebok glory by building Lululemon into a ubiquitous global brand . . . Meers quickly ticks off his plans: additional outlets in Los Angeles, San Francisco and Seattle. A new store in Chicago. Multiple shop openings in New York City and Boston in Q3 or Q4."[21]

To assist his plan, Bob hired a top retail executive named Celeste Keely who had run the Western US for Abercrombie & Fitch. Lululemon's primary strategy was the real estate expansion in the US, which Bob had made a cornerstone of his tenure as CEO. The vision was to build the US in the same mould as Canada.

The expansion looked good, but the new stores were in expensive, high-profile shopping malls, and I didn't know to what extent we'd first seeded cities with a cool, urban street location, or if we'd been proactive in creating excitement or

21. Laura Bogomolny, "Toned and Ready: Lululemon Transitions," *Canadian Business*, April 24, 2006, www.canadianbusiness.com/business-strategy/toned-and-ready-lululemon-transitions/.

building networks in the local yoga and athletic communities. We wanted to ensure the locations were correct for Super Girl customers, and it was at this point the light bulb went on, and we understood the power of showrooms and pop-ups and community we didn't realize we had invented.

We were ready for expansion. New stores would add substantially to lululemon's valuation, as analysts would model out their profit a year in advance and then recommend a higher price for the lululemon stock if we were to go public. The idea of an IPO was still highly conceptual to me, but it seemed Advent and Highland talked about it constantly.

I thought I had made the right moves to succeed in the US. I had hired an experienced CEO, I had Tom Stemberg who seemed well versed in US real estate, and I had Advent who were private equity retail experts. I believed the PE partners when they said lululemon needed another four to five years to mature.

New York City

We'd recently signed the lease for our first store in New York City. Lori Jane Budd—a former track athlete, Calgary lululemon ambassador, and most recently, manager of the highly successful Oakville, Ontario, lululemon store—was on her way to Manhattan to run the new location.

As Lori recalls, "I told Chip that if he ever opened a store in NYC, I was the person to do it. Without hesitation, he responded with 'Great! I will pay you $80,000 a year to manage it.' I was beyond ecstatic at his apparent confidence in me . . . yet slightly overwhelmed, but that night I sat down with my husband and put my one-, five-, and ten-year goals down on paper for the first time.

"I managed the Oakville store for over a year," Lori continues, "and it became one of the top performing stores in the company and produced many managers that moved to other stores and regions. In early 2006, a lease was finally signed in Manhattan, and I was offered the position of store manager. I promoted my assistant manager to take over the Oakville store and planned my move to NYC.

"Bringing this company to NYC exceeded every expectation I ever had. We attended unlimited yoga and fitness classes around the city, meeting instructors, and talking about the brand. There was no middle ground—people either hadn't heard of us yet, or they were already *obsessed*."

To borrow from Frank Sinatra, if you can make it there, you'll make it anywhere. His lyrics were top of my mind as we decided on lululemon's next big expansion. New York City has always been a world leader in retail and apparel—in some ways, taking lululemon to NYC was something we had to do.

Expanding into New York was nerve-wracking, partly because of the high rents. It was a surprise to set up in Lincoln Square and see how little space we could get. Sometimes a company might open in New York, taking a high rent, and not make any money on the location. They would just use it as a marketing ploy to build the brand since New York has that major international appeal. Despite the size of our store, we managed.

If world-class logistics managers knew how the staff at our smallest stores (located in Lincoln Square and West Edmonton Mall) problem-solved, they'd hire them at a salary of half-a-million dollars a year. Our employees were amazing.

Michelle Armstrong

Meanwhile, the question of going public was looming larger by the day. In 2006, just after we'd made the private equity deal with Advent and Highland, Pricewaterhouse-Coopers was brought in to assist with auditing lululemon.

A young woman named Michelle Armstrong was the manager of the audit. She came out to lululemon in March of 2006. We were so impressed with Michelle that we offered her a job as director of finance, to augment Brian Bacon as our CFO. Up to this point, I hadn't put a lot of effort into hiring finance personnel. Working in the stores, I had developed an acute sense of the business and could tell within a few percentage points the exact profit and cash flow of the company. My new partners did not have this same insight, and at $110 million in sales, we could no longer only operate based on my innate sense of numbers.

Much to Michelle's—and everyone's—surprise, the prospect of the IPO came up within a few months of her joining lululemon.

As Michelle puts it, "When I got hired, they told me it would be a two- to four-year time horizon for us going public, but then in August [2006], Bob brought me into his office and said, 'Actually, we're going to start the process now.'"

This wasn't just a surprise to Michelle—most of lululemon was surprised. I wish that I had the type of relationship with Michelle at that time where she would have felt comfortable letting me know the IPO was coming sooner than expected. The world in early 2006 was awash in capital, and there were a lot of parties eager to invest in IPOs. Under Armour had just gone public, as had Crocs, both at high valuations. David Mussafer, Steve Collins, and Tom Stemberg all advised me that lululemon needed to make the move sooner rather than later.

I didn't know that Advent and Highland were already thinking of their exit. I expected Bob Meers would preside over a five-year period of growth, after which we'd presumably open the books and assess our options. I didn't know how closely his profit motive was tied to that of private equity.

Conflicts of Interest

I had been transparent that I was not averse to going public. I thought the IPO and public experience would allow me to be a valuable mentor to my children if they ever, one day, took their companies public.

At a board meeting just before going public, Tom said I had to clean up my personal connections to rid myself of conflicts of interest as a future director of a public board. To clean up, I had to change three things. The first was to let go of my sister-in-law, Susanne Conrad, as a board advisor since she would be a conflicted director as my relative.

"Because I was a family member," Susanne recalls, "there was a fear about optics. I was asked to step down just before the company went public. I would have liked to stay on the board. I think I sustained the company culture at the board level."

Even though we'd lost Susanne from the board, it was still very important to have her as part of the team. I wanted her to coach and develop our top one hundred people every quarter, as her background was executive-level coaching. Working with Delaney Schweitzer's Training and Culture team, Susanne would become one of lululemon's most beloved speakers. The curriculum Susanne developed, 'igolu' (now known as "Lightyear Leadership"), is a comprehensive self-leadership methodology that she delivered to thousands of lululemon employees and ambassadors from 2007 until January of 2017.

As Susanne remembers: "Delaney (SVP retail) and I worked to make lululemon a place where people could come and be with like-minded people, workout, sweat, and make work a place where we could transform some of the most difficult things in life with humour and love."

Susanne had the energy and advocacy I wanted on the board. I was sorry to lose her, but the company was lucky to have her in the years that followed. I asked Rhoda Pitcher, a change-management consultant, to replace Susanne on the board. I was counting on Rhoda to help us protect the company's culture through the coming changes.

The second thing I had to do before going public was sell my 50 percent stake in our manufacturing partner. I was okay with this if lululemon bought my share. The ownership of factories was an essential part to ownership of the vertical model, but Tom and Michael Casey deemed factory ownership was too risky. They didn't want to be in the manufacturing business. They didn't see it as an integral part of the business model but as a distraction.

The third change we had to make was to replace my lawyer, confidante, and our company secretary, Jon McCullough. Tom said we needed an American law firm who understood US public law.

Each of these steps seemed so incremental that there was never one specific moment where I thought to say stop.

The E-Commerce Mediation

Another thing lululemon needed to clean up before our IPO was our e-commerce. I had waited to properly invest in e-commerce while our company was in rapid growth. We couldn't manufacture quickly enough to fill our own stores, so we didn't need an e-commerce store just yet. I understood that e-commerce had come to stay, and I appreciated its power in completing a top-to-bottom vertical model with absolutely no middleman to skim profits.

In 2006, I felt that e-commerce was good for a commodity product—something a customer already understood—while lululemon was primarily touch and feel. At that time, there was no video to educate e-commerce customers on our product. Our value was not in the look of the garment but in the tactile feel and technical features. A photo worked for fashion but not for lululemon. Today, you can ship three or four garments to somebody so they can try them on and return them if they so choose. There was nothing near that level of sophistication in 2006.

Lululemon had its own selection of commodity products, including yoga mats and yoga straps. We also had a few items to sell at a discount. So, I made an agreement with a digital company to sell commodity and discount products online. It was a small agreement with no buyout clause.

If I wanted to regain complete control of lululemon's online products, it looked like we would have to buy them out.

It was clear lululemon was a raging success, so the company asked for $2 million as a buyout. I wasn't convinced this was anywhere near an appropriate price and I refused. We went to mediation, and their ask jumped to $7 million.

Mediation, in my experience, usually splits something down the middle, so by then, it looked as if I would get hit for $3.5 million. I countered at negative $6 million to get the price down to $1 million. Mediation collapsed, and I let it go. My private equity partners pushed Bob to settle at any price because they knew what I didn't; an IPO was imminent, and they wanted a clean slate. The company paid out $9 million.

This wasn't just a lesson in e-commerce, or in being specific in contracts. I needed to grow up and make solid legal agreements.

The Media and Short-Selling

Around this same time, I learned my first—but not my last—lesson in dealing with the media. I'd always been my own PR and brand manager.

Back when I was making technical apparel for surf, skate, and snowboarding, followed by yoga a few years later, the press came to me looking for expert opinions on these markets. Westbeach received free editorial coverage and never had to advertise. Also, everything that was published about my work was always a good story, so when it came to the press, I'd gotten used to good stories.

I never had to be guarded in what I said.

The first time I was "trapped" by a journalist was in 2007, right around the time lululemon went public. We were making a line of clothing called VitaSea, with an eco-friendly, seaweed-based technology called SeaCell. We'd found that using SeaCell fibres in the fabric of our shirts would make the shirts anti-stink, as well as moisturizing for the skin of the person wearing the shirt. On top of that, shirts made with SeaCell just felt great to wear.

I was contacted by the *New York Times*, who wanted to talk about the SeaCell technology.

"Well, have you had it tested?" the reporter asked.

"We get it from a supplier in Germany," I told her. "We've got all the information, all the specs on it."

"How do you know it actually works?" she said. "What kind of testing have you done?"

"We haven't done any technical testing," I said, "other than I wear it every day, and my wife tells me I don't stink anymore. I also think the suppleness of the fabric is beautiful. I really love it."

I didn't realize how the statement could be manipulated . . . but then the article came out. The headline read: "'Seaweed' Clothing Has None, Tests Show." Here's an excerpt of the article itself:

Lululemon Athletica has been a standout performer on Wall Street since it went public in July, thanks to the popularity of its costly yoga and other workout clothes, which are made with unusual materials, including bamboo, silver, charcoal, coconut, and soybeans. One of its lines is called VitaSea, and the company says it is made with seaweed . . . There is one problem with its VitaSea claims, however. Some of them may not be true.[22]

Basically, the *New York Times* was calling us frauds. When I read it, my first thought was that it was mean-spirited. Lululemon was all about love so I couldn't imagine why someone would ever write something like that. I wondered if it was a case of tall poppy syndrome.

The negative article in the *Times* also gave me insight into the game of short selling in the stock market. When the article was published, lululemon was at almost sixty times EBITDA, which is the very top end of stock valuation.

When a company is valued for perfection, anything that goes wrong will drop the stock, even temporarily. I knew lululemon was very heavy on the short-sellers. It naturally happens when a stock is priced that high. People will run algorithms on it and determine the possibility of the stock dropping could be 80 percent. That's the game.

If those prospective short-sellers want to ensure profits, then the smart ones will manufacture a false story that will impact the stock. For example, they might feed fake information to interested journalists. The journalists, in turn, write a high-profile article that damages a company and causes its stock to drop, and the short-sellers reap the rewards. There is so much money to be made I wouldn't doubt a backroom payoff to the writer.

It's interesting to note that the *Times* even admitted they'd gotten the story from a short-seller in that article: "The

22. Louise Story, "'Seaweed' Clothing Has None, Tests Show," *New York Times*, November 14, 2007, www.nytimes.com/2007/11/14/business/14seaweed.html.

Times commissioned its test after an investor who is shorting lululemon's stock—betting that its price will fall—provided . . . test results to the *Times*."[23] I'm sure many people made good money off the stock drop.

Anyway, it didn't take long for our stock to recover. Our overall numbers were among the best in the world, so the drop wasn't a huge problem. In managing the bad publicity, David Mussafer from Advent Equity (who was on our board of directors), stepped up and did a phenomenal job. He'd seen this kind of thing before because Advent had so many public companies that he understood the game well. He understood how to get in, how to respond, and how to talk to the media in the right way.

Overall, with lululemon going public and the article in the *New York Times*, I recognized that the world had changed for me. I saw how easily salacious headlines could increase readership and sales. Still, the incident didn't change my willingness to engage with the media.

Needing More Directors

At the last board meeting before our IPO, Tom told me we needed more board members to fill committees as a public board. Tom, who had been on many public boards, had a deep Rolodex of quality people who were more than happy to come to lululemon. I had none, and I had no advance advice that I should be looking for the right people.

23. Ibid.

CHAPTER 22:
THE IPO

Do not fear failure, but please be terrified of regret. —Deshauna Barber

Lessons from the IPO

Going public was another critical juncture that affected the future of lululemon. Again, for those of you who might be in this position in your own lives, I would like to share my learnings:

1. Have each prospective director explain their theory as to what type of CEO is needed at each approaching growth stage of the company.
2. I didn't control the board, so I should have nurtured and selected my own people to fill board positions and not let PE do it.
3. A founder with more than 10 percent of the company will be a "not independent" director. The other directors are deemed as "independent." To ensure the founder-director does not control the company decision-making, the independent directors elect a lead director. The lead director is essentially the

chairman as he or she represents more board votes. Giving the chairman title to the founder can be nothing but smoke and mirrors.

4. A strategic CEO can divide and conquer a board by undermining the "not independent" founder from the independent board members if the CEO and founder do not see eye-to-eye on vision or operations.

5. A staggered board where only three directors are up for election each year does not allow directors to change with the speed that the world changes. Directors get stale fast. Nepotism and mediocrity set in quickly.

6. With new money in their pocket, the founder now has another job trying to figure out what to do with that money. A founder usually knows one way to turn a profit, and that is in the business they just sold. I recommend the founder invest the money equally with three wealth managers and determine which firm does the best over a three-year period. If instead the founder tries to build a new business or joins other boards, their eye gets taken off the ball. This creates a power vacuum that gets filled quickly by operational directors and management looking for more power.

Becoming American

A final step in the process of going public was officially making lululemon an American company. We registered our business in Delaware. It took me years to understand why this was important. The value of lululemon would be dictated by the demand for its shares. The board wanted to give investors the confidence they needed to buy into lululemon. If lululemon was an American company, under American regulatory laws, it provided assumed security for potential investors. This never made sense to me. Canadian corporate taxes had always been less than those of the US (until, of course, Trump changed the tax rates in 2018 to favour American companies).

Going Public

On July 27, 2007, at 9:30 a.m., I stood on a riser in the NASDAQ Exchange in New York City. Beside me were my family, an assortment of our core staff, and our new board of directors. I took a breath and pressed the button to ring the bell. We'd done it. We'd taken lululemon athletica public.

"I always kind of joked that lululemon was like the sister we never had," my son JJ recalls. "And growing up, I always kind of thought, 'Well, my dad owns and runs a women's athletic apparel, yoga-based business. And that's what he does every day. He gets up, and he goes and makes little black stretchy pants.' I kind of had an understanding, eventually, of what was occurring. It was part of my life growing up. The IPO happened when I was eighteen."

The day of the IPO was huge for us, but I felt as if I'd already experienced it. An entrepreneur is easily able to put themselves five to ten years into the future. They build into the future, and not for the present, so I had already envisioned this for lululemon. It was akin to being a designer. A designer designs a garment but doesn't see it come into the store until eight months later. By that point, the designer has long since moved on to future designs.

Almost as soon as the bell was rung, our stock jumped from its initial price of $18 to $25 a share.[24] As planned, I now owned 30 percent of the company. We marked the day in a memorable way. We'd already arranged it so that Times

24. Steve Gelsi, "Lululemon Athletica IPO Jumps 50%," MarketWatch, July 27. 2007, www.marketwatch.com/story/clothing-maker-lululemon-rallies-50-raises-328-mln.

Square was shut down to traffic during the day on the July 27, which allowed us to stage a massive yoga demonstration right there in the centre.

The demonstration was Eric Petersen's idea, and it went off perfectly. Eric would later say the day of the IPO was among his proudest moments at the company. "Everyone at lululemon felt like they were involved in the process," he commented. "It could have been a divisive time in the growth of the company, but it wasn't."

Lori Jane Budd, who managed our first store in NYC, says: "It was a very exciting time to be the manager of the only store in NYC with all the hoopla surrounding this giant step for the company. After having the thrill of watching the bell being rung, the excitement and traffic increased even more in the store. On the day of the IPO, a banker walked into the store on 64th and Broadway and said, 'Who are you guys?! I just made a shitload of money off you!'"

Giving Back

I also wanted to do something for all of our employees, so we had every electronic billboard in Times Square displaying rotating pictures of everyone working in our stores. If you were working for lululemon at that time, you would have seen your face in Times Square. The whole event brought the company together. It wasn't just those of us down there for the IPO—it was a positive way of enrolling and involving everyone in the entire company in the experience.

July 27 also marked the fulfillment of a promise I'd made to the staff years before. When lululemon was much, much smaller, I'd told a group of our people that if we ever went public, I would give them 10 percent of my shares. I did this, which created thirty or so multimillionaires—most of them women (who have since gone on to build their own businesses).

Coming to New York and experiencing the final stage of our company going public wasn't just symbolic for our staff, it meant that they were now its owners.

The investing world seemed to believe in our new way of doing business. We had a successful formula that was producing the top apparel metrics in the world.

Board Structure

At the time of the IPO, Tom brought forward two possible very experienced and successful directors. The first was Michael Casey, the ex-CFO of Starbucks. The second was Brad Martin, the ex-CEO of Saks. I couldn't have been happier with the quality of people we had on our board.

Michael Casey was elected by the independent directors to the lead director role. This was a nice balance, I thought, between the eight independent, financially minded directors, and myself as a creative and visionary founder.

Michael once told me he took the same route to work every morning, so his mind could focus on what needed to be done that day. When I heard him say that, I chuckled under my breath. I took a different route to work every day. I always wanted to see how the world was changing around me. It seemed we had a nice balance of expertise. Our nine independent directors brought structure and consistency to the board. I brought industry analytics, a five- to seven-year vision, and a deep understanding of what differentiated lululemon and made it special.

Returning to Vancouver

After the IPO in New York, we returned to Vancouver. The atmosphere at the company was very positive—everyone had seen their face on the screens in Times Square, and now most of our staff owned a share in the company we'd grown. This shared ownership changed the whole energy of the company. Across the board, this was a transformative accomplishment, and we commenced our first day as a publicly traded company.

All around, there were small pieces of the business model that seemed to break down as we were growing. I'd been taking extra measures to protect and preserve our culture, including establishing an award called the "Holder of the Flame" to elevate those who stood for transformational leadership.

I felt that everyone had trusted me when I told them that Bob Meers and his team would take lululemon to the next level and had trusted me again through the IPO. If I was going to keep looking these people in the face, I needed to find out where things were breaking down.

The good thing about Bob was that he seemed genuinely excited to work at lululemon. He was a strong leader, and could command attention and draw people in. With our 30 to 40 percent growth each year, Bob's big achievement was recognizing and solving our bottleneck in production capacity.

Unfortunately, solving our production bottleneck was not enough to bring Bob fully into our culture.

As Deanne Schweitzer put it: "Doubts about the future of the company were definitely on a lot of our minds when we started to see how Bob Meers was leading the company, the people he was hiring, and the money he was spending. Bob was spending money in the wrong places and hiring the wrong people—bringing in people who were there for the short term, not the long term. There was a feeling that we were all looking at our watches and wondering, 'How long am I going to last here?'"

Bree Stanlake made this observation: "When Chip was our CEO, it was a period of high growth, but it felt very free, very entrepreneurial in the truest sense of the word. There were some people that Bob brought on who didn't really fit with the culture. It just started to feel like people were there to make money, then leave. It may sound trivial, but some things showed us that they just weren't in line with our culture. For instance, they didn't care about working out. Doing regular workouts wasn't important to them. Being healthy and fit is something that's central to lululemon."

Bob and I still had a good working relationship, so after I studied the growing problems for a while, I spoke to him about the way trust, communication, and culture had eroded over the past year and a half. He was the CEO, and I wanted to empower him to fix the problems. I outlined that things simply couldn't continue to carry on as they had. Bob assured me that now that he'd taken us public and the share price was skyrocketing, the differences could be reconciled.

The Fight in the Air

After a few more months had gone by, I was on a private flight with Bob Meers and David Mussafer from Advent. At one point, Bob and David started raising their voices and, after a moment, David asked Bob to take the heated conversation into the galley. The plane was so small that I could still hear what was being said, but I paid little attention. Bob and David had known one another before Bob came on board at lululemon, so I assumed their argument was personal, given their shift to the galley.

After the flight, Bob told me he would soon leave lululemon. I was shocked. I thought Bob would be around for five years, leading us through our high-growth period. I didn't understand why he was leaving so soon.

At any rate, with Bob's departure hanging in the air, it turned out he already had a successor in mind. Bob wanted us to meet a woman named Christine Day, who was introduced to Bob (and lululemon) by Rhoda Pitcher.

At the end of 2006, Christine had left Starbucks to take a year off. She'd been in Starbucks's international group for three and a half years. She'd been with the coffee giant for twenty years as a troubleshooter, rejigging the foundations for Asia. The time had come for her to spend more time with her family. By September 2007, as her yearlong sabbatical drew to a close, she began to look at what her next move would be.

We contacted her in October and asked her to come and see us before she made any other decisions. The first time I met Christine face-to-face was at a restaurant in Seattle. Rhoda, also a Seattle native, joined us for the meal.

During our meeting, Christine told me that lululemon appealed to her on a lot of different levels. Primarily, she could see how unique the product and its business philosophy were. From Starbucks, she understood the vertical retail model—selling lululemon product in lululemon stores—allowed for our higher margins. The Guest experience was essential, and Christine said she was impressed by the loyalty we'd generated in our customers.

I was excited to get a Starbucks executive, because the company philosophies, locations, employee, and Guest profiles seemed so much alike. I thought she would be a good fit. My only concern was not having an athlete at the helm of lululemon.

Something I didn't know at the time was that Bob was doing everything he could to accelerate his departure from lululemon. A long, drawn-out search for a suitable replacement would only slow that process down, so Bob was highly motivated to hire Christine for the job as COO. She was slated to join lululemon in January 2008.

Christine came in as a COO with the idea of taking over the CEO position from Bob. She'd never held the top job before and would need a little time with us to get the lay of the land. Still, it was good that the best candidate to run a female-oriented company was a well-accomplished woman.

1999 *Standing in the very first lululemon store, Kitsilano*

Chip was so passionate about the concept that I had tremendous faith in his ability to manifest his vision into a great reality.

FIONA STANG
My first yoga instructor

2003 *The image of our original yoga embassador Fiona Stag, featured on the first manifesto bags*

1997 *Sketching the first logo in my daytimer*

2001 *Designer Summer Gray opening the lululemon store on West 4th, Kitsilano*

2001 *Me with Stephanie Bourassa & my future wife, Summer Gray*

1998 *Sarah Bancroft & Eoin Finn (our second yoga ambassador)*

WAKE UP AND REALIZE YOU ARE SURROUNDED BY AMAZING FRIENDS

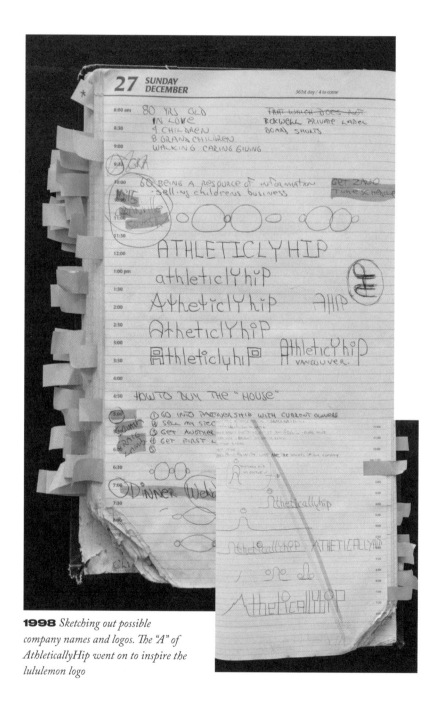

1998 *Sketching out possible company names and logos. The "A" of AthleticallyHip went on to inspire the lululemon logo*

A FEW OF THE THINGS I HAVE LEARNED FROM

CHIP WILSON
BY NOEL FOX

DREAM BIG

When Chip asked me to help with lululemon's marketing back in 1998 the first thing he told me is that he wanted to be as big as Nike.

◄ ♥ ►

TAKE RISKS

I have had the pleasure of working on many very successful marketing campaigns with Chip that upset a few people. Coke is Evil, Naked on Robson, $30,000 Yoga Contest in Yoga Journal for April Fools, Child Labor ad where Chip is at a sewing machine wearing diapers, and the list goes on.

CUSTOMERS FIRST

I was taking a press photo of Chip at the W. 4th lululemon. He only had 5 minutes because he was running late & just as we were about to shoot he started helping an elderly customer. 45 minutes later he finished talking to her and we snapped off a quick photo.

LANDMARK

With out it I wouldn't be as happily married, successful, and content.

2012 *Susanne Conrad from "Lightyear Leadership" leading a lululemon goal coaching session*

2003 *The core Super Girls who set the cultural foundation for lululemon: Delaney Schweitzer, Jackie Slater (employee #2), Karen Wyder, Niki Hatter, & Deanne Schweitzer*

2004 *The Spread Love Van*

1999 *Mocking the "It's Bigger Than I Thought" ad by local gym Ron Zalko's, with our very first designer, Amanda Dunsmoor*

1998 *Our first ad, with ambassador Fiona Stang*

WILL YOU CHOOSE A LIFE OF A GLASS HALF EMPTY OR A GLASS HALF FULL?

2002 *April 20, a day I will never forget. I was lucky enough to marry the best stretch fabric designer in the world, Summer Wilson*

1998 *Me & my sister Noel, opening the second floor store in Kitsilano*

2003 *An early lululemon ad, in the flesh*

2001 *Christmas lineup at our West 4th store in Kitsilano*

DO YOGA - IT LETS YOU LIVE IN THE MOMENT AND STRETCHING RELEASES TOXINS FROM YOUR MUSCLES

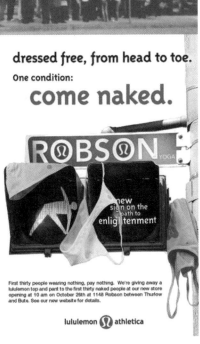

dressed free, from head to toe.

One condition:

come naked.

First thirty people wearing nothing, pay nothing. We're giving away a lululemon top and pant to the first thirty naked people at our new store opening at 10 am on October 26th at 1148 Robson between Thurlow and Bute. See our new website for details.

lululemon ☾ athletica

2002 *This ad got a lot of butts in the store!*

2003 *Our cheeky child labour ad*

2005 *First Japan store in Shibuya*

2002 *The Yoga Pose Off!*

2007 *Going public with Lori Budd, Erin Westelman, Steve Collins, Michelle Armstrong, Karen Wyder, Delaney Schweitzer, Dave Mussafer, Celeste Burgoyne, Mike Tattersfield, Bob Meers, Summer Wilson, Brett Wilson, me, Bree Stanlake, Eric Petersen, JJ Wilson, NASDAQ Suit-and-Tie Guy, Joe Gray, Deanne Schweitzer, and John Currie. Missing: Darrell Kopke.*

2007 *About to make history, with Brett*

FRIENDS
ARE
MORE
IMPORTANT
THAN
MONEY

2007 *In Times Square with Summer*

CHAPTER 23:
AFTER BOB

Give up looking good and pretending you are something other than your core values. Everyone can spot a fake.

Coke and Pepsi

That January, before he left us for good, Bob wanted to remove the first and most prominent branding statement from our manifesto and our shopping bags.

"Coke, Pepsi, and all other pops will be known as the cigarettes of the future. Great marketing, terrible product."

A typical business person would advise against this branding approach because of the risk of alienating people. Exactly! We didn't want anyone who was wearing lululemon to be drinking Coke or Pepsi. It was bad for our brand.

Earlier, in the '70s, I correlated lung cancer with cigarettes before there was real data. I did not allow smokers in the Westbeach store. By driving these customers away, my core customers became more fanatical.

In the '80s, I correlated obesity in the US with Coke and Pepsi. Coke and Pepsi had marketed themselves as the American dream, and I believed it was a primary reason Americans were getting fat. I also knew only a company with absolute integrity could stand up to their massive marketing machines.

I wanted our Super Girl market to know the lululemon brand was not for soda drinkers. If we were aligned with our iconic health-inspired Super Girl, I knew the rest of the world would follow.

After we put our declaration on the manifesto, Coke and Pepsi threatened to drown lululemon in lawsuits. I had always thought of lululemon as a social experiment. I believed our company could be the driver for social health.

"We had absolute conviction in what we were saying," says Deanne Schweitzer. "We had to do a lot of research, due diligence, and legal work to prepare our side of the story and throughout that time we were in the process of going public. I would always follow Chip in focusing on what you believe to be true. In this case, we focused on supporting the claim we had made, and in the end, it was completely supported by facts."

Bob made a point that since people were now much more aware of the health risks posed by colas, the item made the manifesto seem dated. He said we'd already played our part. President Bill Clinton had led efforts to take pop machines out of schools across the US, and I wondered if the lululemon manifesto had played some part in the president's ruling— that is, until I attended the Clinton Global Initiative meeting in New York, sponsored by Coca-Cola.

I never wanted lululemon to appear dated. I deferred to Bob, and the slogan came off our manifesto.

A Cover-up

The manifesto on the side of our shopping bags was such a success that I wanted to take my theories a step further. I couldn't get the entire manifesto on the side of the small shoppers, so I started writing short health philosophies.

When the health philosophies were printed on the side of the shoppers in 2008, Bob thought there would be public pushback and unwanted publicity. He ordered the side of the bags to be covered up with something vanilla. There was some online discussion, but social media was still in its infancy, and the whole incident blew over.

Resetting our Leadership

The CEO transition plan was for Bob to stay at lululemon until the fall, at which point Christine would take over.

In early 2008, Christine moved her family to Vancouver and completed the Landmark Forum. She was officially the first externally hired executive to engage in our newly formalized cultural onboarding.

Within a few weeks of Christine's arrival, Bob was MIA. He was still being paid, but he was absent. After it became clear he wasn't coming back, my instinct was to fire him. Why were we keeping someone around who wasn't doing the job for which we were paying him?

But the board of directors didn't want to fire Bob. As they explained, lululemon had not been public for long. Firing a CEO—even an absent one—would be bad optics. Investor confidence could be affected; analysts and advisors might recommend against buying lululemon shares. It just wouldn't look good if we fired Bob. The company had to suck it up and pay him because the lululemon board did not want to release the news to our shareholders. It made me sick.

We were careful about the public message we released about Bob's departure, simply saying he would "retire" from his position as CEO of lululemon at the end of June.[25] I informally slipped back into the role of CEO, got rid of Bob's hires, and righted the ship. It was a breath of fresh air. The silver lining of our time with Bob was learning what we *didn't* want.

I still didn't know *why* Bob had disappeared. As I thought about it, I was reminded of that private flight that Bob and I had taken with David Mussafer several months earlier. Bob and David had gotten up from their seats and had taken their conversation into the galley for privacy, but their voices carried—especially as things became more heated.

"I did it," Bob kept saying. "I did it, I got the stock to X amount for two months, now pay me."

Since it was a private conversation, I hadn't asked any questions at the time, but now I wondered if Bob had worked out a deal with Advent that enabled him to cash out if the stock got to a particular value for two consecutive months. Perhaps there was a public disclosure about such an incentive package, but it was never brought up in a board meeting to which I was privy. If I had known, I think I would have watched for short-term decision-making.

In February 2008, MarketWatch summarized the situation like this: "All [Meers] had to do was to be on the job when lululemon's LULU, +0.04% share price hit a certain level and its private-equity investors sold a slug of shares . . . this puts management's interests in line with private equity, not necessarily with public shareholders."[26] The same analysis described the inherent dangers of these kinds of

25. Business Wire, "Lululemon Athletica Appoints Christine Day as President, Chief Operating Officer and CEO Designate," lululemon athletica, April 2, 2008, https://corporate.lululemon.com/media/press-releases/2008/04-02-2008-084440140

26. Herb Greenberg, "Lululemon CEO's Sweet Deal." *MarketWatch*, February 25, 2008, www.marketwatch.com/story/lululemon-ceos-sweet-deal.

deals because they "[align] management's interest with the wrong group of shareholders—those who are cashing out."[27]

I realized that Bob had done everything in his power to get the share value to where it needed to be to trigger his exit, and that he was likely incentivized to maximize that share price. The easiest way for him to do this was to open new stores carelessly.

I realized then that it had never been Bob's intention to set lululemon on a course to sustained, long-term growth. He was incentivized for short-term results, also to PE's benefit because they both maximized their share value and cashed out.

In Darrell Kopke's words: "I was with lululemon for the IPO process. Bob Meers was there to protect himself during this process, so he brought in his own people. There was a pure, selfish manipulation of the market for their own benefit. It changed the company from one with a legacy on the health of its community to one that cared only about getting stock prices up to maximize options. I learned about revenue smoothing and presenting oneself on an earnings call to make the stock look good."

In the end, Bob made around $30 million on stock appreciation. Instead of announcing that he was no longer the CEO, he simply walked away. As a result, Christine's rise to CEO was expedited, and her development under Bob was truncated, much like the development of the Super Girls, as we rushed into the IPO.

There was a lot for me to learn from the Bob Meers era. It was also my introduction to the art of looking good to maximize short-term gains.

27. Ibid.

Christine Becomes CEO

Lululemon's shareholders' annual general meeting (AGM) was held in June 2008, and Christine Day was publicly appointed as CEO. It was a boon to investor confidence, with magazines like *Forbes* describing it as a breath of new life for the company.[28]

Unsurprisingly, the US side of the business was struggling, and stores were not hitting their projections.

The first thing we did was coach Christine on our fundamentals. Christine had solid real estate experience from her time at Starbucks, and she knew what a good deal looked like. She reset deal terms, brought the economics back in line, and looked to the streets and the lifestyle centers to complement the mall stores. We also hired store staff from the local communities and invested in their training.

Just like Bob had done with the Coke and Pepsi slogan, the first thing Christine wanted to do as CEO was to eliminate another of our manifesto slogans: *"Children are the orgasm of life. Just like you did not know what an orgasm was before you had one, nature does not let you know how great children are until you actually have them."* We thought she was joking as that particular statement and the greater manifesto were the number one reasons people said they applied to work for lululemon. After we realized she was serious, we took it as a good moment to coach Christine on how tipping-point branding worked.

Using different cultural tools, we had learned ways to be authentic about being inauthentic; we'd found new ways of being open and undefended about who we are and how we protect

28. Melinda Peer, "Christine Day Breathes New Life Into Lululemon." *Forbes*, April 3, 2008, https://www.forbes.com/2008/04/03/day-christine-lululemon-face-markets-cx_mp_0402autofacescan03.html#4425fb639f37.

ourselves. This understanding and training allows us to coach each other in moments where we revert to being inauthentic.

Christine had received one call about the slogan, from one offended person. Her direction to remove the quote was a response based in reaction and not in choice. She may have been new to our culture, but Christine had completed our executive onboarding. With coaching, she quickly came around and withdrew her directive.

The Great Recession

The 2008 economic downturn, now known as the Great Recession, began only a few months after Christine became CEO. This major event—considered the worst stock market plunge since the Depression in the 1920s—had been building since the American subprime mortgage crisis in 2007.

Things only got worse from there, culminating in the Lehman Brothers investment bank collapse in September. Despite massive government bailouts, the damage was done, and everyone was hit hard. The Dow fell 500 points, and there was a massive sell-off of stocks on Wall Street.

It was scary to watch our stocks drop from $45 to $5, almost overnight (especially after we'd gone public at $18). All at once, nearly every company could be bought for cents on the dollar, and everything we felt we'd achieved by going public was suddenly underwater. Nobody knew if anyone, anywhere in the world, would be working the next day.

Times were tough for several months. We didn't have to lay off much staff, but hiring slowed substantially. We closed our stores in Japan, and we saw a much slower holiday season that year.

However, overall, lululemon weathered the storm. Through the worst of the recession, the fundamentals of lululemon seemed to be as strong as ever, and we didn't have to sell our soul as so many other companies did. As we came to the end of 2008, we didn't have to focus our efforts on merely staying alive.

It occurred to me that in past downturns, people had been known to turn to gambling and drugs, but in the new world, people were managing stress with athletic endorphin hits. My theory seemed to be verified as our sales continued to soar.

E-Commerce Revisited and the Lab Concept

The excess inventory triggered by the recession drove us to invest in e-commerce, and our platform launched in April 2009. To supplement it, we sent out widespread email blasts to our customer base whenever we had a new product. E-commerce was very successful for us; even with a limited product line available, we were quickly selling inventory almost as fast as we could stock it. I saw e-commerce as a critical part of the full vertical model I had always wanted.

I was always concerned a pure e-commerce play could undermine lululemon as the vertical model I developed had done to wholesalers. The board was very keen on e-commerce because they could see it working in other companies for which they were also directors. At the time, if I had a choice of e-commerce or owning our own manufacturing, I would have picked manufacturing. But at that moment, manufacturing would not have helped our excess inventory position created by the financial crisis.

The recession may have been the best thing that ever happened to lululemon. We stopped growing, got our processes in place, and reset our foundation for growth. We had nothing else to do. Even during the recession, our stores made their way up to sales of $1,000 per square foot in the US, while maintaining about $3,000 per square foot in Canada (the average retailer does about $650 per square foot).

I had always wanted to recreate the laboratory inside the store like we had in our original Kitsilano location. We had an unused lease in Vancouver, and we had a million dollars in excess fabrics, zippers, and trims. We had an internal "quick turn" pod to turn this excess inventory into cash, but I wanted a fishbowl in which to test new designers.

We hired new designers and turned them over every three months. We let them loose on samples and excess fabric in the floor space of the new building to create street clothing from technical fabrics. With creative freedom, these new designers brought a great dynamic into the brand in a highly uncertain time.

My experience told me we had to go through fifteen designers to find one amazing designer like my wife, Summer, or like Shannon Savage (another incredible designer), a designer who can consistently create multiple new ideas, four times a year. I knew finding a Summer-Wilson- or Shannon-Savage-type creative was more valuable to the bottom line than our CEO or CFO.

We would open more labs in New York City's Soho and eventually a new one in Gastown in Vancouver. It was one more innovation that helped get us through very uncertain times and develop local athletic design talent unavailable anywhere else in the world.

Effects of the Recession

Christine did a fantastic job with real estate deals, resetting our strategies to a fundamental successful formula, investing in e-commerce, and working with the back-end public details and financials. We came out of the recession with increased cash flow and a massive surplus of money.

On March 9, 2009, lululemon's share price was hovering just under $2.25, far less than what it had been just after we'd gone public in 2007. From there, however, our share price began a rise that would steadily climb until 2013.

Analysts at Thomson Reuters were impressed with our performance and the uniqueness of lululemon's position in the market. "Few Canadian retailers have found this kind of success expanding south of the border," Reuters said.[29]

Christine hit the ground running and the next two years were golden.

We didn't have a brand or marketing team because our brand spend was hidden in people development, quality processes, store locations, and anything else "off the cuff" I wanted to do in response to social changes in the world. Everything we did seemed to strengthen the brand.

I kept my desk in the middle of the design area, and we produced our best innovations and looks ever. My wife and I hired a dance designer named Antonia Iamartino to bring femininity to the functional yoga look. This idea put us four years ahead of anyone even thinking of competing with us.

From an innovation end, we set the goal to become the best athletic bra manufacturer in the world by 2013. We contracted the University of Manchester to study breast movement. We produced radio wave bonding seams, laser venting, and cell phone pockets on every garment. I brought silver threads into our garments to kill bacteria and to end stink.

A "home run design" (a design that drives company profits) was the Scuba Hoodie. From my years in the surf, skate, and snowboard business, I knew the hoodie was an iconic garment. My wife, Summer, had made a test version of it in 2001. I wanted to make the best hoodie in the world. The absolute beauty of vertical retailing was that it allowed us to make what no one else could afford. With my friend Elky Hon, we developed a supersoft cotton fabric, thicker than any

29. Reuters Staff, "ANALYSIS-Lululemon Seen Growing in Lucrative Niche Market." *Reuters*, November 2, 2010, www.reuters.com/article/idUSN0116446120101102.

hoodie ever made. When we combined the fabric with a scuba neck and a 2-inch-wide hem at the hood, we had reinvented a classic item. Finally, by inserting the logo on the front seams, we realized that the Scuba Hoodie would account for up to 20 percent of sales during the Christmas 2009 season.

The Oprah Effect

Around that time, we got a call from Oprah Winfrey's people, in preparation for her "Oprah's favorite things" episode. Summer and I flew to Chicago to be in the audience and give out pants. Our share price instantly jumped by $10. We had seventy-five stores in the US, but with Oprah's boost, suddenly millions of Americans heard about lululemon for the first time.

To be honest, I was torn about Oprah's endorsement. I'd become more and more aware of the increasing influence of celebrities on many facets of life. The excitement over what a celebrity was wearing was something I just didn't understand. I also felt it was fake because I thought most celebrities were being paid to wear stuff, just like the Nike endorsements. That's not what we ever wanted to do. When a celebrity would walk into one of our stores in California, our staff would automatically want to give them clothing for free—a practice which I opposed.

Ultimately, we did well in the US because we got back to basics. Instead of opening poorly located stores to push the stock price, we built more studio pop-ups, we developed the local markets, we developed our people, and we focused on education. It took time, but the community was ready for us when we came in, and that was, by far, the most important thing.

We found ourselves in a good position at the end of 2009.

Defining Who I Am

The great years at lululemon, 2008–2010, were an expansive time for me personally because I got to focus on my love of innovation.

To understand me, you would have to know I am an extremely finicky person. Everything about clothing bothers me. If I could spend the rest of my life in a Speedo, I probably would. Every fibre, seam, fit, and colour on most garments irritates me. I'm annoyed by anything un-functional.

I want my clothing to work for me. I want to know exactly how my body is positioned in any sport and I want a perfect ergonomic design to enhance my ability to perform. Pockets must be an exact length, and at the right angle. I must be able to get at my smartphone in two rings. I need a place for my earbuds. My backpacks must have a pocket for everything, and I must be able to get at my toothbrush, Kindle, laptop, phone, lip balm, cards, sunglasses, computer cords, pens, and vitamins in under three seconds.

I have to have a place for my wet clothing, and I need a backpack with breathability for stinky shoes. I want zippers to be positioned perfectly and able to be opened with one hand. I want venting, so air flows through the front, under my arm-pits and escapes out the back. I want manual venting so I can control for sweat and outside weather.

Without my history in athletics, lululemon would never have come to be. When I was a competitive swimmer, the water provided a natural cooling system. After my swimming era ended and I started running or biking or playing squash, my body went into overdrive, and it would take forty-five minutes of perspiring to cool down. As someone who exercises three times daily, the very thought of putting on a non-stretch-cotton collared shirt, tie, and—God forbid—a jacket—was appalling to me. It is no way to dress or live life. I saw no reason to wear clothing that I saw as some archaic mode of dressing. A suit seemed to be a piece of apparel that looked good, but felt terrible while it was on.

The West Coast had no overhangs of the East Coast uniform. Especially in the extreme sports realm.

I am a technical-apparel scientist. I look at the body of every person I see in complete detail, and I log, extrapolate, and run algorithms from the information I absorb. I have done this since I was ten years old. I look at a body and correlate sex, age, sport, muscle, fat, height, race, passion, and colour of clothing.

I look at bodies down to the molecular level in my desire to make the perfect garment. I want to know exactly what type of body performs best for each sport. I want to know exactly how a short, muscular gymnast operates and wears clothing differently than a wiry marathon runner.

I am passionate about solving for testicular compression when on a bicycle or during extended periods of sitting. I want to understand how different-sized breasts affect performance in different sports and what is needed for athletic perfection. I want to know which bodies correlate to which fabrics in winter and again in summer. I was meant to do what I do. I love analyzing why each Olympic sport requires radically different clothing to allow the athlete to perform microns better than a competitor.

I live, eat, and breathe apparel technology. At no time in my life could I do this with more freedom than the years immediately following the Great Recession.

My mind always seems to be in the future. I have a difficult time articulating a fuzzy idea in the present.

I had to marry into humour, and my wife always makes me laugh. I had a poster near my desk that said, "If I could remember your name, I would ask you where I left my keys."

The Olympics

One highlight of our great years was the 2010 Olympic Games, which took place in Vancouver. Seven years earlier, our city had been named to host the event. This was a great guerrilla marketing opportunity for lululemon. I specifically wanted the creative brain of Eric Petersen to maximize on this local opportunity.

Like me, Eric had a very unorthodox and irreverent approach to marketing (exemplified in the Times Square demonstration). I told him I had questionable respect for the International Olympic Committee (IOC). I saw the IOC as an organization that had created a great athletic event, but who contradicted what they stood for with the acceptance of sponsorship money from corporations like Coca-Cola and McDonald's.

John Furlong, a long-time member of the Canadian Olympic Committee, was made the CEO of Vancouver's Organizing Committee (VANOC), which was set up shortly after the city won the bid. John is one of my heroes. I have never seen a person inspire a country and an organization to do so much with so little. Any time John calls me, I am at his service.

I ran into John in 2004 and told him that lululemon was going to put in a bid to provide clothing for the Canadian athletes.

I absolutely did not want to win the bid to sponsor the Canadian team. Sponsorship deals usually come with a lot of IOC regulations that restrict creative freedom. My goal was to let everyone know I would bid as a ploy to have Roots pay top dollar. This money would help VANOC stage a successful Games, and that success would ultimately benefit the City of Vancouver for years to come.

For thirty years, Roots Athletics had outfitted Canadian Olympic athletes, but creating high-performance technical clothing was way outside their wheelhouse. It just wasn't their core business, but they'd had a monopoly on providing clothing for our Olympians because no one else thought to compete for the rights. I figured that if lululemon put in a bid of $2 million, Roots would have to put in a higher bid to be an official clothing sponsor.

We put in our bid, but then the Hudson's Bay Company stepped in with an offer of their own . . . $100 million. This was both to outfit the Canadian athletes and become an official sponsor for three Olympic Games. Their exorbitant bid was one of the dumbest business decisions I'd ever seen. Just like all sponsorships I had experienced, I believed Canadian athletes would end up with mediocre-quality apparel and would have to pretend they liked it.

Laws were introduced to protect the Olympics' paying sponsors and give them special legal protection. Embargos were put on words like Vancouver, 2010, Olympics, Games, winter, gold, silver, bronze, sponsor, Whistler, and medals. The legislation making this special protection legal was supposedly intended to address "ambush marketing" (by which they meant attempts by businesses to associate themselves with the Olympics without becoming official sponsors).

We planned to navigate around the IOC rules and make fun of their seriousness. In December 2009, just two months before the opening ceremonies, lululemon avoided all embargoed words and called the apparel *"Global Sporting Event That Takes Place in British Columbia Between 2009 and 2011 Edition."*

We put the slogan on labels inside of a line of hooded sweatshirts, toques, and T-shirts, which came in combinations of colours representing Canada, the US, Germany, Norway, and Sweden—the countries we expected to have the most visitors at the Winter Games. We also included gold zippers on the Canadian hoodies.

VANOC couldn't ignore what we were doing because they had a legal obligation to protect the IOC sponsors, so they sent us some threatening letters. Despite the letters, VANOC couldn't do anything since we'd been so careful and smart about our wording. Their only real option was to express public disappointment in us.

Bill Cooper, director of VANOC's digital rights management, accused us of bad sportsmanship.[30] Cooper also plugged the "real" merchandise being sold by the Bay.[31]

That didn't matter to us. The uproar caused a lot of media attention, which was basically free advertising for lululemon. Break-even, innovative, controversial marketing won the day once again, and I couldn't have been happier.

Vertical Victory

There was no template for a vertical technical product. There was no how-to manual for lululemon's business model. We were winning because we were inventing daily. We got to leapfrog the retail industry because we didn't know what we shouldn't be doing.

Each day I walked into the office and asked myself, "If I had to compete against lululemon, what would I do?" This allowed me to cannibalize what was working today for what would be best for the future. I was fanatical about building a moat around our success.

We were also open and undefended about our weakness, and we coached each other whenever we found ourselves out of integrity or complaining. We enjoyed feedback because we wanted each other to succeed. This wasn't just internal—this

30. The Canadian Press, "Lululemon scolded for linking clothing line to Olympics," *CBC*, December 16, 2009, www.cbc.ca/news/lululemon-scolded-for-linking-clothing-line-to-olympics-1.843999.

31. Ibid.

was the culture we brought to our customers, which they then brought to their families and to the community. Through our ambassadors and community-building formula, we could see consistent proof of how we were elevating the world from mediocrity to greatness.

Lululemon was firing on all cylinders.

The Founder and the CEO

From 2008 to 2010, Christine and I worked very well together. It was like a great marriage, where each person appreciates the other's differences, synergy exists, and everyone wins. Christine was a pure operator who knew exactly what to put in place to handle our high growth and multiple store openings. I was the brand builder, innovator, and cultural founder. I knew where the market was going, and Christine knew how to build a solid chassis to get us there.

The financial crisis ended quickly. It ended even faster for lululemon because our business suffered only minimally. We'd maintained our status as a cash cow, and we kept to my mandate of no debt and lots of money in the bank. I wanted lots of money in the bank because I knew opportunities would present themselves, and with that money, we could move fast and stay ahead of future competition.

We continued the same incredible sales and profit numbers we had done since inception. We just had to keep doing more of what we were doing and hone our expertise. We were coming to the end of 2010 with no visible competition.

Our stock had climbed dramatically and our shares split. We were all living a utopic life. The Super Girl managers were driving the company. They cared, they had integrity, they were smart and responsible, and every decision they made was for the long game.

CHAPTER 24:
THE FOUNDER AND THE CEO, REVISITED

**Brand and culture are the same thing.
Both need to infiltrate all parts of the company.**

Missed Opportunities

Although we finished 2010 in a position of strength, success, and with "best in the world" business practises, the next seven years were going to be a time of significant change for lululemon. Sadly, this change would include many missed opportunities.

Much of this is the cautionary tale of how "not firing" a manipulative employee quickly led to directors acting in ways they would not have otherwise. To provide context, the following includes highlights from a paper called "Where Boards Fall Short," written by Dominic Barton and Mark Wiseman for *Harvard Business Review.* The reader is encouraged to read the entire paper.

"Boards aren't working," Barton and Wiseman tell us.[32] "It's been more than a decade since the first wave of post-Enron regulatory reforms, and despite a host of guidelines from independent watchdogs such as the International Corporate Governance Network, most boards aren't delivering on their core mission: providing strong oversight and strategic support for management's efforts to create long-term value."[33]

According to Barton and Wiseman, of some seven hundred directors surveyed, there are only a small percentage (34 percent) of directors who understand their companies' strategies; an even smaller percentage understand how their companies create value (22 percent).[34] With these shocking figures in mind, how can boards better serve the companies they lead. The answer, as Barton and Wiseman put it, isn't "good-governance box checking"—something I would see on lululemon's own board in the years to come.[35]

Barton and Wiseman suggest that it is crucial for everyone in a company to understand what a director's duty is. Legally, that duty consists of "loyalty (putting the company's interests ahead of your own) and prudence (applying proper care, skill, and diligence to business decisions)."[36] A director committed to his or her duty does not prioritize short-term financial gain above all else. Rather, the dutiful director should, if necessary, push management to bet on a "credible corporate strategy that will take years to bear fruit."[37]

Another key shortfall Barton and Wiseman observe is that

32. Dominic Wiseman and Mark Barton, "Where Boards Fall Short," *Harvard Business Review*, December 19, 2014, hbr.org/2015/01/where-boards-fall-short.

33. Ibid.

34. Ibid.

35. Ibid.

36. Ibid.

37. Ibid.

public boards don't do enough to attract the right expertise. "If you truly get the importance of thinking and acting long-term, you'll do whatever it takes to attract [expertise]."[38] Here was another failing I would see—the lululemon board of directors had no interest in finding the right people . . . or, more critically, planning for CEO succession.

The plan for lululemon, as Wiseman and Barton have demonstrated, should have been for our board to attract directors with deep, relevant experience, who also think long term. Unfortunately, this was not the case.

Moving My Desk

Our most important Operating Principle had always been "The store Educator is the most important person in the company." They deliver the technology and brand to the Guest. After the Educators, it was the managers, then the CEO, followed by the board, and the shareholders. As the founder, I was at the bottom of that list. If a company wants to deliver amazing value to the shareholder, I believe they must elevate the very people who drive the profits; in our case, the Educators.

One day, a strange thing happened. The board asked me to move my desk out of the design area. They explained this was so Christine could manage and be responsible for results without the messiness of dual direction and interference from me.

I agreed that this was the best next step. I did not want to be the excuse used to explain why management did not hit their numbers or collect their bonuses. I said I needed six months to find the right person to head Innovation— someone as finicky about apparel as I was, who had the same

38. Ibid.

love for small technical details. Probably someone with a background in technical outerwear.

Six months was not soon enough for Christine, so in late 2010 she hired Sheree Waterson as the head of product. I liked Sheree, but she approached design primarily from a fashion viewpoint. I thought maybe she just needed time to prove herself.

In addition to hiring Sheree, Christine also hired consulting companies to look at the way we designed and brought a product to market. These consultants had never seen a technical vertical retailer, and by bringing them in, we essentially paid $2 million to educate *them* on *our* business. The consultants recommended we adhere to "best in practice" operations set out by wholesale companies. I never understood the point of this contract, but I do know that it slowly started to unravel our "best in the world" business practices.

These same consultants soon came out with an "expert paper" telling the world how vertical retailing worked. It was disheartening to me that we had opened our kimono to a group of consultants who would go on to invoice our competitors as they taught them our business model. I thought I was the ultimate consultant, but our directors believed better processes, information, and validation was possible from East Coast apparel consultants who were experts in fashion wholesaling.

The Harvard Business Case

Around that same time, Christine had asked me if Harvard Business School could come in and do a case study on lululemon. She told me they wanted to document lululemon's history, and since we'd never had the time to do so, it seemed like a win-win, and I agreed.

Harvard professors looked at our stores, our past performance, and our history. I took them up the Grouse Grind and answered interview questions about the transition between Bob Meers and Christine Day. That was the extent of my part, and after it was done, I didn't give it much thought.

The business case was published in December 2010 as a series of twenty or so videos, each maybe three or four minutes long, designed to be presented in business school classes.

My heart sunk when I looked at the published business case. The videos gave away 50 percent of our unique culture and business practices, our successful formula, and our operating principles.

Further, the videos were done in the context of Christine arriving at the company in 2008, at the worst of the recession, and fixing everything. Christine was quoted as saying: "The whole organization slowed down . . . because people weren't aligned."[39]

This wasn't a fair or accurate depiction of how things had been going before Christine had arrived at lululemon, or the successes we'd experienced *despite* the recession. In reality, the financial crisis was a positive. It gave us the opportunity to slow our growth, get our feet under us, and create a super solid foundation.

Once that foundation was in place, all we needed to do was open more stores while sticking to our successful formula. Any good operator could do this. Suddenly, the whole case study seemed a brand-building exercise for Christine herself . . . one that could've arguably cost lululemon billions of dollars as our successful formula was handed to the competition.

I wondered how I could have been so short-sighted as not to ensure that I got the final say on the history of lululemon.

39. Michael Tushman, Ruth Page, and Tom Ryder, "Leadership, Culture, and Transition at Lululemon, Multimedia Case," *Harvard Business Review*, hbsp.harvard.edu/product/410705-HTM-ENG.

He who wins the war writes the truth, and the truth that Harvard got was wrong.

I went to Harvard to present my issues with the case study, and they were receptive to my concerns. They were embarrassed by the inaccuracies, so they let me record two additional videos to set the record straight (having said that, I saw the case study presented in Vancouver in 2016, and the new videos were *not* included).

The people at Harvard explained that they'd needed a senior executive at lululemon to sign off on the case study. Christine was the person who'd signed off.

Trimming Expenses, Raising Prices

Christine was adding value to lululemon's stock by trimming expenses and testing the upper limits of what we could charge for our product. I believed this created "bad profit." Our hedgehog, as you may recall, was to have the best black stretch athletic pants. The company priority was changing incrementally to became about quarterly expectations set by the public stock analysts.

For the first time, I wasn't entirely sure Christine and I were pulling in the same direction. It seemed we were cutting costs and increasing prices for the wrong reasons.

As a long-term shareholder, I believed all we had to do to keep our "first in market" advantage was to continually increase quality and keep prices low enough to make it uneconomical for competitors. Our vertical model was unbeatable. We would become a mediocre company only if our quality failed or we increased prices too much. If we increased prices, competitors would enter the market, take market share, and we would make less money.

Advent had sold down their position and needed to attend to other investments. In their parting words, Advent implored lululemon to pursue international as soon as possible. They said we needed to be first in market with our global product. We had invented the break-even showroom/pop-up concept, and we could softly enter Europe and Asia. This would have meant an investment now for future growth with no projected return for at least five years. This was not good for short-term financial reporting.

Gap Athleta, Nike, and Under Armour

In 2010, I believed we owned streetnic (athleisurewear), even with other brands circling in on what we were doing. The Gap was floundering, but it made a great move by buying the infant online competitor Athleta in 2008 for $150 million and adding bricks and mortar stores to build out the Athleta brand.

Athleta didn't concern me as I saw them as a Microsoft compared to our Apple. Lululemon and Apple had that unde-niable, unquantifiable cool factor in their designs, technology, product, and branding.

I didn't mind having Athleta in the market. The Gap was a merchandiser-lead business where decisions were made based on past spreadsheet numbers rather than instant customer feedback. I knew spreadsheets and algorithms showed a big opening in the market. The older women's market was under-served, and Athleta took this position. I knew their consumer was not iconic as a brand driver, and, in my opinion, Athleta would never be a market leader.

In general, I observed that older women preferred looser clothing and were typically larger in size. This meant a 30 to 40 percent increase in fabric with far less profit than lululemon.

There were also the wholesalers Nike and Under Armour to consider. As of 2010, Nike was a footwear company trying to understand apparel, and Under Armour was still making garments with big logos for impressionable teenage boys and insecure men. I knew wholesalers would be very good competitors if they could use their model to produce huge volume and low margin (think of the McDonald's hamburger model). Huge volumes meant they could take away production space from lululemon's fabric and mill suppliers.

For a brief period, I even considered *buying* Under Armour.

For a few years after our IPO, lululemon was worth about twice as much as Under Armour, maybe even three times as much. About 85 percent of our sales went to a female market. Under Armour, meanwhile, was almost all male and did not appeal to the female market. Had we been able to take the Under Armour male brand and market it through the lululemon business philosophy, the result would have been a formidable opponent to Nike.

However, after a meeting with Under Armour CEO Kevin Plank in 2008, I couldn't see Kevin's macho philosophy working with that of the Super Girls. Lululemon stood for soft, rounded edges. We stood for yoga, mindfulness, and for everybody winning. Under Armour, I thought, had an in-your-face image of winning at all costs, male chauvinism, and leaving everybody else in the dust. With those things in mind, I did not pursue the thought of a merger.

In any case, I didn't see Nike or Under Armour as a major concern for the moment, as the expense of developing and running apparel retail stores was not in our competitors' area of expertise.

As 2010 ended, I was thinking more about traditional media advertising than ever before—just because we hadn't advertised in the past didn't mean we shouldn't do so in the future, especially with the changing horizon. Lululemon was still an *underground* brand, known mainly to its customers and employees (and competitors), but not as well known to the world.

If Nike used its worldwide network, it would appear to Asians or Europeans that Nike was first in the market. I thought lululemon needed to build 300 to 400 small break-even community pop-up stores around the world and/or start buying traditional media to inexpensively put our stake in the ground and flex our global e-commerce muscle. We had perfected the pop-up model; all we had to do was put it into action.

Anna Wintour and Jacques Levy

Around that time, Summer and I had a meeting with Anna Wintour from *Vogue* magazine at her office in New York. We were introduced by our director, Brad Martin, the former CEO of Saks. We tried to paint a picture for her of how West Coast technical athletic apparel was starting to dominate fashion.

To provide a couture-related context, I asked Anna to imagine a future where wedding dresses would be made with stretch fabrics and have silver threads for anti-microbial stink control and mesh venting for breathability.

More and more, people were demanding the comfort and functionality of athletic wear in everything they wore, but the fashion scene hadn't yet caught on to this paradigm shift. The fashion scene had always had a very cyclical relationship with itself—the same designers were covered by the same journalists with the same advertisers, year after year.

For the last twelve years, I'd purposely pushed all fashion conversation out of the lululemon dialogue. That meant we were still a mystery to fashion experts.

During our meeting, Anna rightly stated that the mass consumer knew nothing about lululemon and that our success existed only in our own mind.

We needed to advertise in a big, big way, Anna told me.

People needed to know about lululemon before multiple competitors could water down the idea that lululemon had invented a movement—before they could make us just one of many. I'd seen this exact same thing happen in the surf, skate, and snowboard industry, when the market became oversaturated. I wanted lululemon to be known as the inventor of the streetnic business, and I wanted us to be recognized globally. I knew old-school media would attract thousands of unpaid editorials and result in exponential future sales.

There was a little part of me that wondered if Anna was just trying to sell advertising space in *Vogue*, but I had no problem agreeing with her premise, and I couldn't deny the point she'd made.

Then, in early 2011, a man named Jacques Levy joined our board of directors. Jacques had served as CEO of Sephora and had twenty-five years' experience in the high-end retail industry. Unfortunately, Jacques would not be with us long—he lost his battle with cancer less than a year after he joined our board—but in the time we had him, he repeated what I'd heard from Anna: lululemon needed to advertise and bring our message to the masses.

As I mentioned earlier in the book, a personal mandate of mine holds that when I hear something three times, I must do it—almost as if hearing something three times is a sign. Hearing about big advertising first from Anna, then from Jacques, then more and more from my own subconscious as I considered the changing market, prompted me to act. I approached our CEO and board of directors and told them the authentic community way our brand was built had worked for a long time, but we now had to double down. We needed to continue our community branding, but also advertise in a big way. The rest of the world needed to know who we were. We needed to invest now so we could own the future.

The Fearful Board

Grassroots networking and word-of-mouth promotion had worked for lululemon for ten years. Not only had it worked, but it had also contributed to the company's unprecedented success. But I couldn't convince the board to continue widening the moat around our stronghold.

I could not prove advertising would work. This was the second inkling I had that something was wrong. I had always done well at knowing the right time to venture into something new for the future of the company.

Lululemon had a strong board and CEO. It was the perfect combination as far as share ownership and distribution went. I owned 30 percent and $2 billion of the stock. My 30 percent represented the company's voice for brand, vision, and innovation on the board. The other board members represented audit, compensation, governance . . . or in Christine's position, operations.

Michael Casey, the lead independent director, delivered the message: If I couldn't prove the unknown future, then my advertising idea had zero validity.

I sensed something very amiss. I knew lululemon had a financial wizard in Michael Casey as the lead independent director. I also knew he believed his job was to secure the money lululemon had in the bank whereas I wanted to use the free cash to make money for our shareholders. I was okay with Michael being fearful and cautious, as that's what the company needed to balance out the board's diversity. But I wondered if the board was truly diverse.

It occurred to me that the combination of a security-driven lead director and a CEO-operator was not synergistic for the company. I believe the decision to *not* step up advertising cost lululemon $5 billion in market value over the next five years.

Who is John Galt?

Lululemon might not have been investing in big advertising, but that didn't mean we couldn't ask the world one compelling question: "Who is John Galt?"

John Galt was an idea I raised at a creative meeting with twelve people and our CEO, Christine Day, in early 2011. The focus of the meeting was to up the ante on lululemon's shopping bags. The bags had successfully displayed our manifesto for many years, but perhaps the time had come to think of something new.

I'd read *Atlas Shrugged* when I was nineteen and working on the pipeline, but I'd also reread it when I was fifty. It was as I reread the book all those years later that I recognized how much influence the book had had on my life. I'd absorbed the characters' uncompromising quest to make a quality product, their love of their employees, their passion, and their refusal to make money off the backs of other people. I was fascinated by the convergence of both self-interest and providing for the world.

Not long before this creative meeting, Christine and I had done a joint interview. We laughed during the interview because we both said the one person we would want to have dinner with was the author Ayn Rand.

At the meeting in 2011, I mentioned that *Atlas Shrugged* had been an important book for me in laying the foundations of lululemon's culture. I thought this book represented the perfect Super Girl philosophy.

I proposed we might allude to *Atlas*'s influence on our iconic bags. I loved subtle branding. Only highly educated, well-read people and Super Girls would understand if we put "Who is John Galt?" on the side of our bags. This was the kind of marketing no other company would think of doing. The brand team agreed.

A 1991 poll by the Library of Congress and Book of the Month Club found that *Atlas Shrugged* was the second most influential book after the Bible. Another poll conducted in 2007 found that 8.1 percent of adult Americans had read it. Almost none of the young women who worked for us had read it or even heard of it. This was surprising because if there was anywhere a woman was to look for inspiration to be great in business, it was in protagonist Dagny Taggart.

Christine loved the idea of putting the John Galt question on our bags. A few months later, the new bags came into circulation in all of our stores. I thought of this as both a branding strategy and a way to start a philosophical conversation. It would also help us to solidify the people who "got it" as our core customers.

To supplement the bag's release, we added this explanation to our community blog: "Many of us choose mediocrity without even realizing it. Why do we do this? Because our society encourages mediocrity. It is easier to be mediocre than to be great. Our bags are visual reminders for ourselves to live a life we love and conquer the epidemic of mediocrity. We all have a John Galt inside of us, cheering us on."

Although I loved Rand's work, I did not realize how politically divisive she was in the United States. With the 2012 US election on the horizon, right-wing political factions were using *Atlas Shrugged* as a touchstone. This gave the left wing (who I am sure had not read it) all the reason to hate the book, as well as the rest of Rand's work. Many people seemed to think there was an incongruity between a brand influenced by yoga and Rand's objectivism.

I didn't see it that way. Lululemon's philosophy is about

building people up, influencing everyone around you to be great, and elevating the world. *Atlas's* Dagny Taggart is a driven, professional female in her thirties—someone in whom lululemon's ideal customer might see herself reflected.

I also noticed that the loudest complaints seemed to come from people who were not striving for greatness or fighting to do something extraordinary. These people were the antithesis of our iconic customer.

To build a brand, our CEO and directors needed to understand that strong resistance on social media from non-customers actually creates real brand value. Core customers don't want to be lumped in with the loud naysayers, so their loyalty only increases.

Meanwhile, the media had a wide swath of analyses of the bag. The *Globe and Mail* acknowledged the "lively conversation" the bag had stirred up, while *Slate* and *Forbes* pointed out Ayn Rand's status as a Tea Party heroine.[40]

Overall, I was happy with the chatter, but this was also the beginning of social media. Suddenly, anyone with a computer was an expert on any given subject. Endless political debate aside, we were doing something right. We'd sparked a conversation, and we were marketing our brand in our unique way.

Many of our directors did not understand our unique branding. Our branding emanated from my experience in the

40. Simon Houpt, "Lululemon's Ayn Rand Bag Irks Some (Others Shrugged)," *The Globe and Mail*, November 15, 2018, updated, May 8, 2018, www.theglobeandmail.com/report-on-business/industry-news/marketing/lululemons-ayn-rand-bag-irks-some-others-shrugged/article4200710/; Molly Worthen, "Who Is John Galt and Why Is He on Lululemon Bags?" *Slate*, November 18, 2011, http://www.slate.com/articles/double_x/doublex/2011/11/ayn_rand_groupies_yoga_enthusiasts_and_the_american_genius_for_self_absorption_.html; Todd Essig, "Occupy Your Yoga Pants: Lululemon's Toxic Mix of Commerce and Ideology," *Forbes*, November 21, 2011, https://www.forbes.com/sites/toddessig/2011/11/21/occupy-your-yoga-pants-lululemons-toxic-mix-of-commerce-and-ideology/#611893935848.

surf, skate, and snowboard industry where brands were created by being antiestablishment. This created a "tribe" who then created a social movement that others wanted to emulate (this is not really different from the luxury company whose advertised tribe is jet-setting models whose lives are unattainable by 99 percent of their customers). These are the subtleties of how word-of-mouth branding works, as described in the book *The Tipping Point*.[41]

Christine's reaction to this was nothing but weird.

In the board meeting, in front of the directors, Christine told the board she had never seen the shopping bags and had never given approval. The idea that Christine didn't know was unthinkable. I had to take time to check in with myself to ensure I had not made up a story.

I thought it best to talk to the brand team to be sure I wasn't going crazy.

When I brought up Christine's position to lead director Michael Casey, I could sense he didn't believe me. The scenario was bizarre, and so, I thought the whole thing must be a crazy one-off. My integrity took a hit, and the John Galt bags were removed from the stores.

In my opinion, that recall was damaging to our brand because our Super Girls could sense weakness in our stand for greatness. The people from the creative meeting wondered why I didn't stand up for them and why Christine had thrown us all under the bus. I couldn't explain myself.

Christine stood firm in her story and was rewarded with accolades for managing a stable company and a wildcard founder. It seemed the love for a rising stock value compelled the board to err on the side of caution. She went on to tell the media the same story she'd told the board. She maintained that she had no oversight or agreement on the production of the shopping bags over the next several months.

41. Malcolm Gladwell, *The Tipping Point* (2000).

In seeing this, the culture at lululemon changed immediately. The company culture shifted to one where people wanted nothing more than to look good, protect their asses, and embrace mediocrity. Christine had ensured that the employees had no direct access to the directors and the directors were determined not to interfere or examine such things under the guise of good. I was speaking for the employees at the board level, but I sensed I had lost influence.

The culture of integrity was being abused at the highest level.

Jayna Murray

In the middle of an already uniquely challenging year, tragedy struck in one of our US stores. On March 12, 2011, just after 8 a.m., police arrived at our location on Bethesda Row in Bethesda, Maryland. There they found Jayna Murray brutally murdered. Another employee, Brittany Norwood, was still alive after having survived an apparent robbery-turned-homicide.

As the day wore on, Brittany told police that two masked men had broken in, sexually assaulted her, and killed Jayna in a horrific way. It was a terrible thing to happen anywhere, but it hit even harder because it was in one of our stores. This murder was like a home invasion, striking where our employees felt safe.

I had met Jayna just a few months prior to her death. She was a wonderful and authentic person. She was laid to rest in her home state of Texas a week after her murder. I attended the funeral. As a father, I simply could not imagine the anguish and heartbreak her parents were experiencing.

Over the next several days, I thought about how we would get our employees through this seemingly random act of violence perpetrated by men. Fear had rippled through the entire lululemon family. Everything we did at lululemon was about making employees feel powerful, self-motivated, and part of a community. We contributed to the reward offered to find the two assailants, hoping their arrest would be a first step toward understanding what had happened.

A few days later, the story took a strange turn. Police arrested Brittany, accusing her of having committed Jayna's murder and then staging an elaborate cover-up. It emerged that Brittany had been stealing from the store, something Jayna had discovered. Brittany had previously worked at another lululemon store where she'd also been suspected of stealing. No theft had ever been proven, and, as there were no definite grounds for her dismissal, the legal system would have interminably tied us up in litigation had we fired her.

Instead, Brittany was moved to a store where her actions could be better monitored. On the night of the murder, Jayna confronted Brittany with definitive proof that she'd been stealing, and the confrontation turned violent.

I asked myself if there was anything lululemon could have done differently to prevent this. We'd put cash-counting procedures in place and had policies to ensure there were at least two people present. We'd implemented systems to ensure the security and safety of our staff. I just couldn't understand how something like this had happened.

Three and a half months after the murder, the Bethesda store reopened, embracing and showcasing a theme of love in Jayna's memory. Later that fall, Brittany Norwood's trial lasted six days before she was found guilty of first-degree murder. The jury deliberated for less than an hour. She was sentenced to life in prison.

CHAPTER 25:
FRICTION WITH THE BOARD

Those with the most knowledge are the ones who feel they know the least.

By 2011 I knew we were at the start of an exponential change in the way the world dressed. In the early days of pre-Nike, Phil Knight went to Tiger in Japan and marketed America as being a billion-dollar market in running shoes. He was laughed at by anyone who he told this to. Visionaries can see the future before it arises because they are so deep in the subject matter and can see precursors of a trend. I started to understand the technical streetwear market could reach $500 billion inside of the next decade. With competition beginning to circle, we needed to think strategically to stay on top.

No Expansion Permitted

In lululemon's early days, we'd owned 50 percent of our main apparel factory through my partnership with Frankie and Elky Hon. We could rapidly change production to meet immediate needs and style changes, and we were able to cut certain costs out of our supply chain.

The Hons were creative, smart, and diligent. When I negotiated pricing with them, we would look at the market together and determine at what price we needed to sell our product to maximize the volume while still making the best margin.

Further, and maybe most importantly, lululemon's 50 percent ownership of Charter Link cut out our competitors from using the factory. With the changing market landscape and competitors rearing their heads, I revisited manufacturing as a strategic asset.

I knew Taiwan had the three largest technical fabric mills in the world. Of these three, Eclat Textile out of Taiwan was the most innovative and our best supplier. Eclat also happened to be publicly traded. If we applied some of our billion-dollar cash reserve to buy a 50 percent stake in Eclat, we could do at a world scale what I had built with the Hons. If that worked, we could partner with the other two big mills and dig a huge new moat around the production of technical fabric.

Once again, the idea fell flat with the board. Billion-dollar investments in factories and mills were not our core business. Besides, they said, they'd seen nothing yet to indicate any serious competition from other brands.

I was deeply frustrated with my own inability to communicate my experience and expertise to the board. I thought smart, successful directors understood that lululemon made its money from being vertical.

Owning our manufacturing as a way to widen our moat was off the table. I thought about diversifying our product line to keep us ahead of the curve. Nike had recently added apparel to their shoe business, and Under Armour was adding shoes to their apparel line.

For a time, I'd considered entering the footwear market to supplement our own product line. But lululemon had grown so quickly that all our efforts were directed at keeping up with the production of our core products.

The best time to diversify, I thought, was two years before yoga apparel became widespread, when there was still a little breathing room. We were not quite at that point in 2011, but would be soon. The worst thing a company can do is to start planning when the need is already there—a company must invest prior to demand.

I also had reservations about footwear. Running shoes had an odor—rubber, plastic, glue, and leather—that evoked old-school, male-centric sporting goods stores. The shoe smell made me picture industrial light fixtures and dirty sports stores' change rooms that only men found acceptable. This was the opposite of the beautiful design and atmosphere of our lululemon stores, which we'd designed specifically to welcome and appeal to female Guests.

Chemical odor aside, Nike had always done a hell of a job designing and producing footwear and had eradicated the toxic glue smell in shoes. For lululemon to compete in the shoe market, we would have to develop new technology and get ahead of Nike in what they did best. It seemed like a broad, uncertain gamble when most of lululemon's efforts were directed at keeping up with apparel production. Shoes also had the opposite store layout of apparel. Shoes have 30 percent of the retail store up front and 70 percent warehousing in the back, whereas apparel is the reverse.

With e-commerce, I knew we could market shoes to try on in the store and then ship directly to people's homes. This had not been done yet, but we had enough stores to make this business model work. All we had to do was wait until we could identify a shoe technology that would position lululemon as an innovator.

My theory was to own yoga in the eyes of the world. Once we owned this slice of the athletic pie, the customer would give us the right to venture into other areas. Because the Vancouver yogi was also a 10k runner, running apparel was a natural fit.

In 2008, the only female running short was something our design team called the Nike diaper short. This short met the Midwest sensibilities of Americans, but it wasn't attractive. I wanted to create running shorts with a waistband that mimicked my wife's yoga pant design, so I shared my vision with one of the best designers I knew, Shannon Savage. Shannon created an iconic style. The only additions I made were the bar tacks along the back venting, so we could create an industrial trademark to own the look forever.

There was also outerwear, including winter jackets and other seasonally specific apparel, for lululemon to consider. From my days of making outerwear with Westbeach, I considered myself an expert in the field. I knew our business model was perfect for mountain survival apparel. But I didn't like where global warming was heading, and it seemed outerwear was always on discount. I hated discounting.

Global climate change meant one coast was too hot and one was too cold well into December. If the heavily populated East Coast was warm, 30 to 40 percent of seasonal inventory would be unsellable. I decided lululemon was to be the best in the world at mid-layer clothing that could sell from fall to late spring.

What I called Après Yoga, or clothing to get to and from a sweaty endeavor, was a big gap in the market that we could own. Instead of diversifying our line into footwear or outerwear, I strongly felt our focus needed to be on continued design and innovation of our core products.

Unless we redefined lululemon as something other than a yoga company.

Meditation as a Blank Canvas

Through my years as an entrepreneur, especially through the different sports of the surf, skate, and snowboard apparel industry, I'd seen a tendency of crests and descents. Westbeach, like many businesses, had always crested and descended, crested and descended, repeatedly, like a wave pattern, with no real change. The question now was how much this applied to lululemon.

Evolution is crucial to a company's success. Enhancing and evolving the brand by being the future is key, because riding into the commodity market with hundreds of competitors is my definition of failure. It can even lead to eventual bankruptcy or buyout.

I loved the business model of the workout studio where I took my first yoga class. Ron Zalko wasn't one to sit on his butt. He was always evolving, and he was the first with every new fitness trend in Vancouver. He said you shouldn't be stuck in your ways just because they work.

When you're moving forward and ahead of a trend, you can become the coolest gym in town, keep your customers, and charge a higher premium. The coolest, most athletic people want to be in the future right now.

A renewed, refreshed customer response drives your product for the rest of the world.

This made me wonder how lululemon could evolve. My recurring strategy was to take myself out of the competition altogether. I hated how the commodity market revolved around low-paid, uninvolved employees. I knew it didn't fit into our business model. Commodity is a boring business that requires uncreative bureaucrats to run it.

It occurred to me that lululemon might evolve by finding another way to create new meaning, but I needed to determine what that meaning might be. I found the answer in my life as a swimmer, in the lululemon manifesto, in Dad's meditation practice, and in lululemon's yoga roots.

I thought back to 2009, when I was navigating the combined demands of lululemon's meteoric growth. I was working ten hours a day, and exercising two to three hours a day, while being the best husband and father I could. The only time my mind could truly shut down, and become mindful of nothing more than the present moment—was when I was peeing.

I would shut off my phone, go into the bathroom, close my eyes, and find a mental black dot while I did my business. I'd float through that black dot for about sixty seconds, existing in nothing. Coming out of the bathroom, I felt great. It was like I'd rebooted the hard drive of my mind—off and back on again, to realign everything and run more efficiently.

With millennials in particular, I saw the value that mindfulness might add to their lives. Millennials could not see the water in which they were swimming. They had never experienced a digital-free context and held multitasking as a skill to build and be proud of. The lululemon manifesto says, "The mind can only hold one thought at a time." Without the right tools to keep them grounded, I feared millennials would push themselves off the edge.

I wondered if lululemon could own meditation as a concept. Could we bring it to the world, be authentic about it, and invite a generation of people to create new meaning in their lives through our brand?

This wasn't about abandoning yoga or our core products. It was about moving to where the puck was going before it got there. If I could get lululemon to own mindfulness—a concept solidly in line with yoga—I knew our ability to maintain an aura around our brand would continue. We would build a wider moat around the competition and provide superior branding.

I knew I had a wall to climb. At Westbeach, the internal resistance to transform the company from surf and skate into snowboarding had been overwhelming. When I started lululemon, everyone over the age of thirty thought yoga apparel was dumb, but nobody could deny what happened next.

If we could add mindfulness into people's lives with the same success that I'd had with surf, skate, snowboard, and yoga, it seemed we could add between $5 and $10 billion to our market cap before 2015.

It might take a few years to bear fruit, but we needed to prepare for the future. Otherwise, a brand that is not generating new concepts will eventually consume itself.

Even beyond the business opportunities mindfulness offered, mindfulness itself represented to me the final frontier of personal development. Consider this: a runner's high, which occurs after thirty-five minutes of aerobic activity, floods the mind with dopamine. Dopamine locks us into the present by eliminating our past from our thoughts.

As time went on, some athletes realized they did not have to get a dopamine hit from athletics to be present. The runner's high could be achieved by simply choosing to be in the moment. Choosing the present became known as mindfulness. If we understand this, we can choose to be mindful a thousand times a day.

I had a board that was naturally risk resistant and my reputation was now undermined by my CEO, but I remained optimistic. I thought my track record would speak for itself in this case.

In November 2011, I took my proposal to the board. I suggested opening our stores at 9:50 a.m. instead of 10:00 a.m. and inviting customers to come in early and join our employees for a ten-minute, guided meditation session. We might open mindfulness studios in the future, but at that time, all we needed was ten extra minutes in our stores every morning.

From a financial perspective, there would be a small advertising cost to get the word out. There would be the added expenses of having our 300 stores open ten minutes earlier. We would also need to bring in mindfulness teachers and experts to introduce the training, at least until our staff could master the work of being mindfulness leaders.

I calculated an expenditure of $800,000 to be included in the 2012 budget—a modest number, given lululemon's revenue—to get the ownership of mindfulness underway. I proposed a launch date of four months out. I tried to provide some metrics to support my proposal, but there's not much supporting data for any new idea. Fear of an unknown future seemed to freeze the directors. If there were detailed metrics available, that would have meant mindfulness had already arrived on the market, and anything we did with mindfulness would come far too late. I wanted to be ahead of the market.

Once again, the board erred on the side of caution. They pared my request down to $250,000—far too little to provide critical mass for the project to be successful. The board just did not want to spend any money to invest in the business. Once again, Michael Casey made sure the message was clear— lululemon would play it safe and protect the money in the bank.

As the illustrious entrepreneur and author Peter Diamandis said, "The day before something is a breakthrough, it's a crazy idea." If an idea could be quantified, it would have been done already. No one wants to change. Change is hard. But change is the only constant, and today the rate of change is faster than ever. The board may not have meant any harm by their unwillingness to be anything beyond mediocre, but the end result had lasting harmful effects.

The important insight is the directors with a limited mindset who vetoed mindfulness are the exact same directors who would not have invested in yoga apparel. Also, no amount of market research would have told investors the Sony Walkman would have been as successful as it was.

I am reminded of Queen's proposition to bring a seven-minute song called "Bohemian Rhapsody" to the radio, and the old producer that could not see the possibility.

I was beginning to feel uncertain about my role. The board rejected my proposals out of hand. They were making financial decisions outside of the integrity and culture that defined what I felt were the best parts of who we were. They put less money into quality while at the same time increased product prices just because we could. It seemed to me the board was selling our future for instant gratification. They were weakening our foundation while building sandcastles to meet Wall Street's expectations.

We had nine very smart directors who met four times each year. They all continued telling me everything was perfectly fine. "You don't know how a big company operates," they told me. Meanwhile, they applied all the practices beloved by the competition lululemon had spent years crushing. Our unique culture and approach was no longer unique. As 2011 ended, lululemon's stock value kept rising even as we set ourselves up for unsustainability and failure.

Looking back on it, it's interesting to see the way mindfulness exploded. Now, you can subscribe to many online meditation tools. Companies such as Google, General Mills, Target, Virgin, and Intel have all invested heavily in internal mindfulness training for their employees. I know lululemon could have been the iconic leader of this next social movement, which in turn, could have doubled the company's value.

I remember a story of how, in the '70s, Detroit automotive executives took the same road to work every day, and everywhere they looked they saw Detroit cars and concluded business was great. If they had taken a different route to work, through California, for example, they would have seen small, economy-sized Japanese cars starting to appear—cars that would take hundreds of billions of dollars in value away from the Detroit companies.

As 2011 ended, it occurred to me that lululemon's stock

value was rising at the expense of serious reinvestment in the company itself.

My concerns about quality were very difficult to articulate to the board of directors, but I'd spent every day for thirty years (between my time at lululemon and Westbeach) feeling our fabrics, looking at them, stretching them, and inspecting the stitching. Tiny, almost unnoticeable errors to a layman were huge indicators of trouble to me.

Over time, those tiny flaws would accumulate. With no deliberate reinvestment in quality control, lululemon had few employees who could raise a red quality control flag without being fired by Christine.

Our new head of product started meetings late and was not open to coaching about the ramifications of integrity. By consistently being late, she indicated to the entire company that it was acceptable to be late. So much for leading by example. Most meetings started ten to twenty minutes late, while the ten to twenty people who arrived on time sat around waiting. My theory was that if a design meeting started late, then the employees subconsciously believed the thousands of intermediate steps to get product to the stores, could in turn also be late. If delivery to the stores is late, the product doesn't have enough selling days that season and styles must then go on sale to move excess inventory.

Each $1 of sale discount removes $10 from the company's market capitalization. Companies that consistently discount product attract employees of lesser quality and incur higher employee turnover. Higher turnover means higher human resource expenses, training costs, and management issues. Higher turnover results in fewer available people to develop for the management pipeline. This is how integrity works. It's why meetings must start on time.

The Soda Story

Staff at lululemon had always practiced what they'd preached. Nowhere was this truer than in our long-standing manifesto, especially the part about how Coke and Pepsi, and all other soda pops, would be the cigarettes of the future. Lululemon— whether at the Store Support Centre or out at the retail locations—had never been a workplace where you'd see people drinking soda pop or eating junk food—until recently.

In late 2012, Deanne, Delaney, and I went with Christine to Whistler to spend a few days away from the office to examine and discuss lululemon's culture and future. We took Susanne Conrad—our outside development consultant— with us.

While in Whistler, the five of us had lengthy discussions about lululemon, the changes it had undergone in the past few years, and what we thought lay ahead for us. One evening, the subject of seeing Coke and Pepsi cans around the office came up. We discussed what we could do about it, how we could get ourselves back to our core culture.

Seeing cans of pop on people's desks seemed to coincide with the arrival of American middle management. I wasn't the only one who'd noticed it—both Deanne and Delaney had seen it, too. On its own, this may seem like a small issue, but it was fundamental to lululemon's health culture. We were all concerned about the edges fraying.

The answer we came up with seemed straightforward—we would just put the Coke and Pepsi part back in the manifesto. The manifesto was lululemon's guiding light.

However, as Christine told us that night in Whistler, we *couldn't* put the slogan back in the manifesto—we'd signed a binding agreement with PepsiCo, she said, not to disparage them any further.

This surprised me. I knew nothing of that agreement. I

asked Christine if she was sure it existed. She assured me it did. When I got back to Vancouver a few days later, I asked Erin Nichols in our legal department for a copy of the agreement, so I could read the specific clauses. Erin told me no such agreement existed. Later that afternoon, Michael Casey called me, telling me just to drop the whole thing.

Former director of finance, Michelle Armstrong, recalls: "Something happened where all of a sudden there was a competition between Chip and Christine. There wasn't room for both in Christine's mind. It just went downhill from there. I saw some things they disagreed over, and I thought, 'Why would she think that? The guy came up with the idea for the whole company.'"

Further Dishonesty

After the Pepsi agreement and John Galt lies, lululemon became all I did not want it to be. Integrity meant little and fear ruled the roost.

At this point I had zero trust in Michael Casey and Christine Day. I felt a need to be responsible to the shareholders, and I began to consider what had to be done.

Widening Her Own Moat

As the relationship between us deteriorated, I noticed that Christine had begun taking steps to protect her position and the power that she held within lululemon.

For example, the succession pipeline for managers was a cornerstone of lululemon's survival because of Canada's twelve-to-eighteen-month maternity leave laws. Both the maternity leave turnover in a female-dominated company and lululemon's exponential growth demanded it. We had a deeply qualified group of women who had started with the company in the early days, ready to move up as growth required. Their careers had skyrocketed early but were now stalling at the middle management stage.

I thought again of *Good to Great*, and many of Jim Collins's other writings, which underpinned lululemon's foundation from day one. Among Collins's ideas is the concept of the "Level 5 leader" who builds enduring greatness through personal humility and professional will.

In Collins's hierarchy, there are four subordinate leaders:

1. The highly effective individual
2. The contributing team member
3. The competent manager
4. The effective leader

Without the Level 5 leader in the executive position, a company cannot be transformed from good to great. A key distinction of the Level 5 leader is someone who selects, trains, and prepares their eventual successor, ensuring the company will continue to grow and succeed into the future.

I could see that with the exception of Delaney Schweitzer, we had stopped developing Level 3 women for Level 4. We had to have those highly effective senior managers next in line for executive positions.

Christine had hired people into the senior management positions, but they seemed mediocre at best. As Deanne Schweitzer said, "Christine surrounded herself with a core management team composed of older, non-athletic power women instead of Super Girls." Why? I wondered. Lululemon was the iconic public company at the time. Lululemon could have hired the best from anywhere.

Christine's senior-manager hires did not appear to be interested in training their own successors, so a whole generation of Super Girls who'd grown lululemon and formed its backbone were unable to grow. For the time being, there was no position higher than the mid-level management positions they'd already achieved. It seemed Christine's Level 4 managers were killing both the advancement opportunities for the Super Girls and the company itself.

This constrained our Super Girls with golden handcuffs. They were now thirty-five years old with mortgages and kids attending private schools. Vancouver didn't have enough companies that paid what lululemon did. If they quit, where would they go? Once somebody has lived in Vancouver, they aren't willing to leave.

I wondered if Christine had been deliberate about this—if she'd wanted to put a barrier between herself and the next generation of lululemon's leaders. Possibly, Christine was ensuring she would have no direct competition for the CEO position for the foreseeable future.

In 2010, I was clear with the board that Christine should name and develop someone under her to take over should she get hit by a bus or quit. Christine deferred for a year. She was allowed to do this because Michael Casey, chair of the nominating and governance committee, was just a weak person. He didn't push her. Finally, the board, to their credit, later nominated Delaney Schweitzer to be interim CEO should Christine be hit by the proverbial bus.

We did have two excellent people in senior management. One was Kathryn Henry, who had come from a senior position with Gap Inc. and was hired in 2010 as our chief information officer. Within the first few months Kathryn worked for us, she'd turned lululemon's entire IT infrastructure around.

The second person was Delaney Schweitzer, who had worked her way from the bottom to the top at lululemon. Delaney started off as one of our first store managers and worked her way up to become EVP, global retail. In that capacity, Delaney ran all retail operations, e-commerce, store culture, basically anything that made money.

When I made it clear with the board that Christine should name and develop someone to take over if she should quit, get hit by a bus, or go AWOL like Bob had, Christine was adamant that neither had the ability to succeed her as CEO. The truth is that either Kathryn or Delaney would have been excellent candidates. However, Christine apparently felt threatened by both women, viewing them as potential rivals.

Christine had control of Michael Casey, her top outside hires, and CFO John Currie. It seemed she had shifted her focus from building the company to boosting her own financial position. Meanwhile, by refusing to develop a replacement pipeline, she solidified her power over the board by making herself apparently seem irreplaceable.

Despite this, 2011 was a great year in the media for Christine. I had my misgivings, but lululemon's stock value kept climbin,g. She ended the year as *Globe and Mail*'s CEO of the Year, the first woman to earn that honor.

After all, there were nine directors who disagreed with me. These were experienced businesspeople, brought on precisely because they knew things I didn't. Maybe their perspective was correct, and mine was too limited as the founder of just my brand.

You see where this is going. I honestly don't know why I thought they would listen to me—they didn't. The directors disagreed with my assessment and ignored my advice. It was suggested I step down and become chairman emeritus of lululemon. This sham title might have meant something to people who believe I cared about looking good, but it was nothing to me. The directors proposed the wrong suggestion for the wrong reasons, to the wrong person, and I may have been less than polite when I declined.

Trouble in the Stores

Part of every new Store Support Centre hire's onboarding included working an eight-hour shift in one of the retail stores. Through this experience, each employee learned what our Guests thought of the clothing, simply by seeing their facial expressions, body language, and comments when they were trying the garments on—in person. Working in the store, we were also able to see what was staying in the change rooms, and not bought. This type of information doesn't show up in metrics.

As upper management changed, many of the new people didn't want to carry on the tradition of working in the stores. The connection between stores and head office was weakening. But I loved working in the stores. As a result, I never lost my ability to know just by touch or sight the state of lululemon's quality.

At the registers, Guests were now only buying one or two items at a time instead of three. Either our prices were getting too high or reduced quality no longer justified the investment in multiple pieces.

When I talked with our Educators, they reported other small details only they would notice. Returns were higher. Hang tags kept curling. The stitching was of lower quality than when they'd started. From the beginning, I had fostered a culture where even a new hire on their first day felt as if they could talk to me and tell me the truth as they saw it. The Super Girls told me these truths, and my own observation and expertise confirmed them.

This was trouble, but it was almost impossible for me to verbalize these subtle cues to the board. I knew something bad was happening, but with the stock price still rising, I doubted my warning would have much sway.

I first raised my concerns in September 2012. In a lengthy message to Michael Casey, I listed several issues related to culture and quality control that I had personally observed at the store level over the past year. I proposed a "King or Queen of Luon," whose sole responsibility was to eat, breathe, live, and love our Luon fabric. They would maintain quality, and be the third-highest paid person in the company.

I decided to do what I believed was right. I flat-out told the board, "Christine is the wrong person for the CEO job, and she is killing lululemon. Her hires are dependent on her and are not strong enough to speak up. We are not investing in quality processes, and we are going to have a quality disaster. The employees are unhappy, but Christine has built a wall to prevent you from talking to them. You are out of touch. If we can't get rid of Christine now, then the issue is not the CEO, it is the board of directors. Our number one job is to have a CEO who can add long-term value. Our CEO is strangling the golden goose. If you can't see you are complicit in the company's destruction, then for the sake of lululemon, please resign."

CHAPTER 26:
DEPARTURE

Is your twelve-year-old self proud of who you are today?

Maybe the problem was me. If I genuinely believed in the principles of personal accountability and authenticity, I had to consider that possibility.

I continued to believe our directors provided the experience and knowledge the company needed. Most of them had run companies bigger than lululemon. Many were icons of American business. They understood the nuances of being public and how we could avoid being sued in the American legal system. Directors Michael Casey, Marti Morfitt, Emily White, Rhoda Pitcher, Tom Stemberg, and RoAnn Costin told me lululemon didn't need to change.

All we had to do was keep doing what we were doing. Michael told me we had the best CEO possible and we didn't need to develop a pipeline for Level 4 executives. Michael thought it would be too expensive to keep a well-paid competent COO in the second-in-command position until Christine's tenure was up. In retrospect, this was poor corporate governance, and I was saddened by the board's unwillingness to spend money in a fast-growing company to help prevent future disasters from occurring.

A Confrontation

Lululemon's stock value kept increasing and we were headed to a $12 billion valuation in the next year! I believed clothing was a bigger market than shoes, but the tide had turned against exponential growth. I also knew our foundation was crumbling and we had lost the momentum to overtake Nike.

When I was young and held the Canadian record in the 100-meter backstroke, I was visited by Howard Firby, Canada's head Olympic coach. He looked at my stroke and changed my technique to that of the world's top swimmers. As it wasn't effective, I got to thinking that perhaps Howard had gotten it wrong. As I had beat the time of the top swimmers when they were my age, shouldn't they be looking at my stroke and trying to emulate what I was doing?

Consider this as an analogy for lululemon. As we were producing the best metrics in apparel, shouldn't people want to figure out what we were doing right and learn from it? Each time someone with outside experience came in, they wanted to change our model into something that was familiar to them. People should have been coming on board to learn from us, not the other way around.

ABC Pant for Men

In the meantime, I had conceived the ABC Pant for the men's line. I realized we had created amazing stretch pants for women—why not for men? We, too, want pants that move with our bodies. We want to be able to sit at a desk all day or go on an eight-hour flight and not be concerned with our testicle compression. So, we created a warp knit fabric and made it into a design I called the Anti-Ball-Crusher Pant.

This caused a complete rebellion from the head of branding, a hire of Christine's from Procter & Gamble named Laura Klauberg, who was not the best culture fit at lululemon.

The pants were renamed ABC Pants for fear of any social media backlash. This was a missed opportunity for original, irreverent branding that men would have perfectly understood. Five years later, lululemon started calling the ABC Pant the Anti-Ball-Crusher Pant, but by that time I was using the term *Anti-Ball-Crusher* as a descriptive term for other brands. In 2019, lululemon sent an aggressive letter to a company I had invested in to stop using the term (a brave and late attempt), claiming their recent application to the trademark.

The design of the men's line was moving farther away from meeting the masculine and athletic demand from the market. If lululemon had put adequate focus on men's apparel, lululemon could have been worth another $10 billion in 2021. As I've said, lululemon owned 90 percent of the women's market before 2011 and dropped to only 10 percent from 2011 to 2018. Conversely, lululemon had the opportunity to own 30 percent of the global men's business, because no competitor was combining style with technical fabric—yet.

In the early 2010s, I felt compelled to define what a lululemon male was in the following email:

> Our man is not a show-boater or a grand-stander. He has no need for self-promotion or self-marketing. He plays a clean game, led by the desire to win, following the rules of the gentleman's game.
>
> Our man does not have to talk about himself. He has such confidence in himself as a good person, he is smart

enough to know others will do the talking for him: good or bad.

Our person does not need to win with the use of drugs because he competes against himself using his own morals and goals. Overwhelmingly, he wants to have a nice family, a good business and decent friends. He doesn't want to die early or walk poorly because of sports injuries.

He is a decent person who wins by helping others, with no expectation of return. Those he has helped speak well of him when he is not present and would drop everything to be part of his team or to help him succeed in life.

People will give him business because he has integrity and is humble.

To the sport: it is old English/Canadian. The way Steve Nash shows up (even if he isn't that clean). An "aw, shucks" type of guy. Not the biggest or the fastest but certainly the smartest. He leads his teams by example and never talks about himself.

Rugby players/old school hockey players/swimmers/ Tough Mudder participants. We show him doing these sports as it differentiates us from Nike and Under Armour.

Turning our thoughts to the Vancouver male. We know hockey. We know rugby better than the rest of North America, the psychology of swimmers can be exposed.

I believe we can make a connection between Tough Mudder and its required level of cooperation, athleticism, teamwork and what it is to be a lululemon male.

We have to work on these ideas until a new Tough Mudder concept comes, and then commit to owning it.

We need a head of men's design who will lead the pipeline from the psychology of the athlete, through to the product and then to the educators.

Nothing about this can be siloed.

What do you think?

We can define this person using the words above. We need to show the lululemon male in sports but reacting and being the opposite of what Nike and UA would show.

Board Meetings

I take responsibility for the board direction of lululemon. I was as green as they come. I didn't understand board dynamics and directors' motivations and desire for power. Because I had a 30 percent interest in lululemon, good governance dictates the board have a lead director who speaks for all independent directors. The only people the lead does not speak for is a major shareholder and the CEO. If the CEO is in survival mode, the power play is to get into bed with the lead director and take the power from the chairman (me). The chairman's power is in setting the agenda of the meeting and the time spent on each topic.

My biggest mistake was letting Michael Casey, as lead director, and Christine have too much freedom in determining the agenda items and the length of time spent on each. I thought I was being a team player without realizing they were eating up valuable board time.

Now that I am older with more experience, I realize that Christine basically knew little of the company outside of operational metrics. To look good to the directors she steered the meeting away from her weaknesses and toward operations, where she could report with confidence.

With ten competent, time-constrained directors getting paid top dollar, a board should spend most of its time discussing the top three most pressing issues. These issues are usually touchy and fraught with opinion but fuzzy in facts. Decisions from these discussions are the ones for which the company relies on its directors. Like our quarterly analyst reports, the board meetings under Christine and Michael were mostly a waste of directors' productive time.

Australia is the Answer

I could no longer look our employees in the eye. By supporting upper management, I was not upholding the lululemon culture of integrity and openness with which I had led them. I had promised to protect them, and I couldn't fulfill that promise.

I was confused as to how I had lost the power to fulfill my vision. I had no idea how to regain that power.

Maybe I was better at starting businesses than running them, while other people were born to operate companies in more mature stages. Perhaps the lululemon model I'd worked so hard to define, before we even sold our first pair of pants, just didn't work in a larger company. '

If so many of lululemon's directors disagreed with me,

then maybe I should step out of the way and let the directors and Christine prove their long-term value. Our kids were still young, and so Summer and I decided I would step out of daily operations, and we would move to Australia.

"Chip kept taking on a lesser role in the day-to-day operations," says Deanne, who by 2013 had risen to SVP of women's products, "but at least I still felt his presence on the board. I always respected what Chip was up to and what his vision was. Right or wrong, I always felt compelled to follow him. So, as he got less and less involved—and as he and Christine started not to get along—I started to think about my own future with the company."

Delaney, the former EVP of global operations, says, "With a new CEO and new senior leadership, they created the next phase of lululemon. In my opinion, almost a new company. I think for a lot of the original people who started with lululemon, this new vision did not fit with their values, and they subsequently left lululemon."

By the summer of 2012, we were living in Sydney. It was one of the best things we ever did. Summer and I assisted with our boys' surfing lessons, helped with their homework, read them bedtime stories—all the things our commitment to lululemon had left so little time for.

The company at that time was worth about $12 billion, so it put Summer's and my net worth at about $4 billion. I was also still chairman of the board. I was obviously very interested in lululemon's performance in the market because every time the stock went up or down a dollar, our net worth went up or down $40 million.

Since our departure, Summer and I had stepped away from much of what was happening at the company. I hadn't been a part of any of the changes to the lululemon product or the restructuring of the business, but even from afar I could see their struggles.

There was a dichotomy between the company's short-term incentive plan and my own plan as a long-term stockholder with a fifty-year outlook. A CEO's personal wealth lies in their ability to sell their options on a high and to inflate their personal brand to negotiate the maximum compensation at their next job. Christine and Bob had both done this. Bob at least had been transparent about it. When Christine did it, it caught me off-guard, and it hurt.

In *Good to Great*, Jim Collins illustrates how every change to a best process makes the flywheel move more slowly. Lululemon developed systemic atrophy, moving it from great to good. A company of lululemon's size is made up of thousands of processes. If one process changes, then someone must know how to change the three pieces that fit into it. If a CEO changes twenty processes—but doesn't change the three contributing processes—then the system breaks.

The Single-Ball Scenario

While in Australia in November 2012, I bought a pair of our men's shorts, which I immediately and forevermore referred to as the one-ball short. The inner liner pattern was literally so skinny it could hold only one testicle at a time. Men reading this are already wincing. Women reading this—imagine if we put out a sports bra with just one cup in the middle, sized correctly for one of your breasts.

This was a huge issue, and the production run was 20,000 units. The recall would be horrendous, and immediately I sent an email along with photos to Christine. Fifty days passed with no reply, so I sent another email in December. That month I also sent an email to Deanne Schweitzer as head of product. I didn't hear back from her either, and never found out why. She may have been too busy, or there might have been heavy pressure for her to ignore my message.

The new year came and went, and still nothing. In February 2013, I emailed Marti Morfitt, chair of our audit committee, because she was responsible for this kind of oversight. Still nothing happened—I now understand a recall of that size would have upset the 2012 financial statements and forced the company to claw back management bonuses. My view of Marti as both the chair of our audit committee and as a person of integrity instantly collapsed. I recognized she needed to be moved off the board immediately. However, nothing happened until a bigger, more public issue received everybody's prompt attention.

CHAPTER 27:
A PROBLEM WITH THE PANTS

**Designed in Vancouver, made in Vietnam:
I think Apple looked hard at the lululemon
model and labeled their product "Designed
in California, made in China."**

As 2012 turned into 2013, lululemon's sales continued to increase by 30 percent per year. The demand for athletic apparel was exceeding our ability to supply it. Increasing sales can hide all problems. Then, in March, the quality problems I'd been unable to convince the board about earlier came to a very public head.

Quality Control

"Lululemon Has a See-Through Yoga Pants Problem." That was the headline in the Corporate Intelligence section of the *Wall Street Journal* on March 18, 2013. On the same day, *Business Insider* ran the story "Lululemon Pulls Stretchy Black Pants Because They're Too Sheer." A day later, the CBC ran "Lululemon Recalls Pants for Being See-through."

Similar stories ran in the *National Post*, *Globe and Mail*, *Daily Mail*, *Bloomberg*, and *Forbes*—among many others. We had to announce a massive recall of our signature women's Luon pants at a cost of $60 million.

Jill Chatwood recalls:

> I was on maternity leave, traveling in Australia with my husband and children. We stopped in for a visit at the house that Chip and Summer were renting. It was clear to me that Chip had some concerns with how the product team was operating. I confirmed for him that quality was not as strong a focus as it had been in the past and that I, too, was concerned.
>
> Lo and behold, within weeks of that conversation, it was discovered that the consistency and quality of our key fabric, Luon, was compromised. The "sheer pants" emergency was in full swing. Pressure to make financial numbers was winning out over commitment to quality.

I was mortified for lululemon. Solving for sheerness was the functional reason I started the company in 1998! A lifetime of research into how to make best-in-the-world non-transparent black stretch pants all came undone in an instant. Amid all this uproar, the conversations of other big quality issues I had previously brought forward evaporated entirely.

Delaney Schweitzer, at that time head of retail, called me to ask what I thought we should do about it.

"Put a sign on the door saying 'We are closed because we make a terrible product and we will reopen when we figure out how to be the best in the world again.'"

It wasn't my most diplomatic moment, but I was operating out of full integrity. When the cyanide issue with Tylenol happened, Johnson & Johnson took the hit. They announced an immediate total recall, told all customers not to buy their product, and moved quickly to safety caps—and that situation wasn't even their fault. Lululemon owed our customers and employees to be at least as responsible, to have at least as much integrity as Johnson & Johnson.

Instead, Christine blamed our fabric supplier Eclat Textile. They had grown to become our number one fabric and manufacturing partner. She fired our chief product officer, shifting blame in a standard Machiavellian move to protect her own position.

Around this same time, we received an email from Lucy Lee Helm, general counsel for Starbucks. I was a carbon-copy recipient of the e-mail, as was Michael Casey. The letter was addressed to Christine, and summarized Starbucks's concerns about a recent interview Christine had given with ABC's Katie Couric only a few weeks earlier. It flatly contradicted several statements she made in the interview, and called Christine's integrity into question yet again.

Dear Christine,

On behalf of Starbucks, I want to express our deep concern about your troubling comments on the "Breaking the Glass Ceiling" segment of the nationally syndicated Katie Couric television show. What we heard you say about Starbucks personnel practices, and your own career opportunities with Starbucks, are disparaging and simply untrue.

During the course of your interview with Ms. Couric, you described your experiences at Starbucks and, specifically, that the company gave you jobs that "nobody else knew how to do" and that the company "tried to sideline you when you had children." You described one experience in which you perceived you were treated differently than a male colleague and agreed with Ms. Couric that that was a "fairly typical moment" in your Starbucks experience. Your comments imply that your considerable success at the company was somehow limited based upon your gender.

This characterization is not only inaccurate and

untruthful but disparaging of Starbucks and its partners. Starbucks appreciates your many contributions during your employment with the company but frankly you, too, were provided with significant opportunities. Indeed, you progressed significantly in your career at Starbucks over 20 years, from administrative assistant to senior executive levels. You had many leadership roles and received opportunities for learning and advancement across the organization. To suggest that Starbucks somehow mistreated you or failed to accommodate your schedule because of your gender is a serious distortion of the record and one that does a great disservice to Starbucks, its partners, and its legacy of progressive personnel practices. And it does not accurately reflect the career path you achieved at Starbucks, which you have successfully leveraged to "catapult" to an impressive position at lululemon.

Starbucks would prefer to avoid a debate or dispute with you over your statements. But we cannot allow inaccurate, misleading and frankly disparaging comments about the company, its partners, and its human resource practices to go unanswered.

Sincerely,
Lucy Lee Helm
Executive Vice President, General Counsel
and Secretary

cc: Howard Schultz
Dennis J. Wilson
Michael Casey[42]

42. Author's personal records, April 2, 2013, letter from Lucy Lee Helm to Christine Day (cc: Michael Casey, Chip Wilson, Howard Schultz).

With Michael Casey as one recipient of the letter, I thought the support for Christine would finally collapse. After all, the number one job of a board is to hire a CEO and ensure a CEO succession pipeline is in place. I think the board was afraid that firing the CEO would draw publicity that would adversely affect lululemon's short-term share price and possibly their own reputations.

A meeting was held in Sydney, Australia, during which the board asked me to come back to Canada and help fix the problems. With our chief product officer gone, the lululemon product team also phoned my wife, Summer, asking her to come back and help.

Christine then provided the directors with a document that set out the terms of my return in an attempt to protect her job and to keep me at arm's length. It included five Operating Principles, each designed to limit my ability to do meaningful work or affect meaningful change within the company. In response, the board directed Christine to make space for us in the company because of all the challenges they were facing. Summer and I agreed right away. We were lululemon's biggest cheerleaders—we always will be—so we uprooted ourselves from our new life in Australia, returned to Vancouver, and got to work.

Meet the New Boss...

It only took a few weeks to find out how bad things had gotten. The signs were everywhere.

For example, over a period of thirty years, I had collected samples of clothing from all over the world. Each garment had a special button, zipper, technical apparel solution, or other unique aspect I wanted to keep "on file." We used this library, which could easily have filled a museum, to visually and tactilely inspire designs. It was easily worth $100,000, but its worth to lululemon was a million dollars.

When I went to design the season's next line, I discovered most of our best samples had disappeared. I told Marti Morfitt that we had a major theft issue on our hands. She was unable to look me in the eye as she said the issue wasn't important enough for the Audit Committee to investigate. My heart sank when she told us Christine had sold 95 percent of the samples to create space.

Still, it was good to be back. I don't think Summer and I were alone in feeling that way. Legacy people—those who truly understood the company—were happy to see us, and we were very glad to see them. The design team was excited for lululemon to once again be design-led instead of merchant-led.

"I was focused on keeping the business going," says Michelle Armstrong, "so I didn't even notice the circumstances that brought Chip and Summer home early. My team and I were incredibly grateful when they came into the office to support us. Our merchandising team was so excited to learn the original Operating Principles from Chip, as many of them were new to the company and had not come up with him leading the product team. Summer had an incredible talent for giving feedback in meetings, and her taste and perspective were highly-valued."

Deanne Schweitzer says:

When we called Chip and told him we had a massive quality issue in our signature fabrics, I assume he felt that his company was being fucked up and he needed to get back ASAP and fix it. We had also gone from a culture of responsibility and accountability to a lot of finger-pointing.

I was in a new role for the company at the time, SVP of women's. When Chip and Summer came into the office, I personally welcomed their expertise. They were both attending our design meetings and grounding us in what made a lululemon product. Summer would also attend fittings with the designers, which was just as valuable. The designers loved her perspective, and I loved the extra set of eyes.

Prior to their sabbatical, Chip had written Operating Principles for the company. Many people had never worked with him before, and they were thrilled when he presented all the Operating Principles. The Product team felt energized after those presentations.

None of this went over well with Christine. As an executive at the time, I felt the tension between Chip and Christine when Chip returned. Without saying anything, I also felt I was placed on an unspoken 'Chip team.' It was a stressful time.

"It was very clear that upper management was not happy to have Chip and Summer back on the scene," says Jill Chatwood. "This was the beginning of the end for Christine. There was an awkward divide because you were on Chip's team or Christine's team and you really didn't get to decide which team you were on. The division at the top caused fractures within the product team. The environment was tense, with direction and redirection occurring daily."

This was possibly my worst time working in lululemon. I sat in the production area struggling to find and fix quality issues every day. I had the authority to make changes, above whatever power Christine still had. However, Christine's weak team in upper-middle management still had control of their various departments. Whenever I would lay out a plan with a coworker, they had to get approval from one of Christine's people. It purposely frustrated the recovery system and put those Super Girls in a tough position.

Meanwhile, Christine seemed to spend every moment at work trying to get rid of me. I spent any time I could spare trying to get rid of her. I was trying my best to save the company. It was the absolute worst.

Family Business

While I was settling in, Summer made her own contribution to lululemon's future—or at least she tried to. While in Australia, she had developed a fabric she called "technical cashmere" that had a luxurious feel but could endure the same five-year quality standards we demanded of athletic apparel. She offered it to lululemon as a way of bringing a new innovation into an already stagnating line—a move with the potential to add $2 billion to lululemon's stock value over the next few years.

She didn't want any payment for her design or ideas since our share of the money this innovation could make lululemon was spectacular. Her only concern was that lululemon might accept the fabric, only for Christine or the directors to do nothing with it. They had already shown an unwillingness to put money toward innovations or invest in the future. To cover herself, Summer said she wanted to reserve the right to use technical cashmere if lululemon chose not to.

Summer and I weren't the only Wilsons to come to lululemon's rescue. A year earlier, JJ had been hired in marketing at a menswear company called wings+horns. This was a dream job for him! JJ simultaneously celebrated the passions and interests we shared while also building an identity of his own. "I loved my job at wings+horns," JJ recalls. "I'd created something for myself separate from lululemon and the Wilson family name."

Not long after JJ started there, he was asked to come back to lululemon to work on the men's design team. Lululemon's ethos had emanated from our earliest connections with yoga.

The original male yogis were often small and slight. As lululemon had been using women's fabrics, the style and feel had been feminine. In 2008, we declared men's apparel as the next big business. We knew we could get men's sales to $1 billion by 2011. (In the end, it would take lululemon until 2020 to hit $1 billion in men's business.)

Because our head of product wasn't familiar with the men's market, she didn't know how to build the foundation for exponential growth. I maintained that lululemon's men's business needed to become ultra-masculine as a counter position to effeminate yoga. I had asked the head of brand to focus on professional ice hockey and rugby teams as our new target. We needed to align the men's market with Canadian sports we knew well, and in which we could be authentic. I asked for a design head from a West Coast surf, mountain, or snowboard company as our head of men's product—somebody that understood men and would drive masculinity at all levels.

Instead, the head of product hired a fashion-focused men's design director from New York. This was the opposite of what was needed. The result was an inappropriate product that was feminine and technically deficient, and as a result, lululemon lost five years of men's growth and billions of dollars in market capitalization.

This was the state of the men's design team when JJ was asked to come aboard. It was difficult for him to say no to this opportunity, so he accepted out of loyalty to the company.

We all learned quickly the level to which that loyalty was not reciprocated.

Showdown

In mid-April 2013, I had a talk with Christine. I had no plan going into this conversation. It was 5 p.m., the end of the workday. She and I were in her office. I was just trying to reestablish a working relationship with her.

This difficult, cut-the-shit conversation had been a long time coming. We had worked together well once, both bringing different strengths to the table. A lot had changed since then, but I had hope that we could reestablish that excellent working relationship. The time had come to clear the air.

I looked at her and said, "Christine, you put a lot of good things in place for lululemon, but you never had a vision for the company. Other than a three-year operational, strategic plan, who are we? We've got competition growing every day—how are we different from them?"

I summed up by saying, "You're a world-class chief operations officer. But you're a terrible CEO."

She cried and turned away—an unprofessional reaction that seemed fake. She'd cried wolf one too many times whenever pressure was put on her. The next day, Christine announced her resignation.

Sort of. To a point.

CHAPTER 28:
DAMAGE CONTROL

Now I understand that instead of recruiting greatness in the form of Howard Schultz, the founder of Starbucks, as a director, I got Howard's support staff. I believe Michael and Christine were at odds with Howard as a purpose-driven founder and they thought they could do better with lululemon. I understand why Howard had to return to the CEO position three times to "right the ship."

To understand what happened for the next few months at lululemon, you have to understand Christine's "resignation" as CEO. She announced her resignation immediately, but I believe it was a ploy, a power play intended to bolster her ego and—ironically—protect her position in the company.

The board, worried about the optics of losing two CEOs in such a short span of time, talked her into staying on. A little bit later she resigned "for real," but still stayed on until the board found a replacement. This process took a very long time, owing to her failure to have developed great employees under her and the directors not monitoring their number one job. During this time, Christine remained CEO.

That's the context of the next couple of years at lululemon, and with that context, what follows will make a little more sense.

Well, it doesn't make sense, but at least you'll be able to follow the plot.

Resignation of a Sort

Christine's resignation shocked the board. Despite my constant urging, the directors had done nothing to plan for her departure. I believed we would rebound from her immediate removal, especially if we replaced her with Delaney Schweitzer. Another possibility would have been to make me interim CEO, like when Bob went AWOL five years earlier.

The board did neither of those things. Afraid of any public announcement that would make Wall Street nervous, they convinced Christine to stay on for an undefined interim period while they quietly searched for a new CEO. They bent over forwards for Christine, which improved nothing for the company, the board, or for her.

The situation did not improve. In June, she tendered her resignation anyway—just in time for the first-quarter conference call. She stuck around long enough to hurt my family, but not short enough to do the company any good. I'm not saying this was spiteful and personal, but it sure felt that way from our perspective. She did agree to stay on until the board found a replacement—which proved difficult as she put out word that I was challenging to work with.

In its present form, I knew lululemon could not take advantage of the next two to five years, which would be the inflection point of the most dramatic change in the way people dressed in the history of the world. The company did not have a succession pipeline in place for the top five executives, and it had not invested in infrastructure.

"This was a personal decision of mine," she said in a brief statement. A few months later, in an interview with *Fortune*, Christine said she left lululemon because her vision hadn't matched mine, and that I loved disruption and clash.

The morning of Christine's final departure, lululemon stock was at an all-time high. When the announcement went public, shares dropped by nearly 15 percent.

It was exactly as the board had feared. Whether or not we recovered, and how quickly, would depend on who we brought on to replace her.

In October, Summer received a letter from Christine. She thanked Summer for assisting lululemon's product design on a "volunteer basis." She then went on to say that Summer's continued work with Cirqq Designs—a company Summer had incorporated to protect her intellectual property—could lead to a conflict of interest.

"We do not feel it is appropriate for you to continue your volunteer work with lululemon, and we hereby confirm the termination of any such arrangement," was Christine's final word on the subject. Christine did not want innovation or Summer's new fabric or designs. She had essentially fired Summer from her volunteer position. Given that Christine had resigned months prior, it was frustrating that she still had that level of control.

A week later, Summer crafted a response to Christine, with input from our lawyers. She expressed regret that anything she was doing could be construed as a conflict of interest.

Summer also emphasized how—in addition to her volunteering in design—she had offered to give lululemon the right to use Cirqq's new fabric, without any cost or obligation. An offer which Christine turned down.

"Our family has the most to gain from any benefit that I can give to lululemon," Summer added, "and the most to lose by anything I could do to hurt it." As I said before, every dollar lululemon went up or down affected us by $40 million. Only someone with an ulterior motive might suggest that Summer was in a conflict of interest.

In Summer's own words: "That whole time was quite emotional because there were people in the business that were so great, and still wanted the business to be great, and I think people were really excited when Chip came back to help. I think we were sad because there was a noticeable shift in the business. A shift away from the culture, and people were disappointed. They were disappointed that lululemon had this mark against it in terms of the quality."

Christine didn't stop with Summer. That same month, JJ was also sent packing with a letter echoing the same idiotic concerns. I say idiotic because anybody could look at the situation and see the reality. There could be no conflict of interest between the Wilson family and lululemon. We owned so many shares in the company that a dollar change in the stock price meant millions to us. Anything we did to hurt lululemon would hurt us.

As JJ says: "I had left my dream job to go back to lululemon, a company I would have done anything for, to only a year later be told by HR that, 'You, as a member of the Wilson family, are no longer allowed to be a part of this.'"

At that point, I'd had enough. I again told the board Christine was the problem and pointed to the recent disasters that had occurred under her leadership. She had lied so many times to me, to the board, to our employees, and to the public. "If you don't fire Christine immediately, then you are the problem."

I honestly don't know why I thought the board would suddenly see the light and listen to me. They reached the predictable decision—Christine could stay until they found a replacement. I could not work under those conditions, so once again I stepped out of direct, ground-level work and tried to reinvent myself as a more effective chairman of the board.

Failure on Every Level

At some point during all of this, the SEC started a review of lululemon's internal documents, looking for information about the see-through pants issue. During this process, they came across a document about the one-ball short issue I had discovered in 2012.

That fall, they called me down to Seattle to discuss the documentation. This put me in between a rock and a hard place. The SEC would ask me how serious the one-ball situation was. If I was truthful to myself and said I thought it was extremely serious, a five-year legal case was the most likely outcome. I would spend years in court, doing depositions, and maybe getting sued by the board, when I could be at home with my kids. I would have to fly to SEC offices and courtrooms and my focus would be pulled into the legal hairball instead of on my family, and on moving lululemon forward. If I agreed with the lululemon board that everything was fine, none of that would happen.

At least that's what the board told my lawyer, and that's what my lawyer told me. Nobody fed me a script, exactly, but it was heavily implied. They even sent Marti Morfitt (who had hidden the emails I sent to her) to sit in the back of the interview, as a reminder of what the board wanted me to do.

I justified it to myself. I also looked at the overhaul lululemon had just done with their quality control process because of the see-through pants debacle. If I spoke to the full extent of the one-ball short situation, the SEC would ultimately demand that we make the changes we were already making. It would be a lot of bother and expense—and significant hits to our stock price—for improvements lululemon had put in motion.

Ultimately, I agreed with the board. I said that I had sent the emails but had overestimated how big of an issue there had been. I said, now fully understanding the situation, I no longer considered the shorts a problem. There is so much failure in that.

Most importantly, I failed. From my point of view, I was not living in integrity when I spoke with the SEC. I told the truth as a board member doing his fiduciary responsibility to side with lululemon's leadership. But from my personal perspective, I was doing a disservice to the brand and to myself. I knew the board's approach was wrong, aimed at looking good and saving their reputation at the cost of the values I had sought to instil in lululemon from day one.

It occurred to me later that I failed in another way, too. If I had been honest and lived in integrity, the SEC investigation would have forced lululemon to clean house. The stock price would have fallen—temporarily, but a lot, and the board would have lost its worst members. They would have had to oust Christine immediately, instead of waiting months for her replacement. It's possible the government would have forced out a few of the other most dysfunctional board members. Had I been willing to swim that rough water for three to five years, I might have filled those emptying seats with people who understood and believed in what lululemon was meant to be. It's possible I could have saved the company instead— from what it became.

But I didn't. Although worse things happened to me personally not long afterward, this was my lowest point in the whole story.

The Interview

With Summer and I both removed again from the day-to-day management of lululemon, we at least had more time to focus on launching a new initiative based on one-minute mindfulness exercises. Summer and I sought to develop a free digital platform offering training to individuals, schools, and companies. We were wealthy, creative people with no creative outlet, and we wanted to do something more for the world.

On November 5, 2013, the *Bloomberg* business show "Street Smart" interviewed us at their New York studio. The anchor was Trish Regan, an experienced journalist who'd appeared on CNBC, CBS, and Fox, among others.

As was expected, the interview started with Trish asking us to define mindfulness.

Then came the switch.

"I want to segue into another story," Trish said. "You're the founder [of lululemon], you're a former designer...what's going on with the pants?"

My initial response was to focus on the unique challenges of producing a technical fabric. "When you push technology," I replied, "something's going to happen every now and then."

Trish pressed a little harder, asking me about complaints of pilling on the fabric.

My reply: "There has always been pilling. The thing is that women will wear seat belts that don't work, or they'll wear a purse that doesn't work, or quite frankly some women's bodies just actually don't work for it."

Trish: "They don't work for the pant?"

Me: "No, they don't work for some women's bodies."

When Trish tried to pigeonhole our exchange by saying, "Interesting, not every woman can wear a lululemon yoga pant," I immediately replied, "No, I think they can. I just think it's how you use it." I thought this clarified my remarks.

Summer and I left the studio feeling good, but the next morning the real trouble started. *Bloomberg's* editors had spliced and diced the footage, turning my simple comments into the antithesis of everything I stood for and everything the women of lululemon had built.

Coverage and commentary about that interview ranged from the malicious to the outright bizarre. Very few people expressing their opinions took into account my life's work of empowering women and encouraging health, fun, and personal growth.

I didn't know what to do. I didn't have a blog or a website. I wasn't on social media. I had no idea how to connect directly with the Super Girls without going through the filter of traditional media—or worse, a lululemon PR machine controlled by Christine. I couldn't trust either of those not to warp my meaning and intentions even further.

If I'd had a direct outlet to the world, I would have put it out there immediately. I did record an internal apology-slash-explanation video for our staff, but nobody was happy with how that turned out—least of all me.

For the record, then, here's what I meant.

I knew from working in the stores that something about our perfect fit hadn't been working and I couldn't put my finger on it. I didn't say that in the moment, but after the social media backlash from this comment, I had an "aha" moment. Some women had been buying our Luon pants not just for athletics, but as a compression garment, like Spanx. But lululemon pants, and Luon fabric, specifically, were designed for athletic use, not compression.

A new product need was emerging. Women wanted garments to reframe their bodies while they were training and sweating to improve their bodies. I could sense something was happening to the integrity of the pants, but the real information was emerging slowly and only after women had owned the pants for six months or more.

So, when asked why lululemon pants pill, I considered my own market research. I had studied every person's body and clothing for as far back as I could remember. I had a lifetime of gathered information. I hear fabric crinkle. I feel other people's bad quality clothing, and I feel sorry for people wearing stiff, uncomfortable fabric. I smell the odor from polyester fabrics. I cringe at hiked-up pants, poor-fitting bras or plumber's butt. I understand the correlation between every athlete's body and the millimeter of fabric required to make every type of fabric work.

I calculate the exact perfect athletic garment for each body, and then I correlate it to the average, so that I can make and sell the greatest quantity to the most people. I cross-reference the cost of fabric per body, and I determine if there are enough consumers of that body type to design a style and make enough pieces to make money. I assess the cost of marketing to each segment group, for which there could be 40 billion permutations and combinations.

With the pilling, what I eventually discovered was that some customers were buying the pants two to four sizes smaller than necessary, with body-shaping in mind. The pants still looked great, but there was more stress being placed on the fabric and seams than what we'd originally designed it for. If the fabric is stretched far enough and meets a sharp object, fractures can occur.

I did not mean to say that women who aren't a size 6 shouldn't wear our pants. I meant that our pants are highly technical and precisely designed. A woman who is a size 12 should wear our pants in a size 12. A woman who is a size 6 should wear our pants in a size 6. Lululemon was one of the few companies that did not adhere to vanity sizing. Vanity sizing occurs when a company of questionable integrity labels a size 10 to be a size 8 to make a woman feel good about herself.

I am not surprised that what I said in the interview would be a controversial statement. It was controversial purely because making it controversial sold advertising for *Bloomberg* and because it was the beginning of cancel culture.

From the *Bloomberg* moment on, nothing would be the

same. My comments were the antithesis of everything I stood for and of everything the women of lululemon and I had built. The ramifications for the company, for my family, and for everyone involved were catastrophic.

I made a mistake, and I was going to pay heavily for it.

One media blunder. That's all it took. One media blunder and a lifetime of dedication to women was out the window. With those words and that sound bite, I was ruined. I chose the words that I used, and in doing so, I'd created an opportunity for the CEO and the board to shift the conversation away from their part in the quality issue and over to the "wildcard founder" who was sinking the ship.

As Ayn Rand said, "I can ignore reality, but I cannot ignore the consequences of ignoring reality." A new game was being played, and I was unknowingly sitting in the stands.

I absolutely believe that both Christine and the board had been waiting for this chance to take me off the field. I am certain this was done with a degree of malice and intention. That said, I can only place the responsibility for what happened on myself. By then, any illusion I had of sincere partnership was my fault, and mine alone.

The silver lining of the *Bloomberg* interview was in discovering the distinction that women wanted athletic compression tights that would also body shape. I communicated this idea to David Mussafer. The lululemon product team did superb work and perfected a new fabric. They densified the fabric thread count and stitches per inch on seams. In my opinion, this solved the pilling issue and allowed women to buy their true size.

The Board Finally Seizes an Opportunity

The December 2013 quarterly board meeting took place in our Vancouver head office. Even though I'd set the agenda, it was only at the beginning of the meeting that I spotted a last-minute addition—some kind of report by Christine about the *Bloomberg* interview. I wasn't sure what to make of it, but I knew it couldn't be good.

We went through the routine agenda items, and then came the *Bloomberg* report. Christine had worked hard on it. She'd brought in an outside consultant—at a cost of at least $30,000—and put six internal lululemon staff to work to create a statistic-heavy report (numbers and statistics being the board's first language) about how I had become a detriment to the company.

I'd expected something bad, but the amount of sheer labor, effort, and expense Christine had put into this—within a company she had already announced her intention to leave—caught me off guard. Still, I didn't immediately feel threatened. I believed the board was smart enough to see through her. When she was finished, I asked how they had conducted their statistical analysis, and what kind of people they had surveyed to reach their conclusions. Christine and her consultant replied that they had surveyed a broad range of demographics across North America—a few thousand people in total.

In all lululemon's branding and design, in everything we did, our focus was on one person: the Super Girl. In my opinion, there was no point in asking a broad group of demographics what they thought. I said as much.

"You're telling me," I said, "that you're actually surveying people who may not even like our company or care about our products, and you're having them drive the decision-making process for our core customer?"

I intended this as a rhetorical question, to demonstrate the problems in the analysis.

Not that it mattered. This was the end of 2013, a time when social media was coming into its own. The directors used online comments as the way to run the business, and

Christine had her opportunity to prove I was who she wanted me to be. The outcome of the meeting was the decision to remove me as chairman. Michael Casey would take my place.

This was a recipe for disaster. Was this what they wanted to do? I guess they wanted to get me out of the picture, and they needed an "official" way in which to do it.

The *Bloomberg* interview gave the board the ability to reframe me as the weird uncle that the family had to put up with, but wished it didn't. Reframing me in public provided a diversion for poor governance, poor quality, and declining stock value.

"The way lululemon handled Chip's *Bloomberg* interview was deplorable," says Jenna Hills. "Or better put, the way the company didn't handle the uproar was. We didn't stand for him. I certainly didn't say or do enough. Fear won that battle, and it put a lid on the potential of leaders all over the world. Suddenly, there was an intolerance for making mistakes. Not to mention that it gave rise for all the haters to hate."

I didn't get angry or emotional at that meeting, but I was perplexed. Something had happened, and I didn't understand what it was. I also felt powerless and sad—sad for the shareholders and sad for myself, but more so for the employees. They had spent years pouring their hearts and souls into a company, and these newcomers had changed it into something different, something bad.

CHAPTER 29:

THE INTERVIEW

A refrigerator can brand harvest when the foundation has been built. It takes a futurist to build a company for 100 years.

After the meeting was over, I went home and talked to Summer.

Lululemon's official statement was that I had resigned as chairman of the board.

It was at this time that the history and culture of lululemon went mainstream. Store managers were no longer in control of their windows for fear of social media backlash. The full manifesto was eliminated from the website, and the story of how the company was named became a liability. The transformational leaders created out of our development program were too vocal and too strong to fit into a company now run by fear. Many great employees were exited or quit, and the intellectual knowledge of the company dropped significantly.

The directors knew that because they had stopped reinvesting in the quality processes of the company, there would be hard years ahead. The directors needed to show the public that I was the reason behind the next terrible five years so that they could survive and make themselves look good.

Sizing

While we're discussing sizing, I do want to share my insights on this topic. The current media position is that an apparel brand is against specific markets if it does not make product for everyone. In lululemon's case, it was ostracized for not making sizes larger than 12.

I think people just do not understand the business of apparel. Thirty years ago, all cotton and polyester was $2 a metre and it did not really matter if a pattern was a size 4 or a size 10. With technical apparel, the cost can reach $25 per metre. Consequently, the cost difference between a size 6 and a size 14 can be double.

Diane von Furstenberg gently explains how the expense of her fabric does not allow her to make large sizes without charging for the extra cost. It is easy for a woman to say this to women but impossible for a man to say this to a woman without causing judgment and upset.

To provide context, a small luxury bag can cost $1,000, and a large bag can cost $5,000. As a larger bag requires more leather and takes additional time to sew, the cost is more. Or take a simple everyday purchase: if a person buys a large bag of carrots, the price is naturally double that of a small bag of carrots.

Social media is an outlet for people to state their views but it's also a negotiation tool. A forty-five-year-old person who is a size 16 is essentially saying she wants a size 4 high-school student to subsidize her size 16 purchase. I don't believe in forcing a small person to pay for a large person's size. On a side note, I believe as a 220-pound man I should pay double a 110-pound woman on a plane as the fuel cost is the under-lying expense.

Via algorithms, everything we do digitally is tailored

to our specific individual tastes. We are offered preselected brands from the data we provide. We are targeted by age, race, religion, geography, sexual preferences, income, and education level. Every brand you own is a brand you have specifically been targeted for.

The fact is people's bodies change drastically as they age. It is insane to think one brand can make an infinite number of patterns to cut fabric. Competition is effective in segmenting the population, so each market gets the attention they deserve.

Aftermath

As of mid-January 2014, traffic and sales trends were decelerating meaningfully. Operating lululemon with nobody from Vancouver on the board or management is like running Brooks Brothers from an ashram in Big Sur. That's how I felt as we were looking for Christine Day's replacement. The board was under immense pressure to announce a new CEO. They had failed at their number-one job of ensuring succession, but at this moment, that was beside the point.

With the little power I had left, I was adamant that the upper levels of management would return to our foundational concepts. This meant our new CEO would have to understand fully how our culture ensured our best-in-the-world metrics.

One possible contender for the CEO role was Jerry Stritzke, who'd joined the lululemon board of directors in 2012. Jerry had a background with Coach, Inc. and Victoria's Secret, which gave him much of the operational experience we required. Jerry and five lululemon people attended a course in Vancouver called "Creating a Leader" run by Werner Erhard and Michael Jensen. Jensen had joined the faculty of the Harvard Business School in 1985, founding what is now the Negotiations, Organizations, and Markets Unit. I believe Erhard and Jensen's world-class, three-page document on integrity should be framed and hung in every home and office (the document is available in the afterword to this book).

Ultimately, Jerry felt that his Christian beliefs conflicted with the leadership-based concepts of Erhard and Jensen. The conflict for Jerry was so severe that he'd quit the seminar two days early. As far as the employees and I were concerned, this eliminated him from being our next CEO even though he might have been great. The board thought I was nuts, but I knew the employees needed the right cultural person after two CEO-operators.

Again, I put forward Delaney Schweitzer, but the board had little interest in a CEO who might be perceived as a "Chip ally." Sadly, Delaney didn't stand a chance.

Finally, after thirteen candidates had either declined or been rejected, the CEO head-hunter delivered a wildcard candidate. Laurent Potdevin was a mediocre-at-best candidate to take over a public company of this size.

We'd already put him through two interviews, but his appointment to CEO seemed a foregone conclusion with absolutely no one else in the pipeline. The pressure was immense for the board to announce a new CEO.

I clarified that I wanted Laurent to take the Landmark course before he started with us.

With Laurent, I wanted to know upfront if he would fit with lululemon's unique culture.

"We'll make sure he does the course," the board assured me. "It'll be one of the first things he does when he comes on."

Until Laurent had committed to guided transformational development as part of due diligence and onboarding, I wouldn't vote for him. Eventually, I was confronted by the board. "Look, Chip, if you don't agree with the rest of the board, then it's going to be all of us against you, and we're going to vote him in anyway." I didn't want the optics of having a new CEO voted in by a divided board, so I acquiesced.

Looking for a CEO under pressure is incredibly expensive to a company, and I would say the poor CEO transition cost lululemon another 5 billion in market cap over the next ten-year period.

Kit and Ace and the New Dynamic

My family, at least, had moved on from 2013, and from lululemon. Early 2014 saw the beginning of Kit and Ace.

Summer had ideas and designs for T-shirts, partly inspired by the technical cashmere she'd conceptualized a year or two earlier. As Summer says: "We really started it as a hobby . . . I thought, well, why don't I just hire a few people. I'll get another designer, and I'll bring along a fabric person, and we'll probably need somebody to help us with some logistics, and we'll work in the heritage building."

It was all simple and straightforward.

"This was about the size of the business I wanted to have," Summer says. "Just one shop, getting the assortment right."

As Kit and Ace got started, my son JJ also became prominently involved with it. He had been raised with Westbeach, and then when lululemon started, he'd always worked in the stores. From there he got a retail business degree from Ryerson University in Toronto, spent a summer at Advent Equity in their retail department, and lastly, returned to lululemon in 2014.

JJ was also the perfect age to understand the new social media and e-commerce landscape, so Summer brought him on as a partner, working on that end of the brand. I was proud to see it working as a true family business.

Dinner-table discussions revolved around lululemon and Kit and Ace, but I had a lot to think about on my own: what had happened to me, what was happening with the company, and what I could do about it. What was my responsibility? Was I being a leader? Was I giving without the expectation of return? Was my vision for lululemon too much at odds with the direction upper management and the board wanted? Was my identity as a person too wrapped up in it all? Could I recreate myself to live outside of lululemon?

CHAPTER 30:
END OF THE ROAD

Michael Jordan said he was at the top of his game when the Chicago Bulls disbanded, and he was sad and disappointed he did not get to do all he had wanted.

I knew if I blamed other people, I lost the power to change a situation. Blaming does nothing to shift a power balance. A rule I've always adhered to is: if I ever complain twice about something, I either must act or shut up. The time had come for me to apply this rule to my present situation with lululemon.

For starters, I'd never taken the time to write the story of lululemon. Under new management, lululemon's PR and social media machines were reframing the company's foundations and history. Often with social media, once anything is documented on a digital platform, it may as well be true.

Now that I had "resigned" as chairman, the dynamic had changed. I could make it my mission to hold the lululemon board and upper management accountable for its appalling performance since 2011. And although streetnic apparel and stock markets had grown exponentially, even as late as January 2018, lululemon was still valued at the same amount it had been valued five years prior. This lost growth would forever keep lululemon at half the value it could have been.

Preparing for Battle

The company was no longer an agent for change or a social experiment, but maybe, just maybe, that could be fixed. I thought investors would want to know how lululemon could again recreate the world of technical apparel.

The challenge that I encountered was that the lululemon shareholder base was primarily comprised of financial institutions who would sell if the company didn't fit into their short-term growth parameters. Institutions will not work to change the rules of how directors are elected. Activists gain little from agitating as the company does just well enough to not be worth the effort, and it cannot be broken up into smaller, more profitable entities.

Lululemon's governance structure doesn't allow shareholders to change the directors as fast as the world changes. This has created nepotism and a "leave it be" mentality. A principal foundation of lululemon culture had been to view everything as though "nothing works." Within this context, we never rested on our laurels, and we were willing to abandon what looked good to perfect and ensure a better future.

I had a problem, and to solve that problem I had a plan. In 2014, the lululemon stock was weak. With the stock continuing to drop, lululemon couldn't attract quality directors or a quality CEO. I saw no upside for lululemon to continue in its present form and thought the only way forward was to sell half my shares—and, effectively, two board seats—to Advent and shake up the board.

Through Dave Mussafer, Advent expressed the same

concerns as mine—lululemon had too many old, ineffective directors. David explained to me that Christine had made no money during her time at Starbucks. At lululemon, she was given three-year short-term options with no incentive to add value for the long run. With a great company like lululemon, she took the opportunity to cut the expenses of quality, people, and product and then raise prices. These actions did not affect short-term value as our world-class brand would stay strong for years ... even as its cultural foundation was crumbling.

At this point, I turned to a book called *Boards That Lead*, by Ram Charan and Dennis Carey, published by Harvard Business Review Press. In Chapter 4, Charan and Carey say: "In our experience, as many as half of Fortune 500 companies have one or two dysfunctional directors ... It becomes a drain for everyone involved—except the dysfunctional director." The chapter adds that these kinds of directors too often refer to what their own companies have done and that the best course of action for dealing with them is to remove them from the board. Not an easy process, Charan and Carey acknowledge, "since few directors readily exit on their own accord."

Still, these are wise words. Of the three director positions up for reelection that summer, one belonged to Michael Casey, the new chairman of the board, and one belonged to RoAnn Costin.

Both RoAnn Costin and Tom Stemberg were direct investors in a Boston-based company called City Sports, which was a vertical-retail yoga clothing company in outright competition with lululemon. I had raised my concerns about this, but this only made me an enemy of Tom Stemberg.

The core of the lululemon board was comprised of Tom Stemberg's business associates. The legal opinion the board received was: "You can have people on the board that have a conflict of interest if the board knows it's a conflict of interest, and if they agree that it's not going to affect the value of the company adversely."

In 2014, Tom Stemberg wasn't up for reelection, but RoAnn was.

I released a public statement saying I would use my 30 percent of shares to vote against Michael and RoAnn's reelections, and I encouraged other shareholders to do the same.

As part of my statement, I said, "I am concerned that the board is not aligned with the core values of product and innovation on which lululemon was founded and on which the company thrived." I added that for far too long we'd been focused on short-term profits at the expense of long-term vision and value.

Advent convinced me to sell my shares by saying they would come in and do a director review. With this "independent" assessment of the board, they would find a "nice" way to approach three to four directors and ask them to step down.

On August 11, 2013, I sold half my shares to Advent International. Advent also offered to buy Kit and Ace. I agreed it was a good idea, but it wasn't my company to speak for—it was Summer's and JJ's. They declined the offer, and I supported their decision.

"The timing didn't seem right," Summer said. "There was a lot of flux at lululemon, and they had already told me very clearly they didn't want the idea. Kit and Ace had been open only a few months. I felt responsible to the people who had come on board at Kit and Ace and was unsure of their future with a possible change of ownership."

Kit and Ace's growth brought speculation that it was poised to compete with lululemon. The *Financial Post* said, "[while] Kit and Ace is still in its infancy, it will probably appeal to a core segment of lululemon consumers."

Kit and Ace used natural fibers, while lululemon used synthetic. Lululemon was made for sweat and for working out, and Kit and Ace was made for those same people who wanted technical apparel that they could wear to the office.

Besides, as they'd done with mindfulness, lululemon had already taken a pass on the technical cashmere and the designs that formed the foundation of Kit and Ace. Lululemon's *real* competition was represented in the billion-dollar opportunities to compete properly against Nike, Adidas, and Under Armour.

Unfortunately, lululemon's board of directors had a different take on the situation. I discovered this at a board meeting in late 2014.

The Meeting

The annual general meeting took place at a hotel in downtown Vancouver. As I walked in that morning, I didn't realize I had already lost.

Shortly before the meeting convened, David Mussafer took me out in the hall.

"There's something you need to know," David said. "The board is going to set up a special committee to run the company." He explained this "special committee" would consist of all directors except me. The "official" board meeting would last about two minutes, then the special committee would take over. Since I would not be part of that committee, I wouldn't be needed after the first two minutes were up. They weren't kicking me off the board, but they were making me 100 percent ineffective.

The reason for this was Kit and Ace.

As the board saw it, my connection to Kit and Ace constituted a conflict of interest. Obviously, I found this ridiculous. To call it a conflict of interest when Tom Stemberg and RoAnn Costin were investors and on the board of City Sports, a direct lululemon knockoff, only added to the insanity.

Advent didn't help me either. They were upset that Summer hadn't agreed to sell Kit and Ace to them when they'd offered. They said they lost face with their investors.

Advent's so-called "independent study" on board composition showed that I was, in fact, the person the directors believed did not work nicely with other directors, and no changes were made. Unbeknownst to the board, I also had an independent assessment done that proposed the removal of five board members for conflict of interest and for not having the expertise needed to be a director of a global apparel company.

It is clear to me now that Advent created a Trojan horse to remove me. When I offered to sell them half my shares to come in and help me change over the board, it was in their best interest to work with the existing board. My presence on the board wouldn't work for their short-term PE interest, as my long-term views would conflict with their need for short-term gains. Advent needed board control and passive, uniformed institutional shareholders to fulfill their strategy.

I was given an opportunity to say my piece. I took it, reiterating the advice I had been giving the board for years. We needed to invest in the long-term health of lululemon, to return to the core principles that made us different from the competition. We needed a competent CEO who would protect lululemon from mediocrity and a board willing to steer the company in the right direction.

It had about as much impact as all the other times I'd said it. If anything, it just alienated the board against me more.

When I was done, David said, "Chip's going to be leaving now."

And that was that.

In 2007, Amazon recruited a coach to remove Jeff Bezos from Amazon. Apple fired Steve Jobs and Musk was relieved of the CEO position in his first two companies. You might see a pattern between visionaries and fearful directors.

CHAPTER 31:
LOST AND FOUND

It is the optimists of the world who can change it. An optimist may not always be right, but a pessimist never accomplishes anything.
—Tim Draper

The first thing I did after leaving the conference room was call my wife.

"I-I think I'm off the board," I said to her. Ever supportive, she offered to pick me up, but I said, "No, I think I'll just walk home."

I kind of remember walking home, along a route I'd done on foot and on my bike many hundreds of times, but I was in shock. The life I had built was over, and my mind was spinning trying to figure out exactly what had happened, how I had lost control. I was in a daze.

People ask me how that felt. Imagine being a father at the beach with your child. You're building a sandcastle together, having a wonderful time at the beach. Because you love sand-castles, you get hyper-focused on the shape, the architecture, the sheer beauty of making the sandcastle perfect—but at some point in it all, your child has wandered into the waves.

You see signs here and there—people are screaming, there's a lifeguard giving a small human mouth to mouth—

but you're so focused on the details of the sandcastle that you don't understand the larger picture until you suddenly realize your child is dead.

There's grief, overwhelming grief at times, but more than that there's guilt. How could you have let that happen? What kind of parent are you? How could you let your child down like that, let down the rest of the family who also loved this precious child?

Unlike the parents of Jayna Murray, I have never had to experience losing a child—but I think that's the closest way to describe how it felt.

Feelings

In the darkest moments, it's even worse than that. It's more like lululemon is my child, given to foster parents who just want to collect a check and have no interest in her well-being.

The second thing I did was to sit with Summer at the corner table of our kitchen, looking out at our beautiful view of the water. We sat there while I talked and mused. Summer was in listening mode, because she understood that I think best when I talk out loud. I took her through every detail of the meeting, registering how unbelievable it was to me that they could run the company without me. We were both in shock. Even the house seemed to be quieter than usual.

The third thing I did was to get up and do the Grouse Grind and bring my mind into the present instead of continuing to spiral in my confusion and anger. It might have been the only thing that could help get my mind straight and clear, focused on the most important thing—being with my family and fully present for dinner that night.

Things were foggy for a while—so long I can't really remember exactly how long. I had some really bad days, and even worse nights. It was only when I chose to take responsibility for it all that I really started to see a path forward.

That responsibility took shape in two ways.

First, I reimagined the entire situation as something for which I was 100 percent responsible. I had been viewing it as something the board had done to me.

Yes, the board had set me up and taken me down in a move I might have recognized if *The Prince* or *The Art of War* had been on my pipeline reading list. I chose to sell to private equity, and I let important cultural decisions slide. I let PE take us public before the company was ready. I had checked out of quarterly analyst meetings, and allowed a thousand other small things that resulted in Machiavellian maneuvers being able to work.

The other responsibility I took was to lululemon's people. The company still had thousands of employees who—rightfully in some ways—felt I had abandoned them, and Guests who didn't know why the quality of our pants and their brand experience had deteriorated so quickly. I decided to write a book, to provide context for those passionate people still at the company. So many great employees departed to new emerging companies as lululemon in its mediocrity lost its institutional knowledge.

Ties That Bind

I stepped off the board so I could speak publicly about lululemon. Lululemon states publicly I do not speak for the company, but I am the founder and largest individual shareholder, and I will speak when I want. I have a commitment to my family to ensure value in our investment.

I see my job as being a polite but insistent thorn in their sides. I'm not there out of anger. I've moved on from that, and I'd like to be more cooperative, but communicating with liars is not the best use of my time. I will wait until specific directors have offboarded before I reengage.

So, I hold them accountable in the ways I can.

Hopefully, knowing that I'm there watching keeps directors from abusing lululemon too terribly. The current CEO, Calvin McDonald, is doing a good job. He's an athlete and committed to long-term success. His public communication shows me he is running the company to be inclusive to all. The company is now being led by the lowest common denominator of the physically and mentally unhealthy. The definition of a brand is that it targets a specific customer and if it does not focus, a company risks becoming a drugstore chain or the Gap. This should not be surprising to history buffs of lululemon, as the former lululemon chairman Glenn Murphy was CEO of the Gap and Shoppers Drug Mart.

In 2020, lululemon spent $500 million buying a digital product called Mirror. By the time lululemon renovated stores to market the product, hired and trained people, and fired the founder of Mirror, the investment was $1 billion.

Losing $1 billion is equivalent to two years of lululemon sales. This purchase shows the disconnect between the business model lululemon is best-in-world in and the knowledge of the CEO and directors. No one was fired.

I talked to the CEO of Mirror who told me her experience was horrible. She said her vision for Mirror was stripped away immediately and she was relegated to a meaningless job and then fired. I think this says a lot about lululemon's ability to work with founders and creators. I believe this is a precursor to lululemon's ability to substantially shift who it is in the marketplace. The directors now have such massive fear of buying another company, it leaves their only option to continue to buy back its shares with its war chest of cash rather than investing properly.

Creating a Powerful Story

It's easy to think of CEOs and directors as manipulative people trying to gain power. Instead, I choose to reframe them as entrepreneurs. Their business wasn't in creating products or building up people. It was in finding things people had built, and then exerting control to extract value for their own purposes. When I think of their short-term, highly profitable business model based on lack of integrity, it makes me laugh because it would've been impossible for me to recognize.

Private equity directors probably do add value, certainly to the bank accounts of their shareholders or to their personal brands, at least in the short term. They didn't know how to get the best out of a creative founder and I did not know how to keep power to offset naturally occurring, risk-averse directors. My single biggest mistake is not keeping "B" class shares to control board voting as Phil Knight did at Nike. I build my life and my business on the premise of trusting people, training them, and developing them, then getting out of the way. It worked well for young Super Girls, but once I reached seasoned executives, it was a different situation.

An analogy to lululemon is Boeing and their quality disasters. When Boeing merged with McDonnell Douglas, board dynamics shifted to McDonnell Douglas's culture and strategy of cost cutting. Boeing changed from a creative engineering company with safety as its number one priority and value, to a finance company. Quality people and product took a back seat to profit margins and quarterly reports. Quality continued to slip—and people started dying in the 737 MAX.

My point being, there is no difference between the mindset of the Boeing board and the lululemon board. In this analogy, lululemon directors killed its consumers.

It's the law of attraction. The board could not and has not been able to attract a futuristic creative as a director. In lululemon's desire to promote diversity and inclusion, I find it frustrating that the lululemon board is unable to round out the board with the company's most important and required skill set.

I haven't left the company entirely. Lululemon is the embodiment of my lifetime of experience, so I will never be completely uninvolved. Even if my heart wasn't so tied to the company, the people, and the Guests, my pocketbook is still firmly attached. As of this writing, Summer and I still own 8.5 percent of lululemon. When the stock fluctuates by a dollar, we gain or lose $10 million. I'm linked to lululemon the same way a parent remains linked to a child with a drug problem—even when they're heading in the wrong direction and there's nothing I can do, even if I've had to cut them off so they don't hurt the family anymore, the love never ends and I still want what's best for them.

After stepping off the board, I had two proposals from global companies to partner in taking back control of lululemon. It would have required a year of sixteen-hour days and taking on debt. I did not need another dollar in my life, and my personal life was my priority.

After reading the *Elon Musk* book, I get where it is the individual that needs to fulfill on the unknown future, and to accomplish great leaps, control needs to be concentrated in one person. A great company has to deliver a product to the consumers they need before they know they need it.

I have focused, like all good people would, on my family. I had time to take my boys to school and back every day, throw the football, go snowboarding, and walk with them in the park. They would do their homework in my office with me in the evenings—hours I will treasure forever that I might not have done had I still been working on lululemon.

2012 *Family: Tor, JJ, Duke, Brett, Summer, & Tag*

CHAPTER 32:
THE PERSONAL SIDE

Fully accepting the life you have lived is the first step in creating a new future.

Muscular Dystrophy

Three years after completing the Ironman in 1983, I found I could not swim across the pool. I was diagnosed with FSHD, a form of muscular dystrophy that causes muscle wasting. I went into denial until 2018 when I stubbed my toe and fell flat on my face, twice, in five minutes. I snapped into action and set up a $100 million fund to provide grants and solve FSHD by December 31, 2027.

In 2024, I invested $30 million of the $101 million to the XPRIZE Healthspan contest to restore muscle, brain, and immune function by at least ten years by 2030.

I had made good on all the goals I'd set for myself as a young man, and accomplished the most important things Summer and I set out to do when we were first married. But all I see is possibility. I could see the company I wanted to own across the sparkling ocean and into Vancouver's snow-capped North Shore mountains.

CHAPTER 33:
THE FUTURE OF ATHLETIC APPAREL

Design your life and goals as though you have amnesia.

Back when I did the Ironman, I realized I wasn't truly happy just designing and selling fashion clothing. I'm at my happiest when I'm working specifically with high-quality, technical, athletic apparel. Now that I was no longer with lululemon, I wasn't working with apparel at all. Kit and Ace was sold and I was focused on creating a world-class real estate company and family office.

Arc'teryx had been on my radar to buy since the fourth year after starting lululemon. Almost since its inception, Arc'teryx held the title of the world's best technical outdoor jacket brand. Ironically, it seemed to have gotten this reputation almost by accident.

Arc'teryx got their start by making the world's best "life or death" climbing harnesses before deciding to go into apparel. In their ignorance of how to make apparel, Arc'teryx did what they knew best—they made outdoor jackets like they made climbing harnesses. The designs were overbuilt, with military-level quality control. The construction was superior to previous jacket construction and was consequently very expensive.

However, living in Vancouver and snowboarding at the nearby ski resort of Whistler, I noticed that mountain guides were almost all exclusively wearing Arc'teryx jackets. Arc'teryx had exactly the same design ethos as lululemon, but from a different context. I remember thinking that if I could buy Arc'teryx and implement lululemon's innovative retail formula, Arc'teryx could be just as valuable as lululemon.

Every couple of years from 2004 onward, I returned to the idea of buying Arc'teryx. But lululemon was a rocket ship. We could barely hire and develop people fast enough to keep up with the demands of the business we had . . . we couldn't possibly take on Arc'teryx, too. It was one of life's great opportunities, but one I was outwardly resigned to letting go of.

Finally, in 2018, though I still owned 22 percent of lululemon, I decided to return to my plan of actively acquiring Arc'teryx. I hired an investment banker to investigate a bid.

Arc'teryx had been sold a few years earlier to a sporting-goods conglomerate out of Helsinki, Finland, called Amer Sports. In addition to Arc'teryx, Amer owned a number of other impressive global brands including Salomon in France, Atomic Skis in Austria, Peak Performance in Sweden, and Wilson Sports in Chicago, to name a few. However, I knew Arc'teryx could not fulfill its potential with its ultraconservative approach to business.

Amer tangled their public financials in a way that made it hard to evaluate and, consequently, difficult to take over. But after thirty years in the apparel business, I can observe a store for ten minutes and estimate what yearly sales and profit are with less than a 5 percent margin of error. I knew Arc'teryx still had great upside from within the crowded group of Amer brands.

I became more and more excited about getting involved.

The size of the deal was going to be over USD $5 billion. I knew I did not have the expertise to succeed alone in a deal as complex as the one that was proposed. I determined I would need to find a world-class private equity firm and a partner in China. Unbeknownst to me, the same week I was working on my offer, an offer to acquire Amer came in from a consortium that consisted of Anta Sports, the Chinese leader in sportswear and athletic shoes; FountainVest Partners, a private equity firm from Hong Kong; and Tencent Holdings, a Chinese multinational investment-holding conglomerate. Together, they'd made a bid at USD $40/share, or USD $5.9 billion. I was so bummed, as it looked like I had missed my window.

But then I thought, wait a minute. FountainVest is a solid private equity company with a history of taking long-term positions. Tencent's massive private equity arm is no different. Both were interested in long-term stewardship of Amer—not a quick and profitable turnaround.

Anta was an even bigger prize. They were a shoe company that in 2020 operated close to 20,000 stores plus 1,500 vertical Fila-brand stores and had just won the rights to develop Descente within China. Its chairman, forty-eight-year-old Ding Shizhong, had built the company with his family from the ground up. He was advised by President Xi himself to stop producing shoes for other companies and start his own brand. Chairman Ding and his team ended up becoming the most knowledgeable team in China as far as technical apparel and shoes. They were my kind of people running my kind of company.

I surmised Anta would make a move onto the global stage, with the Amer deal as their first step in that direction. I went to see their logistics and infrastructure, and Chairman Ding showed me one of four warehouses, each four football fields' worth of logistic automation—a computerized room that looked like something out of *Star Trek* with almost nobody in sight. They had the infrastructure, were in the right business, and understood vertical from top to bottom. Clearly, they were the partner for me to get into business with.

We sat down in my Vancouver offices and they offered me a 10 percent stake in the consortium. I countered by saying I needed to invest $1 billion or 20 percent to create enough of a stake that I could prioritize my time and energy to it. Anything less, and I wouldn't really have skin in the game. It would be too easy to shift my focus to my other projects.

They took a leap of faith and brought me on board, probably because they needed a solid North American partner. The consortium knew Arc'teryx was the crown jewel in their Amer buyout, and that having a partner in Vancouver would be vital.

So there I am, at the age of sixty-eight with my sole job to support and expand upon Chairman Ding's vision. I, and my son JJ, who is a board observer, have a strong belief in companies owned by entrepreneurs who have large ownership positions. I travel and visit the different companies and engage deeply with them to find out what's strong, what's weak—and what parts of their culture are vital to what they do. In this role, I get to think critically about organizational structure while working in the technical athletic apparel industry.

I believe that Amer creates the best possibility in the world today for elevating the lives of twenty- and thirty-year-olds through sport. I see the future and it is outdoors. The world of technical apparel has gone from surf in the mid-'70s to skate, then snowboard, then yoga, and now COVID put the outdoor market on steroids.

Family and Pipeline

I want to support and spend time with my family, and I'm doing a lot of that. We work together to meet our goals as individuals, as a family, and as part of the enterprise that is the Wilson family. It's my joy and commitment to teach my boys how to contribute to the world.

Beyond that, I work hard to observe the rule of "Seven Generations." This is an Iroquois concept that has a leader make decisions for the seventh generation, yet to come. I make sure my decisions stay focused on long-term stability.

The Wilson 5 Foundation

Beginning in 2007, our family and directors did all we could to bring quality education to every child in Ethiopia by 2030, with our charity Imagine1day (IOD). Governance, wars, and famine made our goal a challenge. We merged IOD with Water Charity, and have shifted our focus from being a small fish in a big pond to a bigger fish in a small pond.

Looking at the Pacific Northwest, and our lives, I realized that movement, the outdoors, and Vancouver's beautiful system of parks were all central to our lives. I then thought about how the broad expanse of British Columbia is one of the only untouched places remaining on Earth. Despite its enormous size—bigger than Texas—it's just the kind of small, local pond I was looking for.

There are some other stretches of wilderness in places like central Africa, Borneo, West Australia, and the Amazon, but those are just going to get hotter as the years go by. British Columbia is at risk of falling victim to what happened in the area around Yellowstone National Park. Beautiful as it is, so many people have moved into the surrounding area and overrun the natural beauty—and the flora and fauna—of the place.

We wanted to avoid that, to keep the most beautiful parts of our amazing region pristine forever. We want to avoid, to paraphrase Joni Mitchell, paving paradise and putting in a parking lot. With that vision clear in our minds, the next step was figuring out how.

CHAPTER 34:
LESSONS APPLIED

A leader creates a future that would otherwise not have occurred.

I just read the *Elon Musk* book by Walter Isaacson where Walter talks about the type of personality that is required for greatness. Very few people understand how hard it is to create a future that would otherwise not have occurred. Considering a global population bell curve, on one end are 5 percent who are willing to risk it all and build wonderful companies and on the other end are 5 percent who are fearful of change and will fight all levels to keep the status quo.

I am struck by how most of the risk takers fail, have lost all their money, and, because they have families to support, can no longer fulfill their dreams. I wonder as I walk through the world how many superb people there are as managers of top restaurants, or banks, or forestry divisions who, with just a little bit of better timing, could have been Elon, Steve, Jeff, or Bill Gates.

CHAPTER 35:
LULULEMON 2025

However good or bad a situation is, it will change.

The Pareto principle holds true for lululemon. Eighty percent of their sales derive from seven products conceived before 2011. The foundation set in place was so good, mediocre success was guaranteed. When I left in 2014, lululemon was in four countries, omnichannel and e-commerce were well-developed, and RFID tags were managing inventory. We had already committed to growing the men's line to $1 billion in sales by 2020, but had failed.

CHAPTER 36:
TO THE HORIZON

Do not be afraid of death. Be afraid of a life half-lived.

Final Word

As a young man up on the pipeline, I used to imagine what a successful life for me might look like in its final quarter. I would visualize myself at eighty-five, sitting at the Thanksgiving table surrounded by my children, grandchildren, and a few great-grandchildren. Everybody would be making jokes at my expense and laughing at me, because that's the kind of relationship I would genuinely have with all of them. I'm the patriarch of a fun family where everybody is living a fulfilled and happy life.

Outside of the family, I would have done something that moved the world forward—left it better than I found it. Above all, I would be living in the moment because I was enjoying the present without shadows from the past or fear of the future. I could die happy—knowing I was all used up.

I didn't get here by accident. I got here because I live my

life to the fullest and I continue to give without expectation of return. I attract amazing people into my life. People like my wife, my children, and my friends—who make me laugh.

In closing, I'll offer this: don't waste a second of your life. You only have 40,000 days to live. The longer you live, the quicker time goes by. To a toddler, ten minutes feels like ten years. To a ninety-year-old man, ten days feels like half a second. I am honored you took part of your life to read this book.

Examine who in your life is eating up your precious seconds. Who around you complains, but doesn't act?

Ask yourself, "What is my real passion? Where do I thrive? Where can I give the most back to the world?"

We get too hung up on what our social values and morals say we should do, what our parents, society, or friends say we should do. For this reason, I'm always impressed by people who live their own great life.

So how about you? What will you do with the days you have left? What can you do today that moves you away from mediocrity and toward greatness?

Peace, love, dove, and Hare Krishna, all you groovy cats,

Chip

INTEGRITY
WITHOUT IT, NOTHING WORKS
BY MICHAEL C. JENSEN
Note: Reprinted in whole with permission

INTEGRITY, MORALITY AND ETHICS, DEFINED

INTEGRITY: A state or condition of being whole, complete, unbroken, unimpaired, sound, in perfect condition.

MORALITY: In a given society, in a given era of that society, morality is the generally-accepted standards of what is desirable and undesirable; of right and wrong conduct, and what is considered by that society as good or bad behaviour of a person, group or entity.

ETHICS: In a given group, ethics is the agreed upon standards of what is desirable and undesirable; of right and wrong conduct; of what is considered by that group as good and bad behaviour of a person, group or entity that is a member of the group, and may include defined bases for discipline, including exclusion.

INTEGRITY OF AN ORGANIZATION, DEFINED
An organization (or any human system) is in integrity when:

1. It is whole and complete with respect to its word. This includes that nothing is hidden, no deception, no untruths, no violation of contracts or property rights, etc.

2. That is to say, an organization honours its word:
    • *Internally*, between members of the organization, and
    • *Externally*, between the organization and those it deals with. This includes what is said by or on behalf of the organization to its members as well as outsiders.

'ONE'S WORD,' DEFINED
A person's word consists of each of the following:

1. **What you said**: whatever you have said you will do or will not do, and in the case of do, doing it on time.

2. **What you know**: whatever you know to do or know not to do, and in the case of do, doing it as you know it is meant to be done and doing it on time, unless you have explicitly said to the contrary.

3. **What is expected**: whatever you are expected to do or not do (even when not explicitly expressed), and in the case of do, doing it on time, unless you have explicitly said to the contrary.

4. **What you say is so**: whenever you have given your word to others as to the existence of some thing or some state of the world, your word includes being willing to be held accountable that the others would find your evidence for what you have asserted.

5. **What you say you stand for**: What you stand for, whether expressed in the form of a declaration made to one or more people, or even to yourself, as well as what you hold yourself out to others as standing for (formally declared or not), is a part of your word.

6. **The social moral standards, the group ethical standards and the governmental legal standards of right and wrong, good and bad behaviour**, in the society, groups and state in which one enjoys the benefits of membership are also part of one's word unless: a) one has explicitly and publicly expressed an intention to not keep one or more of these standards, and; b) one is willing to bear the costs of refusing to conform to these standards.

CAUSES OF THE 'VEIL OF INVISIBILITY' AROUND INTEGRITY

1. "Integrity is a virtue"

For most people and organizations, integrity exists as a virtue rather than as a necessary condition for performance. When held as a virtue rather than as a factor of production, integrity is easily sacrificed when it appears that a person or organization must do so to succeed. For many people, virtue is valued only to the degree that it engenders the admiration of others, and as such it is easily sacrificed especially when it would not be noticed or can be rationalized. Sacrificing integrity as a virtue seems no different than sacrificing courteousness, or new sinks in the men's room.

2. Self deception about being out-of-integrity

People are mostly unaware that they have not kept their word. All they see is the 'reason,' rationalization or excuse for not keeping their word. In fact, people systematically deceive themselves about who they have been and what they have done. As Chris Argyris concludes:

"Put simply, people consistently act inconsistently, unaware of the contradiction between their espoused theory and their theory-in-use, between the way they think they are acting and the way they really act." Because people cannot see their out-of integrity behaviour, it is impossible for them to see the cause of the unworkability in their lives and organizations—the direct result of their own violations of the Law of Integrity.

3. The belief that integrity is keeping one's word

The belief that integrity is keeping one's word—period— leaves no way to maintain integrity when this is not possible, or when it is inappropriate, or when one simply chooses not to keep one's word. This leads to concealing not keeping one's word, which adds to the veil of invisibility about the impact of violations of the Law of Integrity.

4. Fear of acknowledging that you will not be keeping your word
When maintaining your integrity (i.e., acknowledging that you are not going to keep your word and cleaning up the mess that results) appears to you as a threat to be avoided (like it was when you were a child) rather than simply a challenge to be dealt with, you will find it difficult to maintain your integrity. When not keeping their word, most people choose the apparent short-term gain of hiding that they will not keep their word. Thus out of fear we are blinded to (and therefore mistakenly forfeit) the power and respect that accrues from acknowledging that one will not keep one's word or that one has not kept one's word.

5. Integrity is not seen as a factor of production
This leads people to make up false causes and unfounded rationalizations as the source(s) of failure, which in turn conceals the violations of the Law of Integrity as the source of the reduction of the opportunity for performance that results in failure.

6. Not doing a cost/benefit analysis on giving one's word
When giving their word, most people do not consider fully what it will take to keep that word. That is, people do not do a cost/ benefit analysis on giving their word. In effect, when giving their word, most people are merely sincere (well-meaning) or placating someone, and don't even think about what it will take to keep their word. Simply put, this failure to do a cost/benefit analysis on giving one's word is irresponsible. Irresponsible giving of one's word is a major source of the mess left in the lives of people and organizations. People generally do not see the giving of their word as: "I am going to make this happen," but if you are not doing this you will be

out-of-integrity Generally people give their word intending to keep it. That is, they are merely sincere. If anything makes it difficult to deliver, then they provide reasons instead of results.

7. **Doing a cost/benefit analysis on honouring one's word**
Conversely, people almost universally apply cost/benefit analysis to honouring their word. Treating integrity as a matter of cost/benefit analysis guarantees that you will not be a person of integrity.